T·H·E
Royals

JEANNIE SAKOL & CAROLINE LATHAM

W H ALLEN
PLANET

First published in the United States by Congdon & Weed, Inc.
A subsidiary of Contemporary Books, Inc. This edition
published in 1988 by Planet Books, a division of W H Allen & Co Plc

Printed and bound in Great Britain by
Anchor Brendon Ltd, Tiptree, Essex for the publishers
W H Allen & Co Plc, 44 Hill Street, London W1X 8LB

British Library Cataloguing in Publication Data

Sakol, Jeannie
  The royals.
  1. Great Britain. Royal families
  I. title   II. Latham, Caroline
  941.085'8'0922

ISBN 1-85227-031-4

Note

ACKNOWLEDGEMENTS

We couldn't have done it without the help and encouragement of many good friends and professional colleagues:

Special personal thanks to Ann Morrow for her brilliant suggestions and for hospitality far beyond the call of friendship, and to Diane Oliver and her Celebrity Service "family" for their cheery welcome and generous assistance.

Thanks also to Robin Janvrin, Press Secretary to The Queen, and his efficient staff at Buckingham Palace; to Al deSousa and Deborah Moseley of the Central Office of Information; to Brian Gearing, Kathy Smyth, and Christine Phillips of the *Radio Times*.

Gratitude for help with our necessarily voluminous research also goes to Lucinda Adeney, Sylvia Anderson, Eve Arnold, Jane Astell, the Countess Bathurst, Elizabeth Bennett, Sue Cloke, Jonathan Driver, Gay Fenn-Smith, Caroline Hamilton-Fleming, R. J. W. Gieve, Jonathan Gili, Catherine Hart, Camilla Henderson, Anna Hickman, Joyce Hopkirk, Shelagh and Phil Johnson, Robert Lacey, J. A. W. Lee, Eric Lobb, Julie McCann, Jacquelyn Seabrook, Juliet Simpkins, Richard Stephenson, Peter Thompson, Trevor Turner and Andrew Wiles.

Special thanks to the British Information Service in New York, particularly Stewart Grainger, for patiently providing us with excellent research and background materials; and to Vartan Gregorian and the New York Public Library, always hospitable to writers.

The authors' personal thanks go to Jim, Anthony, Louis, Joe and Vinnie of Carbon Copies Corp. for photocopying materials of every conceivable size, shape or condition without complaint. And especially we thank Anthony Kellar, whose Hudson Valley Express sped material back and forth over the miles separating the authors.

Other invaluable help was provided by Elizabeth Cranin, Dejuana Durham, Missy Saron, Douglas H. Flynn, Shirley Giovetti, Lou Madeoli, Pat Miller, Leif Pedersen, Margie Ponce, Dermot Purgavie, Doreen deRosario, Miriam Sakol, Jane Seigelman, Marie Saxon Silverman, Stephen M. Silverman, Miraed Peake Smith, Jack Strang and Jason Wolin.

Finally, our thanks to our agent, Alice Fried Martell, for helping us turn fun into profit, and to editor Nancy J. Crossman, who never flinched—even when she saw the size of the manuscript.

A

Abdication Address of King Edward VIII

King Edward VIII signed the Instrument of Abdication on 10 December 1936. That night, he broadcast the following address to the British people:

At long last I am able to say a few words of my own. I have never wanted to withhold anything, but until now it has not been constitutionally possible for me to speak. A few hours ago I discharged my last duty as King and Emperor. And now that I have been succeeded by my brother, the Duke of York, my first words must be to declare allegiance to him. This I do with all my heart. You know the reasons which have impelled me to renounce the throne, but I want you to understand that in making up my mind I did not forget the country or the Empire which, as Prince of Wales and lately as King, I have for twenty-five years tried to serve. But you must

A rare collector's plate commemorating the abdication year, or "Year of Three Kings".

believe me when I tell you that I have found it impossible to
carry the heavy burden of responsibility and to discharge my
duties as King as I would wish to do without the help and
support of the woman I love. And I want you to know that
the decision I have made has been mine, and mine alone. The
other person most nearly concerned has tried up to the last
to persuade me to take a different course. I have made this,
the most serious decision of my life, only upon the single
thought of what would, in the end, be best for all.

This decision has been made less difficult for me by the
sure knowledge that my brother, with his long training in the
public affairs of this country and with his fine qualities, will
be able to take my place forthwith without interruption or
injury to the life and progress of the Empire, and he has one
matchless blessing, enjoyed by so many of you and not
bestowed upon me, a happy home with his wife and children.
During these hard days, I have been comforted by Her
Majesty, my mother, and by my family. The ministers of the
Crown and, in particular Mr. Baldwin, the Prime Minister,
have always treated me with full consideration. There has
never been any constitutional difference between me and
them and between me and Parliament. Bred in the
constitutional tradition by my father, I should never have
allowed any such issue to arise. Ever since I was Prince of
Wales and later on when I occupied the throne, I have been
treated with the greatest kindness by all classes of the people
wherever I have lived or journeyed throughout the Empire.
For that I am grateful. I now quit altogether public affairs and
I lay down my burden. It may be some time before I return
to my native land, but I shall always follow the fortunes of
the British race and Empire with profound interest, and if, at
any time in the future, I can be found of service to His
Majesty in a private station, I shall not fail. And now we all
have a new King. I wish him and you, his people, happiness
and prosperity with all my heart. God bless you all! God save
the King!

Abdication of King Edward VIII

Not long before he died, King George V said of his eldest son and
successor, "After I am dead, the boy will ruin himself in twelve
months." In fact, it took only eleven. Although the new King tried to

convince his ministers to allow his marriage to twice-divorced Wallis Simpson, he failed to persuade them.

Much has been written about the events leading up to the King's decision to abdicate. Most analysts agree that the crisis was precipitated principally by the King himself. Constitutionally speaking, the King did not need Parliament's consent to marry the bride of his choice. But in a practical sense, he did need their approval, since a British King at odds with his government would have posed insoluble problems, as the King himself was quick to recognize.

Although individual government ministers were sympathetic to the King's situation, collectively and officially they had no choice but to disapprove of a marriage to a twice-divorced American. It went against tradition, it would offend the moral standards of a large part of the country's citizenry, the prime ministers of the dominion governments advised against it, and it would be unrecognized by the Church of England, of which the King was the secular head. According to the standards of the Church the King would have to swear at his coronation to uphold, his marriage to Wallis Simpson would be unlawful, and any children of the marriage, the lawful heirs to the throne, would be considered illegitimate.

Some advisers urged the King to consider a morganatic marriage, one in which Wallis Simpson would become his wife but not the Queen of England. Edward VIII rejected the idea because he wanted to give the woman he loved the status of a queen. Other advisers suggested patience and discretion. After the King had been crowned, when his reign was well established and his popularity unshakable, when the government and the public had become used to the notion through years of discreet togetherness, he might succeed in getting Parliament's consent to the marriage. But the King insisted that he could not, would not wait. He wanted to marry Wallis as soon as her divorce was final, the following spring, just in time for a joint coronation of the King and his new Queen. Advisers also suggested that the King should not attempt to force the issue, but to win supporters one by one on a personal basis and to trust to their support some time in the future when the matter had to be decided publicly. But the King made no effort to persuade anyone to his point of view: not his ministers, not his friends in the government, not his staff, and not even his family.

Once the issue was publicly raised, it obviously had to be resolved quickly. The country, still suffering the depths of the worldwide depression, could not stand the uncertainty. The King's subjects staged demonstrations for and against his proposed marriage, and the government feared widespread riots if the situation were to drag on. After only a few days of consultation, the government ministers told the King they could not possibly support the marriage. The King quickly responded with the decision to step down from the throne.

On 10 December 1936, at 1.52 p.m., King Edward VIII gave his assent to the Act of Abdication and stepped down from the throne. His brother Bertie, the Duke of York, immediately became King George VI. Prime Minister Stanley Baldwin explained the whole story to the House of Commons later that day, and the former King made his broadcast to the people that night. Wallis Simpson listened to the speech on the radio from a villa in France, where she was in seclusion.

Queen Mary later spoke to the English people on the subject of the abdication: "I need not speak to you of the distress which fills a mother's heart when I think of my dear son who has deemed it his duty to lay down his charge. I commend to you his brother, someone who so unexpectedly takes his place."

Aberystwyth

Prince Charles spent his third year of college at Aberystwyth, learning to speak the Welsh language. It was The Queen's idea—good training, she thought, for the young man who was soon to be invested as the Prince of Wales. The registrar of the college later commented, "If he'd been thoroughly stupid, it would have been awful. But he kept up with his British history and studied Welsh history and literature, as well as the language. No one but a gifted mimic could have learned to pronounce it so well."

During his investiture, Prince Charles greatly endeared himself to the Welsh people by making a short address in their own language.

Jennifer Adams

Jennifer Adams is the superintendent of London's Central Royal Parks. She looks after the gardens of the royal residences at Buckingham Palace, Clarence House, and Kensington Palace, as well as Hyde Park, Green Park, and 10 Downing Street. Among her tasks are ensuring that the gardens at Buckingham Palace look their best during the garden-party season, allowing grass to grow tall around the shores of the lake to give cover to nesting waterfowl, and keeping the royal larder stocked with the fresh baby shrimps that constitute the steady diet of the Queen's flamingos and give them their wonderful rosy colour.

Marcus Adams

Marcus Adams was a favourite photographer of the Royal Family in the 1920s and 1930s. Some of his most enchanting pictures are of the young Princess Elizabeth, with golden curls and a happy smile.

Edward Adeane

Edward Adeane served as Prince Charles's private secretary from 1979 to 1984. A former barrister specializing in libel, he is a bachelor and the son of Lord Michael Adeane, once a private secretary to The Queen, and great-grandson of one of Queen Victoria's private secretaries. He started his royal career as a page of honour to The Queen and became a close friend of Prince Charles, sharing his interest in shooting and fishing.

Lord Michael Adeane

Lord Adeane was The Queen's private secretary from the time of her coronation in 1953 until his resignation in 1972. His grandfather Colonel Arthur Bigge was one of Queen Victoria's secretaries. Once considered one of Britain's top marksmen, Adeane also graduated with honours from Cambridge. He described his duties as private secretary by saying, "One minute you are writing to the Prime Minister. The next you are carrying a small boy's mac."

Always the suave courtier, he is well characterized in a story told by Prince Philip's biographer, Basil Boothroyd. When Boothroyd buttonholed Adeane outside Buckingham Palace to ask for some information for his book, Adeane talked for a while without showing the slightest sign of impatience, but finally said courteously, "I do hope you'll forgive me, but I just heard that my house is on fire."

Admiralty Arch

The centre gates of Admiralty Arch, at the head of The Mall, are opened only for royal processions.

"The Adventuress"

"The Adventuress" was Queen Mary's nickname for the American divorcee, Wallis Simpson. The Queen had refused to receive Mrs. Simpson, but the Prince of Wales got around this by bringing Mrs. Simpson to the wedding of his brother the Duke of Kent and introducing her to the entire Royal Family as his "great friend". Queen Mary remained unimpressed.

Afghanistan

Princess Diana's stepmother once said of her, "If you said 'Afghanistan' to Diana, she'd think it was a cheese!"

Afternoon Tea

The Royal Family enjoys its afternoon tea. At Buckingham Palace, tea is always brewed by The Queen, using loose Darjeeling tea (one spoonful per person). Milk is served in a silver jug that is shaped like a cow and has been in the family for six generations. Usually, there are also muffins, watercress sandwiches, Dundee cake, and bread and butter.

The Queen likes to drink her tea lukewarm in a large cup. The Queen Mother, another devoted tea drinker, has been known in an emergency to use a teabag—much to The Queen's disapproval.

Against The Grain

Against The Grain was the horse ridden by Princess Anne in her debut as a racing jockey on the flat in the summer of 1985. She raced in the Farriers' Invitation Amateur Riders' Stake at Epsom and took fourth place.

AIDS

In the spring of 1987, Princess Diana visited the AIDS ward at London's Middlesex Hospital. She made a point of being photographed shaking hands with all of the patients on the ward. Said one of them, "The Princess shook my hand without wearing gloves, and that meant more to me than anything." The photos were published under such titles as "The Hand of Hope", and did much to convince the public that AIDS cannot be transmitted through casual social contact.

Captain Alistair Aird

Captain Alistair Aird is the comptroller of The Queen Mother's household. He manages her money, pays her staff of forty, and decides the appropriate time to redecorate her houses.

Lord Airlie

Lord Airlie is the Lord Chamberlain, or the official head of The Queen's Household. Lord Airlie is closely connected to the Royal Family. His grandmother was a lady-in-waiting to Queen Mary, and his father was Lord Chamberlain for King George V. His younger brother married Princess Alexandra. His wife is an American heiress who is one of The Queen's ladies of the bedchamber. A former banker, Lord Airlie supervises all royal functions and the running of all the royal residences.

Albert Memorial

One of the most familiar landmarks of London is the Albert Memorial in Kensington Gardens, a monument built by Queen Victoria to commemorate her grief over the death of her Consort, Prince Albert. It consists of a huge bronze statue of Albert (thirty-seven cannon were melted for the metal) under a stone canopy topped by a tall spire. There are granite steps, life-size statues of camels and elephants, and countless square feet of Venetian mosaics.

The Albert Memorial was completed in 1872, and it is now beginning to crumble; however, the government has the necessary funds committed for its restoration. Commented the chairman of the Royal Fine Arts Commission, "Whether people like it or not, public affection clusters around it. It's probably at the peak of its artistic appreciation."

"Alexandra's Band"

In the 1950s, the vivacious young Princess Alexandra was a media darling, rather like Princess Di and Sarah Ferguson thirty years later. She and her group of aristocratic friends were labelled "Alexandra's Band", and their clothes, social doings and romances were extensively reported in the popular press. After the Princess married sober Angus Ogilvy in 1963, "Alexandra's Band" ceased to play.

Alice in Wonderland

Alice in Wonderland was a childhood favourite of Prince Philip. Princess Margaret, on the other hand, disliked it intensely and found it too disturbing—even after she had grown up.

"Alla" (Mrs. Clara Knight)

Clara Knight, nanny to Lady Elizabeth Bowes-Lyon, was still practising her profession when her old charge gave birth to Princess Elizabeth. So she was asked to take charge of the nursery, and she stayed to see both Elizabeth and her younger sister Margaret Rose into their teens. She was called "Alla" by a child who couldn't pronounce Clara, and the name stuck for the rest of her life.

She never married; the "Mrs." was the old-fashioned courtesy title given to nannies and housekeepers. Clara Knight died in 1946 still with the Royal Family. To the end, her life had been dedicated to her career and "her children".

America's Bicentennial and The Queen's Visit

Britain's close relationship with the United States was colourfully illustrated by The Queen's six-day visit to America during the 200th anniversary year of the Declaration of Independence. With typically understated humour, Queen Elizabeth said in Washington, "It has not altogether escaped my notice that there is some sort of a celebration going on in America."

In Philadelphia, Her Majesty presented a gift from the British people, a seven-ton Bicentennial Bell bearing the inscription "Let Freedom Ring" and cast in the same London foundry that produced the Liberty Bell. At President and Mrs. Ford's state dinner, The Queen's "suggested" guest list included Bob Hope, Muhammad Ali, Helen Hayes, and Telly Savalas of TV's *Kojak*, a Buckingham Palace favourite. In New York, Mayor Abraham Beame, who was born in London, made The Queen an honorary citizen of the city. Governor Hugh Carey joined the royal couple at a Waldorf Astoria luncheon given by the Pilgrim Society of the United States and the English-Speaking Union. The royal party visited George Washington's 1776 Harlem headquarters and Bloomingdale's department store, then went on to Boston and the Old North Church made famous by Paul Revere's legendary ride.

Hardy Amies

Hardy Amies has been designing daytime outfits for The Queen since the time of her 1948 tour of Canada. Fashion observers credit him with helping her dress more simply and elegantly. He says, "The Queen's attitude is that of any rich woman: a millionairess of position who does not like to be exploited." Amies was made a Commander of the Royal Victorian Order in 1977.

Mabel Anderson

Mabel Anderson was one of a long line of Scottish nursery maids to serve the Royal Family. Originally hired as second-in-command to Nurse Helen Lightbody when Princess Anne was born, she stayed with the Royal Family until all the children were adult.

Animal Companions

The Queen Mother

Bobs	her first Shetland pony
Lucifer and Emma	her pet pigs
Caroline Curly Love	a favourite dove in childhood
Bali Hai	a racehorse that was presented to her while on tour in New Zealand and which turned out to be a stakes winner
Geordie	a favourite corgi

Prince William

Smokey	his pony

Duchess of York

Peanuts	her favourite pony
Peggy	her English sheepdog
Nigger	her first pony

The Queen

Burmese	the horse she rode on ceremonial occasions
Susan	the corgi of corgis
Whiskey	another corgi
Crackers	yet another corgi
Sugar	one more corgi
Dookie	surprise—a corgi!
Shadow, Spark, Myth, Fable, Diamond	corgis all
Bustino and Shirley Heights	her stallions at stud

Prince Charles

Harvey	his golden labrador
St. David	the horse that refused a cross-country jump twelve times
Happiness	his best polo pony
Allibar	a favourite horse, died in 1981

Prince Andrew
  Frances   his black labrador bitch

Queen Alexandra
  Facie and Punchie   her favourite dogs, buried at
                                                Sandringham

Princess Margaret
  Ching   a Tibetan lion-hound
  Caspar   a chameleon
  Johnny   her sealyham
  Pipkin   her dachshund

King George V
  Charlotte   his parrot, which ate with him

Princess Anne
  Wise Old William   a very special horse
  Random   her Gascony hound
  Apollo   her corgi

King Edward VII
  Persimmon   his Epsom Derby winner

King Edward VIII
  Rifle Grenade   the horse on which he won a
                                                point-to-point race in 1921
  Pet Dog   the horse he rode to victory in
                                                the Welsh Guards Challenge Cup

Princess Diana
  Tigger   her Jack Russell terrier

Annabel's

Annabel's is the exclusive nightclub in London's Berkeley Square
much favoured by young royals and Sloane Rangers.

Annigoni

Pietro Annigoni was the Italian-born portrait painter who created one
of the most popular portraits of The Queen. He later said he had had
trouble getting the expression he wanted on her face until he asked
her to imagine she was looking out of the window over the park in
sunshine. Suddenly her face took on just the right look of quiet
happiness mixed with a touch of nostalgia.

  One of Annigoni's trademarks is that he always includes some small
portrait of himself in the background of his paintings. In his portrait
of The Queen, he is shown rowing a boat in the distance; in the

portrait he painted several years later of Princess Margaret, his profile is hidden in a pile of leaves.

In 1969 Annigoni painted a second portrait of The Queen, this time for the National Portrait Gallery. This was not so popular with the public, and critics said it made The Queen look too careworn.

Annual Rent

Among the tokens of rent Prince Charles is entitled to receive every year from inhabitants of the Duchy of Cornwall are:

- Two white greyhounds
- A pound of pepper
- Caviar from a Cornish sturgeon
- A salmon spear
- A grey cloak
- A leg of mutton

The Answered Wish of King George V

According to an account by Queen Mary's lady-in-waiting, King George V remarked, some time in the early 1930s, "I pray to God that my eldest son will never have children, and that nothing will come between Bertie and Lilibet and the throne."

Archbishop of Canterbury

The Archbishop of Canterbury is the spiritual leader of the Church of England, but The Queen is the temporal head. The current Archbishop is Dr. Robert Runcie, who conducted the marriage services for Prince Charles and Prince Andrew.

Armorial Bearings of Her Majesty The Queen

Quarterly: first and fourth, gules, three lions passant guardant in pale, or (England); second, or a lion rampant within a double tressure flory counter-flory, gules (Scotland); and third, azure, a harp or stringed argent (Ireland); the whole encircled with the Garter.

Crown

A circle of gold, from which issue four crosses pattée and four fleurs-de-lis, arranged alternately; from the crosses pattée arise two golden arches ornamented with pearls, crossing at the top under a mound, surmounted by a cross pattée, also gold, the whole enriched with

precious stones. The cap is of crimson velvet, trimmed with ermine.

Crest
Upon the royal helmet, the Crown proper, thereon a lion statant guardant, or, royally crowned, also proper.

Supporters
On the dexter a lion guardant, or, crowned as the crest; and on the sinister a unicorn, argent, armed, crined and unguled or, and gorged with a coronet composed of crosses pattée and fleurs-de-lis, a chain affixed thereto passing between the forelegs and reflexed over the back of the latter.

Motto
Dieu et mon Droit.

Louis Armstrong

Jazzman Louis Armstrong was a favourite of many members of the Royal Family. In a concert attended by King George V, "Satchmo" called out to the always proper and slightly frosty King, "This one's for you, Rex"—and the King actually smiled in return. Years later, when Princess Margaret was in the audience, he announced, "We've got one of our special fans in the house, and we're really gonna lay this one on for the Princess."

Antony Armstrong-Jones

Antony Armstrong-Jones is a photographer who has chronicled many warm moments within the Royal Family. The money he now receives as fees for the reproductions of these photos goes into a trust fund administered by the National Fund for Research into Crippling Diseases. He is probably best known, however, as the former husband of Princess Margaret. They were married in 1960 and divorced eighteen years later. At the time of the marriage, he was given the title Earl of Snowdon, and his present credit line reads merely "Snowdon".

He has won acclaim for his photos of old people and hospital patients, and he produced several award-winning TV documentaries on the same subjects. He also has designed a number of objects, ranging from spectacles, to the setting of Prince Charles's investiture, to an aviary at London Zoo. (Said the *Daily Express* caustically, "Mr. Armstrong-Jones must now be ranked as one of the leading bird-cage designers in the country. Not an overcrowded profession.")

Antony Armstrong-Jones was born on 7 March 1930, in London. His Welsh father was a successful barrister, and his mother, formerly Anne Messel, was descended from a German banking family. He was the second and last child in the family; his older sister, Susan Anne, later married Viscount de Vesci. When Tony was four, his parents were divorced. His mother soon remarried, to the Earl of Rosse; a year or so later, so did his father, to the actress Carol Coombs.

At the age of sixteen, while he was at Eton, Tony was stricken by polio, and he spent more than a year in a wheelchair. He spent two years at Jesus College, Cambridge, but failed to complete his studies in architecture. After a sort of apprenticeship to a society photographer called Baron, Armstrong-Jones set up his own studio. With the help of the right connections, he began to photograph various members of the Royal Family. Thus he met Princess Margaret, and by 1958 they were seeing one another regularly. On the very day that Peter

The Earl of Snowdon
with some of his photographs.

Courtesy of the British Information Service.

Townsend, Margaret's old flame, made public his own engagement, the Princess agreed to marry Antony Armstrong-Jones.

Five months after his divorce from the Princess, Tony remarried. His second wife is Lucy Lindsay-Hogg, a production assistant at the BBC, with whom he became involved at the time he and Margaret separated. They have a daughter, born in 1979. He still regularly sees David and Sarah, his two children from his royal marriage.

Lady Sarah Armstrong-Jones

Lady Sarah Frances Elizabeth Armstrong-Jones is the daughter of Princess Margaret and the Earl of Snowdon, born on 1 May 1964. Petite like her mother, Sarah attended Bedales School and Camberwell School of Art. She has travelled widely with both her parents, and was chief bridesmaid at the 1981 wedding of Lady Diana Spencer to Prince Charles. (She was also the only bridesmaid at the wedding of Princess Anne to Captain Mark Phillips.)

When Lady Sarah entered her teens, Princess Margaret announced firmly through a spokeswoman, "She will not undertake public engagements or take on official duties. She is an entirely private person and not a member of the Royal Family." Princess Margaret has since stressed this in private on many occasions, as although she is royal, the Earl of Snowdon is not, and they cannot therefore bestow royal titles on their children.

Sir Peter Ashmore

Sir Peter Ashmore served as The Queen's Head of Household from 1973 to 1986. As such, he was responsible for the day-to-day functioning of the entire support staff of The Queen, whether she was at home in one of her palaces or on tour.

Sir Frederick Ashton

Sir Frederick Ashton was a highly acclaimed choreographer and former dancer long associated with the Royal Ballet. He was a great friend of The Queen Mother, and for her eightieth birthday, in 1980, the Royal Ballet performed his original ballet *Rhapsody* in her honour at Covent Garden. The crowd waved balloons and shouted, "We love you, Queen Mum."

Assassination Attempts

During the Trooping the Colour ceremony in 1981, The Queen was trotting along The Mall on her favourite parade horse Burmese, accompanied by troops of the Household Division and bands playing martial airs. Suddenly, a young man with a gun stepped out of the watching crowd. For ceremonial reasons The Queen was riding alone, and no one could protect her. The man pointed the gun straight at The Queen and fired six times. Although The Queen did not know it at the time, the man had loaded the gun with blanks. She bravely calmed her horse, who was upset by the smell of gunsmoke and the sudden noise, and rode on to complete the ceremony. The young man was immediately arrested. He was seventeen-year-old Marcus Sarjeant, whose motive for the act was never fully understood. Sarjeant was sentenced to five years. The Queen later said philosophically, "If someone really wants to get me, it is too easy."

The Mall has been a dangerous spot for royals. In 1974, Princess Anne's car was driving along it when a man swerved his car in front of hers and tried to kidnap her. Before he was subdued, he wounded her detective, a policeman, her driver and a passer-by. The attacker said he was trying to draw attention to the need for more government support for mental health programmes. Prince Philip, who was in Indonesia with The Queen at the time, remarked, "If the man had succeeded in abducting Anne, she would have given him a hell of a time while in captivity."

David Attenborough

David Attenborough was a producer at the BBC when the *Royal Family* film was made, in the spring of 1969. Attenborough was known to be sceptical of the idea of a popular film about the life of the Royal Family, fearing it would somehow reduce their glamour and thus their magic. "Never let them inside the hut," he cautioned.

"The Aunt Heap"

"The Aunt Heap" was the slang description used by Edward VIII when he was Prince of Wales for Kensington Palace, for many years the home of a number of elderly royal aunts.

Auxiliary Territorial Service (ATS)

The Auxiliary Territorial Service (ATS) gave young women of Great Britain a chance to serve their country during World War II. By driving officers' cars and even heavy trucks, they freed able-bodied men to fight. Princess Elizabeth, who had longed to do something for the war effort, was finally accepted as No. 230873 Second Subaltern Elizabeth Alexandra Mary Windsor early in 1945, the last year of the war. She wore her khaki uniform proudly, and learned to strip an engine and change a tyre. She also learned to get along with the other young women in her unit and insisted on being treated as "one of the girls".

Charles Aznavour

The records of romantic French singer Charles Aznavour are favourites of The Queen Mother and can nearly always incite her to dance.

B

Badminton Horse Trials

The Badminton Horse Trials are the most competitive of the three-day riding events in Great Britain, and are always held in early April on the estate of the Duke of Beaufort, the Master of The Queen's Horse. The course is a little over four miles long and very challenging. Princess Anne used to compete at Badminton, but in recent years she has eased off the demanding training required for such arduous events and is more likely to be found in other types of competition. Her husband, Captain Mark Phillips, still occasionally rides at Badminton.

The Queen presents a trophy at the Badminton Horse Trials.

Bahamas Mama

In February 1982, the Prince and Princess of Wales holidayed in the Bahamas for ten days before returning to London to await the birth of their first child. Diana, six months pregnant, sensibly opted to wear a bikini so she could soak up the precious sun. Unfortunately, a photographer snapped her on the beach, and the pictures were published in two tabloids, under the caption "Bahamas Mama". Both papers later apologized for their intrusion on Princess Diana's privacy.

Courtesy of the British Information Service.

The Queen at Balmoral with Prince Edward, Prince Philip, Prince Charles and Prince Andrew.

Balmoral

Balmoral Castle, the privately owned retreat of the Royal Family in Scotland on the banks of the River Dee, is situated in a premier salmon-fishing spot in Aberdeenshire. Built in 1855 for Queen Victoria and Prince Albert, and designed in large part by Albert, it boasts tartan wallpaper and carpets, busts of Queen Victoria and her Prince Consort, and a piper to play the guests out from dinner every night. (In the morning, the pipers wear Balmoral tartan kilts, but for evening they change into the more formal Royal Stuart.) King

Edward VII crossly called Balmoral "the Highland barn of 1,000 draughts", but the present royals love it, draughts and all. Balmoral has no large rooms for state occasions; it is a place where the Royal Family can have complete privacy, surrounded by the wild scenery of the Cairngorm Mountains.

The royals usually arrive in Balmoral in mid August, when the weather is usually at its best, and stay for about ten weeks. Prince Charles and Prince Andrew have always enjoyed hunting, fishing, and deer stalking. The Queen walks her corgis and visits her Highland cattle. Prince Philip goes carriage driving. The Yorks like to sail on nearby Loch Muick. Diana, not as much of an outdoor enthusiast, simply enjoys the scenery.

When the weather is fine, everyone meets for a picnic lunch. Prince Philip designed a special van to get the food to the picnic site and keep it at the right temperature; sometimes he also takes command of the barbecue grill. They all meet again for a formal dinner, convening for drinks at 6 p.m. Long quiet evenings are passed playing Scrabble, charades or Trivial Pursuit. Once a week a film is shown, and in September everyone goes to the Royal Highland Gathering in Braemar to watch the Highland Games.

At the end of the Balmoral season, the royals hold the annual Ghillies' Ball for the staff and estate workers. Male royals traditionally wear full Highland dress, the women white ball gowns with tartan sashes.

"Bambino"

Queen Mary often referred to her grand-daughter Princess Elizabeth as the "bambino", and much enjoyed the time she spent playing with the little girl with the grown-up manner.

Banana Skin

During the 1969 investiture of the Prince of Wales at Caernarvon Castle, a young man threw a banana skin under the hooves of the horses pulling The Queen's carriage. No harm was done, but the angry crowd turned on the perpetrator. He was rescued by the police and eventually fined £3 for insulting behaviour.

Barley Water

The Queen is a devotee of barley water, which she drinks to settle her digestion and also as a weight-watching aid. For those who would like to try it, here is the recipe:

5 oz pearl barley
4 pints boiling water
Rinds and juice of 2 lemons and 6 oranges
As little sugar as necessary, to taste
A tiny splash of rum

Simmer the barley and water over low heat for about an hour. Strain the water into a jug and add the sugar, the rum, and the rinds of the fruit. When completely cool, strain again, add the lemon and orange juice, and store covered in the refrigerator.

Barbara Barnes

Barbara Barnes was the nanny initially chosen by the Prince and Princess of Wales to look after baby Prince William and later his brother Prince Harry. Barbara had been working for the Honourable Colin Tennant but became available when the Tennant girls, May and Amy, went away to boarding school. The Tennants recommended her, through Princess Margaret, to the Waleses.

Nanny Barnes preferred to be called "Barbara". A great believer in fresh air, she had the boys outside in all weather. After five years, Nanny Barnes left, amid rumours that Princess Diana was unhappy to see how attached the little Princes had become to their nanny, with whom they naturally spent much more time than they could with their mother or father. Rumour also had it that Prince Charles thought the boys ought to have a stricter upbringing.

Baron

Baron was the Manchester-born official photographer for Queen Elizabeth's coronation. Subsequently, he was noted for his pictures of the Royal Family and of well-known stars of the theatrical and ballet world. Born Sterling Henry Nahum, he was severely wounded in World War II in the Italian campaign. A close friend of Prince Philip, Baron was at the height of his fame in the 1950s, when he took on as an apprentice the young Antony Armstrong-Jones. He died suddenly in 1956 at the age of forty-nine.

Hector Barrantes

Hector Barrantes is the dashing polo player from Argentina with whom Sarah Ferguson's mother ran away when Sarah was thirteen. Barrantes seems to be as hot-tempered as he is dashing. In 1983 he

was barred from the international polo field for the entire year
because he had impetuously punched a rival player in the nose and
knocked him off his horse.

As stepfather to the future Duchess of York, Barrantes presented a
bit of a protocol problem in her wedding arrangements. He holds a
commission in the army of Argentina, lately at war with Britain over
the Falklands, a war in which the groom had fought on the British
side. However, in spite of no formal peace agreement having been
signed, an invitation to the wedding was sent. Wearing morning
dress, he sat in the place that protocol demanded, in the row just
behind his wife, who was in the front row as the bride's mother.

Hector and Susan Barrantes live on a thousand-acre farm in
Argentina. Of course there is a polo field, and Hector maintains a
string of sixty ponies.

Stephen P. Barry

Prince Charles's personal valet from 1969 to 1981, Stephen P. Barry
violated the royal protocol that restricts disclosure of personal
experiences by royal servants. Barry wrote two volumes of memoirs,
entitled *Royal Service* and *Royal Secrets*. Both books were published in the
United States, but British publishers, in deference to the Palace,
refused to print them. Barry, who reportedly earned more than a
million dollars from his books, died of AIDS in London in October
1986, at the age of thirty-seven.

"Bat Lugs"

"Bat Lugs" was the nickname given the future King George VI when
he attended the Naval College at Osborne. The nickname referred to
the fact that his ears stuck out prominently. His grandson, Prince
Charles, has the same feature, and his schoolmates often called him
"Jug Ears".

BBC Coverage of Royal Travels

In 1987, BBC court correspondent Michael Cole described what it's
like to cover the royals on tour:

> On the recent visit to four Arab countries by the Prince and
> Princess of Wales, I had with me a cameraman, a sound
> recordist, a lighting technician, a picture editor, a producer,
> and an engineer responsible for transmitting our stories by

satellite back to London. Had we been preparing a thirty-
minute programme on the tour—as we often do—we may have
had a second camera crew... Most of the cameramen, for
television, newspapers or magazines, carry small aluminium
stepladders to get above the crowds. On the move—and
they're always on the move—they look like a convention of
window cleaners training for the Olympic 100 metres.
Inevitably, I carry my cameraman's ladder *and* his tripod. I'm
usually beside him as he films, whispering occasionally in his
left ear to point out what he may have missed.

Beards

The Queen, The Queen Mother and Princess Margaret are all known
to detest beards. When Prince Philip came back from a trip wearing
one, it disappeared promptly. When a member of The Queen's
household came back from a holiday with a new beard, Her Majesty
took one quick look at him, went on writing, and said firmly, "That's
coming off." Prince Charles went through a brief bearded period;
when he finally shaved it off, he sent little bits of it in tiny boxes to the
people who had been particularly unkind about it. His aunt, Princess
Margaret, for example, had refused to kiss him as long as he was
bearded. A brief exception to anti-beard sentiment was made for
Prince Andrew, when he came back from fighting in the Falklands
with a beard and still received kisses all round. (Of course, he shaved
the beard off as soon as he reached his home at the Palace.)

The only bearded royal is the Queen's cousin Prince Michael of
Kent, who is thought to retain his beard because it makes him look
very much like his grandfather, King George V. It is not known
whether any of the royals are willing to kiss him.

Sir Cecil Beaton

One of the Royal Family's favourite photographers, Sir Cecil Beaton
was internationally acclaimed in the realms of fashion, art, interior
design and film sets. He won Academy Awards for the sets and
costumes of *My Fair Lady* and *Gigi*. Beaton photographed the Royal
Family from 1939 to 1970, starting with the Queen Mother and
ending with Prince Andrew as a small child. His photographs
emphasized the regal bearing, the majestic settings and the somewhat
aloof beauty of the royal women, and many observers credit these
photos with helping to restore the public's belief in the monarchy
after the crisis of King Edward VIII's abdication.

Colin Beckwith

Colin Beckwith is the flying instructor who taught the Duchess of York to pilot a plane.

Beefeaters

These men, who guard the Tower of London and the royal jewels, have the official title of Yeomen Warders of the Tower. They were first established by King Henry VIII in the sixteenth century, when he left behind a detachment of twelve men to guard the Tower after he gave it up as a permanent residence in favour of something a little more comfortable.

The nickname Beefeaters had its origin in 1669. Cosimo, the Grand Duke of Tuscany, was visiting England at the time and wrote of the Yeomen Warders, "This magnificent body of men are great eaters of beef, of which a very large ration is given them daily at the Court, and they might be called beef-eaters."

Max Beerbohm

Max Beerbohm was a satirist and caricaturist at the turn of the twentieth century who was fond of using the Royal Family as targets. His drawings include pictures of Queen Victoria making her son Edward wear a dunce cap and stand in the corner when he visited her at Windsor, with The Queen looking remarkably like a toad. He wrote a ballad about the life of King George V and Queen Mary, in which members of the Household argue:

HE: Last evening I found him with a rural dean,
    Talking of District Visiting
    The King is duller than the Queen.
SHE: At any rate he doesn't sew;
    You don't see him embellishing
    Yard after yard of calico
    The Queen is duller than the King.

Belgian Suite

In Buckingham Palace, the Belgian Suite is traditionally reserved for visiting heads of state. Prince Andrew and Prince Edward were both born in the Belgian Suite.

Madame de Bellaigue

Antoinette de Bellaigue taught Princesses Elizabeth and Margaret French literature and history for six years, from 1942 to 1948. The wife of a Belgian nobleman, the Parisian-educated "Toni", as the Princesses called her, escaped Belgium just ahead of the German invasion and made her way to friends in England, who recommended her to the Royal Family. She later wrote about her impressions of her pupil who was to be Queen: "Queen Elizabeth II has always had from the beginning a positive good judgement. She had an instinct for the right thing. She was her simple self, *très naturelle*. And there was always a strong sense of duty mixed with *joie de vivre* in the pattern of her character."

Benenden

When she was thirteen, Princess Anne was sent away to school at Benenden, in Kent, where she stayed for five years. There she made many friends and continued to take riding lessons and compete in horse shows. Among the pupils at Benenden was Princess Benedikt of Denmark.

Benetton

Benetton is an Italian-based chain of fashion boutiques that has spread all over the world. Princess Diana is known to shop there, and she once tried to return a jumper she decided she didn't like to the shop where she had bought it, in Knightsbridge. The clerk, who failed to recognize her, refused to accept the jumper without a receipt, and the Princess had to leave with it still in her hand. Later the shop found out who she was, wrote a note of apology, and offered to exchange the jumper.

Betrothal of Elizabeth and Philip

The engagement between Princess Elizabeth and Philip Mountbatten was announced by her parents on 8 June 1947, in the following bulletin: "It is with the greatest pleasure that the King and Queen announce the betrothal of their dearly beloved daughter the Princess Elizabeth to Lieutenant Philip Mountbatten, R.N." In actual fact, Elizabeth and Philip had become privately engaged at Balmoral the previous autumn. Her father liked Philip and considered him a good Consort for his daughter, but he had thought Elizabeth was still a bit young to marry, especially since wartime restrictions had kept her from seeing anything of the world. A trip to South Africa for the King and Queen and the two princesses had already been set for early 1947, and the King asked his daughter to wait to announce the engagement until after the tour.

Princess Elizabeth and Lt. Philip Mountbatten, R.N., at the time their engagement was announced.

Courtesy of the British Information Service.

One question often posed about the engagement is who made the actual proposal. The last female reigning monarch, Queen Victoria herself proposed to her future husband, as protocol demanded. Did Elizabeth feel she must do the same? Neither she nor Philip has ever gone on record with an answer to this question, but Palace insiders agree that it was probably Philip who popped the question. He was never one for strict protocol, nor was he, even in his younger days, a meek or submissive personality. And Elizabeth at that time was still a young princess—just nineteen—who'd had little experience of independence.

"Biggles"

Sarah Ferguson's pet name for Prince Andrew before their marriage was reported to be "Biggles". The origin of the name is the hero of a series of boys' stories about a pilot and his crew in wartime.

Birkhall

Birkhall was the Scottish retreat of the previous Duke and Duchess of York before he became King George VI; thereafter, of course, the family stayed at Balmoral. The Queen Mother still stays at Birkhall while the rest of the family is at Balmoral. She enjoys its charm, with walls full of Landseer paintings of stags and old cartoons of previous statesmen.

Birkhall is a large, white, Queen Anne house that Queen Victoria once used to accommodate poor relations. The Queen Mother has given it a lovely garden, some of which she planted herself, and a cosy atmosphere. The royals often gather at Birkhall for tea when they are at Balmoral, drinking many cups of The Queen Mother's delicate Earl Grey to wash down a slice of Black Bun, her favourite teacake.

Katharine Birks

Katharine Birks is the Canadian public relations consultant who represents Capt. Mark Phillips. When he visited Canada in the summer of 1987, the two were seen dining privately at a remote inn in Ontario. Rumours started to fly about the attractive blonde and Princess Anne's husband, but Miss Birks denies that theirs is anything other than a professional relationship.

"A Bit of a Twit"

In a television interview, David Frost asked Prince Charles how he would describe himself. Quipped the Prince, "Sometimes, a bit of a twit."

Manolo Blahnik

Manolo Blahnik is the trendy international shoe designer who made
the coral-coloured shoes that Princess Diana wore with her going-
away outfit, as well as Sarah Ferguson's wedding shoes. Both women
still send for shoes from his Chelsea shop.

Alistair Blair

Alistair Blair is an English fashion designer. Just after he showed his
first collection in 1986, his publicist Susannah Constantine (a
girlfriend of Princess Margaret's son, Viscount Linley) introduced
him to a friend. She needed a dressy day outfit quickly, for an
unspecified occasion! Blair whipped up a navy blue suit with mid-calf
skirt and a purple blouse to set off her red hair. Two days later he saw
his new client, Sarah Ferguson, on television with her fiancé Prince
Andrew. Since then, Blair has dressed the new Duchess of York for
most of her public engagements, and he made most of her clothes for
the Yorks' first long state visit, the Canadian trip in the summer of
1987.

Blair loves his work but doesn't make the mistake of regarding it too
seriously. "We're not curing cancer," he says, "it's only playing around
with women's frocks."

The Blood of the Bambergs

In 1962, less than two years after the marriage of Princess Margaret
and Antony Armstrong-Jones, playwright John Osborne caused a
sensation with his play *The Blood of the Bambergs*, which revolved around
a "royal wedding". The setting was Westminster Abbey on the
wedding eve. When Palace officials run onstage with the news that
the groom has been killed in a car crash, a press photographer who
resembles the dead prince is brought in as a substitute and the
wedding proceeds. One London critic described Osborne's attitude as
"negative patriotism", a viewpoint he had already established in 1956
with *Look Back in Anger*.

Bloodhound

The yawl *Bloodhound* was Prince Philip's pride and joy, a sailing boat
that he liked to captain himself. He bought the boat in 1962 as an aid to
relaxation when away from official duties. But in 1969 the *Bloodhound*

Courtesy of the British Information Service.

The Duke of Edinburgh out for a sail with the young Prince Charles.

was sold, as part of a general trend towards economizing to help the Royal Family live within its budget.

Bloomingdale's

When The Queen visited New York in 1976, she accepted a formal invitation from Bloomingdale's president Marvin Traub to stop off for a special shopping trip at the famous store. On 9 July, the royal entourage, in sixteen limousines, pulled up at the door and The Queen stepped out on to a red carpet across the pavement. American designers were presented to The Queen, while board chairman Lawrence Lachman introduced Prince Philip to such American merchandise as the talking calculator, the pet rock and Famous Amos chocolate chip cookies. The twenty-five-minute tour went off without a hitch. According to Maxine Brody, author of *Bloomingdale's*, one disappointed little girl in the crowd of thousands trying to get a glimpse of The Queen asked, "But where's her crown?"

Blotting Paper

The blotting paper The Queen uses at her desk is always black, so that no one can inadvertently learn what she has written. As an additional precaution, it is changed every day.

Suzanne Blum

Maître Suzanne Blum was the late Duke and Duchess of Windsor's lawyer for many years, from the time when she met them in Portugal during World War II. When the Duke lay near death, he asked Maître Blum to look after the Duchess, a charge she faithfully carried out until the Duchess's death in 1986. Blum was named the principal executor of the Duchess's estate, and it was she who decided that the Duchess's jewellery should be put up for auction. After several meetings with Nicholas Rayne of Sotheby's, she chose that prestigious firm to conduct the sale.

Sir Anthony Blunt

Sir Anthony Blunt was the British art historian who late in life was revealed to have been a Soviet spy. While a fellow at Trinity College, Cambridge in the 1930s, he was one of the disaffected young men led by Guy Burgess into espionage for the Russians. His career as an art historian reached such heights that he was appointed Surveyor of The King's (later The Queen's) Pictures in 1945 and received a knighthood in 1956.

In 1979, seven years after he retired, the incredible truth was revealed: he had arranged for the flight of the notorious Burgess and his cohort, Donald Maclean, to Russia in 1951, and his 1964 confession to British authorities was hushed up to prevent scandal. Known as the legendary "fourth man" of the Burgess-Maclean-Philby spy ring, Blunt was stripped of his knighthood in 1980 but was not prosecuted. He died in 1983 at the age of seventy-five.

"Bobo" (Margaret MacDonald)

Margaret MacDonald, nicknamed "Bobo", has been with The Queen since her childhood. She joined the household of the then Duke and Duchess of York as a nursery maid when their second child was born. Her job was to look after four-year-old "Lilibet" so that Nanny Knight could devote herself to young Princess Margaret. Bobo has been in the Royal Household ever since.

She is still The Queen's official dresser. Although she is these days too feeble and arthritic to jump around sorting out the dresses, hats and gloves herself, she supervises the younger women who do the work, and has an encyclopaedic memory for details such as how many pairs of white gloves The Queen currently has and where they are stored. (The Queen can go through four pairs a day.) It is Bobo who tells The Queen to put on her "wellies" and take an umbrella when it is raining, to dress sensibly when she goes to exotic foreign countries, and to eat her breakfast every morning. Palace insiders say she is The Queen's closest confidante.

Body Shop

Body Shop is a London salon that sells skin-care products and cosmetics designed by Barbara Daly, who did Princess Diana's make-up for her wedding. In an interview, Daly explained how she advised the Princess to stop wearing pink blusher, which clashed with her fair complexion, and switch to soft shades of peach and coral. She also demonstrated how eye shadow in tan, caramel or rust would bring out her blue eyes more than blue eye shadow would. Last but not least, she showed the Princess how to use a darker shade of blusher at the tip of her nose to make it appear shorter. The Princess continues to be loyal to Body Shop products, even buying them for Prince Charles.

The Bond Street Association

If you want to shop where the royals do, go to Bond Street. The Bond Street Association represents the largest concentration in London of

Cartier on Bond Street, holder of a Royal Warrant from The Queen.

Courtesy of the Bond Street Association.

shops and services holding Royal Warrants. Founded in 1924, the Association includes such well-known royal favourites as Cartier, Benson & Hedges, H & M Rayne and Asprey. Director Trevor Turner is a walking encyclopaedia of the area's links with royalty, which date back to Sir Thomas Bond, private banker to King Charles II. In the eighteenth century, the Prince Regent's fashion adviser, Beau Brummell, lived in Bond Street, where he had his shoes polished with champagne. The Queen was born a few steps away, in Bruton Street, and she and her sister Princess Margaret took swimming lessons at the nearby Bath Club.

Rear Admiral Sir Christopher Bonham Carter

Rear Admiral Sir Christopher Bonham Carter was for many years a close adviser to the Duke of Edinburgh, and was the man who handled the Duke's finances.

Basil Boothroyd

Author Basil Boothroyd wrote an authoritative and meticulously researched biography of the Duke of Edinburgh. Entitled *Philip: An Informal Biography*, it was published in 1971.

Borscht Diana

According to a 1986 French cookbook on the subject of favourite royal foods, Princess Diana loves beetroot soup (borscht) and even has a version she makes herself. Here's the recipe:

> Peel and grate 1 lb beetroot. Dissolve a chicken stock
> cube in 4 cups of boiling water. Add the beetroot and cook for
> 15 minutes. Stir in ½ tablespoon of sugar and the
> juice of 1 lemon. For an elegant presentation, either purée or
> strain, and serve very hot topped with a spoonful of single
> cream.

Lavinia Bowes-Lyon

Lavinia Bowes-Lyon is the daughter of The Queen Mother's brother, David. She was born in 1930, making her the same age as Princess Margaret. The two cousins were close companions in their youth.

Bowes-Lyon Cousins

In 1987 it was revealed that The Queen's cousins Katherine and Nerissa Bowes-Lyon had been mental patients at Royal Earlswood Hospital from 1941. Nerissa died in hospital in 1986 and is buried in a public grave marked only by a plastic tag. Three of The Queen's cousins-in-law were mental patients at the same institution: Etheldreda, Idonea and Rosemary Fane. The Queen Mother had always said that her nieces were dead, but according to one report she found out the true story in 1981 and has since sent money to buy them birthday and Christmas presents. It is speculated that the young women, who are said to have the minds of six-year-olds, were put into the institution by their mother, The Queen Mother's sister-in-law, when the accession of King George VI to the throne made it likely that the family secret would be uncovered.

Boy George

In 1983, at the height of their popularity, Boy George and Culture Club were introduced to Princess Margaret at a charity affair. She was clearly heard to say, "I won't be photographed with that over-made-up tart." Boy George did not go on the record with his opinion of Princess Margaret's make-up.

Patricia Mountbatten, Lady Brabourne

Patricia Mountbatten Brabourne is the daughter of Lord and Lady Louis Mountbatten. She and her younger sister, Pamela, have been friends of The Queen since their childhood. Patricia organized a Girl Guide troop at Buckingham Palace so that Elizabeth and Margaret could become members. Since Patricia was also the cousin of Philip Mountbatten, she remained good friends with the Princesses after her marriage. When Patricia married Lord Brabourne in 1946, Princesses Elizabeth and Margaret were both bridesmaids.

Patricia and her husband were badly injured in the explosion of the terrorist bomb that killed her father in 1979 while the entire family was holidaying in Ireland. Members of royal families from all over Europe attended Lord Mountbatten's funeral at Westminster Abbey. Lady Brabourne's son, Nicholas, and her mother-in-law had a joint funeral, which was attended by Prince Philip and Prince Charles, who was the boy's godfather. Paul Maxwell, the fifteen-year-old friend of Nicholas who was also killed by the bomb, was buried near his home in Enniskillen, Northern Ireland.

Bradley's

Bradley's in Knightsbridge is the biggest lingerie shop in Britain. It furnished the trousseau of Princess Anne with broderie anglaise. With prices ranging from £15 to over £1,000, it attracts women of all sizes, incomes and social standing.

Jennifer Elkan, the owner of Bradley's.

Courtesy of Jennifer Elkan.

Brenda and Keith

The satirical British publication *Private Eye* has invented names for all the members of the Royal Family, as they might be in an ordinary English family. The Queen is Brenda, her husband is Keith; Prince Charles is Brian; Princess Margaret is Yvonne. It is reported that Her Majesty and Prince Philip sometimes use these nicknames in humorous moments.

Brentford Market

The Brentford Market is where The Queen sells her surplus fruits, vegetables and cut flowers from the Windsor estate. Her Windsor acres are so productive that they can supply all the fresh vegetables served there and at Buckingham Palace, with some left over. The Brentford Market also gets most of The Queen's annual mushroom crop, which flourishes thanks to the rich fertilizer produced by horses kept at the Royal Mews.

The British National Anthem

The words and the tune of the national anthem are anonymous. They date back to at least 1745, when the nation was roused to patriotic fervour on behalf of the Hanoverian monarchs as they faced the threat of the Jacobites and Charles Stuart, the "Young Pretender". After a worrisome defeat of the Hanoverian army by the Jacobites, the song was publicly performed on 28 September 1745, at the Theatre Royal in London's Drury Lane. The event's immediate success made it customary to play the song there nightly, and within a few years the King was greeted with the song wherever he made a public appearance.

The tune of the national anthem has proved so popular that it is the basis of many songs in other countries, such as America's "My Country, 'Tis of Thee", for which the lyrics were written in 1831, and even of classical compositions by such masters as Haydn, Beethoven, Weber and Brahms.

HMS Bronington

The *Bronington* was the command given to Prince Charles during his service in the Royal Navy. In February 1976 he took command of the 365-ton vessel, with a crew of five officers and thirty-four men. The *Bronington* was named after a village in Wales.

Buckingham Palace

Buckingham Palace is located on forty-five acres of beautiful lawns and gardens, and costs about £2 million a year to keep up. An artificial lake covering five acres has a small island in the centre, where royal

View of Buckingham Palace from The Mall.

Courtesy of the British Information Service.

children have always liked to play. Grown-up royals, however, confess that Buckingham Palace is not their favourite residence. It is too formal, too official and too inefficient.

Buckingham Palace, built in 1703, was first the London home of the Duke and Duchess of Buckingham, and was later the birthplace of fourteen of George III's fifteen children. In the next reign, George IV commanded John Nash to remodel the house to be the King's home, not a palace. However, the work was not completed until 1837, the last year of William IV's reign, who succeeded his brother George.

Aerial view of Buckingham Palace.

Courtesy of the British Information Service.

Queen Victoria was the first sovereign to live in Buckingham Palace. She moved in in 1837, aged eighteen, when she became Queen. As her family grew, she had the palace enlarged and in 1850 the two wings were joined by a centre block. This meant that the main entrance had to be moved, and it is now known as Marble Arch.

It was only in 1913 that the centre block was faced with Portland stone, so characteristic of London buildings, and the balcony erected. The whole of this work was done in the three summer months while King George V and Queen Mary were away. The first royal appearance on the famous balcony was on 4 August 1914, when George V and Queen Mary came out as a gesture of support to the people at the beginning of World War I.

Buckingham Palace today is The Queen's London home, the centre of her state entertaining and ceremonial functions and the administrative centre of her Household. Many royals have thought poorly of its qualities. King George VI called it an icebox, and his brother, King Edward VIII, claimed it had a dank and musty smell.

"Bud"

When the young Princess Elizabeth heard that her new baby sister was to be named Margaret Rose, she said decisively, "I shall call her Bud." Asked why, the Princess answered, "Well, she's not a real rose yet, is she? She's only a bud."

"Buffy"

When The Queen Mother was a girl, her younger brother and closest companion David was unable to pronounce her name, and turned it into the family nickname "Buffy".

Buick Limousine

Because Wallis Simpson adored Buick cars, King Edward VIII bought a sleek black Buick limousine in 1936. She rode in it on her trip to France, just before the King decided to abdicate.

Lydia deBurgh

Artist Lydia deBurgh's portrait of The Queen, painted in 1959, was commissioned by the government of Northern Ireland and is the first portrait of a reigning British monarch to hang in the Irish Parliament.

Burmese

For seventeen years, from 1969 to 1986, The Queen rode the black police mare Burmese for the annual ceremony of Trooping the Colour. Burmese was born at the Royal Canadian Mounted Police breeding centre in Canada on 21 May 1962, and she was trained by the Mounties for police work. Showing herself to be exceptionally able and intelligent, she was promoted to be the star of a travelling show put on by the Mounties; after the show had been staged in England in the spring of 1969, Burmese was given to The Queen. Her first job was Trooping the Colour that summer.

Burmese was trained for sidesaddle by a niece of the Royal Equerry, Miss Sylvia Stanier, and every year Miss Stanier would return for a

Painter Lydia deBurgh with her portrait of The Queen.

few days of sidesaddle riding to get Burmese ready for the big event. The day before the ceremony, Burmese was washed with an apple-scented shampoo; she was brushed to a shining gloss, and her hooves were oiled. Then she and The Queen would set out for their day of parade.

Burmese retired from active duty in early 1987, although she still sometimes helps out with crowd control at Changing of the Guard ceremonies. Palace insiders say her ears prick up when she hears the "Colonel Bogey" march.

The Bury

The Bury was the English country home of the Earl and Countess of Strathmore, where their daughter, Lady Elizabeth Bowes-Lyon, spent much of her early childhood. Located at St. Paul's Walden in Hertfordshire, the Bury was built in Queen Anne style of soft red brick and covered in ivy. The interior, with fine Adam ceilings, was picked out in delicate colours. The nursery had the traditional coal fire and brass fender, and The Queen Mother still insists that fairies live in the wood at the bottom of the garden.

Business in the Community

Business in the Community is an organization that is trying to revive some of the depressed areas of Inner London. Its president is Prince Charles, and he takes his responsibility seriously. He frequently tours parts of the inner city, and he is very successful at fund-raising for the group. His friend Dr Armand Hammer has contributed generously. Regenerating the inner cities and providing jobs for their inhabitants constitute some of the Prince's top priorities.

R. A. Butler

R. A. Butler, a distinguished figure in British politics for decades, was expected by many to become Prime Minister during the 1940s or '50s, but somehow that position always eluded him. Nevertheless, he was for years one of the leading figures of the Conservative Party. Always called Rab, Butler was Master of Trinity College at Cambridge when Prince Charles studied there. He put forth his thoughts on his royal student and his background in a newspaper interview: "The Queen and the Duke are not university people—they're horsey people, commonsense people. The Queen is one of the most intelligent women in England and brilliant in summing up people, but I don't think she's awfully interested in books. You never see any lying about her room when you go there, just newspapers and things like that. Whereas Prince Charles has a tremendous affinity for books—they really mean something to him."

Butler received a life peerage as Lord Butler of Saffron Walden in recognition of his long career of public service. He died at the age of seventy-nine in 1982. His funeral was attended by Margaret Thatcher, Prince Charles and Princess Alexandra.

Y Bwthyn Bach

In Welsh, Y Bwthyn Back means "the little house". It was a charming little playhouse given to Princess Elizabeth in the 1930s by the people of Wales and set up in the grounds of the Royal Lodge at Windsor, where she often stayed as a child. The little house, too small for an adult to stand inside upright, had a thatched roof and its own little vacuum cleaner, and Princess Elizabeth was responsible for keeping it clean and tidy.

C

Caernarvon Castle

Caernarvon Castle stands on a site in Wales that has been fortified for more than nineteen hundred years. The present structure, considered one of the finest examples of mediaeval military building in Europe, was begun in 1283 by King Edward I, using drawings by the chief household architect of the Count of Savoy. Work continued until 1330, but the internal design was never completed. King Edward clearly intended the castle to play a special role in his conquest of the Welsh. It was also planned as a fitting palace for his son, Edward II, who was born in the castle in 1284. In 1301, Edward became the first English Prince of Wales, a title that ever since has been given to the King's eldest son.

The design of Caernarvon Castle echoes that of the Roman walls at Constantinople, and the great eagles that crown the parapets are appropriate symbols of royalty. The inside of the castle is in ruins, but some restoration of the old stonework is being undertaken sporadically. The castle is separated from the old town of the same name by a large ditch, for purposes of fortification. Caernarvon is considered a Royal Borough, and its constable is the Earl of Snowdon. It was the site of the 1969 investiture ceremony confirming Prince Charles as the Prince of Wales.

The California Rain

Since The Queen's schedule is locked into place months in advance, she often has to carry out her ceremonial duties in a downpour. In 1983, when she visited the California coast, heavy rains fell every day, and the storms grew so severe that she was unable to stay on the royal yacht *Britannia* as scheduled, but had to go to a hotel. At the state

39

banquet hosted by the Reagans, The Queen joked, "I knew before we came that we had exported many of our traditions to the United States. I had not realized that the weather was one of them."

James Callaghan

James Callaghan (later Lord Callaghan), who succeeded Harold Wilson as Prime Minister in 1976 and stayed in office three years, often talked with The Queen about farming as well as matters of state. He later said that she offered him great "friendliness", as distinct from "friendship", which he cautioned one should not expect from royalty.

Calypso

The Royal Family has always been a favourite subject of West Indian calypsonians. Royal marriages, love affairs and supposed scandals are discussed in frank—even lewd—lyrics. For example, when The Queen found an intruder in her bedroom, Trinidad's Mighty Sparrow immediately wrote a calypso about it, in which The Queen "confesses" to Prince Phillip, "My dear, I took him for you." When Princess Margaret married Antony Armstrong-Jones, Sparrow's song began, "I wish I was a cameraman." An earlier calypso about Margaret called her "Loving sister of Queen Lilibet" and added, "She ain't married, she ain't tall, Like to dance, like to sing, Like to try out anything, If she been boy, she been King." On The Queen's 1983 visit to Jamaica, she was greeted by, "Long time Gal, we never see yuh."

Canada Welcomes the Duke and Duchess of York

The first extensive state tour undertaken by the Duke and Duchess of York was a twenty-five-day trip to Canada in the summer of 1987. According to rumour, the Duchess was extremely nervous before they started out, perhaps because Canadian newspapers called her such names as "Rowdy Fergie" and "Big Red". But when the couple arrived in Toronto, the Duchess of York looked happy and composed in her red and white outfit, featuring a white hat trimmed with a red maple leaf, the official symbol of Canada. The tour included a ride in a birchbark canoe at Thunder Bay, a rodeo at Medicine Hat on their first wedding anniversary, the gift of a buffalo skull from an Indian tribe, and a few days' private retreat at a cottage in remote Ontario.

Canterbury Cathedral Trust Fund

The Canterbury Cathedral Trust Fund, which raises money for the upkeep and restoration of the Cathedral, which was heavily bombed during World War II, is presided over by Prince Charles. To help raise money, he agreed to write and deliver the commentary for a thirty-minute television special on the Cathedral, first aired in 1977.

Car Mascot

Any car in which The Queen travels bears her own car mascot attached to the bonnet. The mascot is a solid silver statue of St. George on a horse, looking down at a slain dragon.

Cariad Bach

Cariad Bach means "Little Darling" in Welsh. It is the name the Welsh people gave Prince Charles at the time of his investiture as Prince of Wales, when he delighted them by addressing them in their own language.

Arthur G. Carrick

In 1987, Prince Charles quietly submitted one of his watercolours to the selection committee for the prestigious Royal Academy's summer art show. The picture was entitled "Farm Building in Norfolk" and signed "C"; the attached form identified the artist as "Arthur G. Carrick". Arthur and George are among the Prince's long string of Christian names, and the Earl of Carrick is one of his titles. The picture passed the selection process that rejected about 90 per cent of the entries, and it went on display at the Royal Academy in June 1987.

President Jimmy Carter

It is said that The Queen Mother disliked Jimmy Carter because he was too forward. Despite her warmth, she does not care to be touched and is the sort of person who asks permission before she does anything as intimate as removing a thread from someone's lapel. President Carter apparently kissed her too warmly.

Barbara Cartland

Barbara Cartland is a royal step-grandmother. Her daughter Raine,

Countess of Dartmouth, became Princess Diana's stepmother when she married the Earl of Spencer. Known to the publishing world as the Queen of Love, Barbara Cartland has sold more than 450 million copies of her romantic novels.

Casa Antica

The Prince and Princess of Wales often ski in Switzerland at Klosters, where Diana's favourite disco is Casa Antica.

Sir Hugh Casson

Architect Sir Hugh Casson was the President of the Royal Academy until his retirement in 1986. He frequently advised The Queen on all matters artistic. The current President of the Academy is Roger de Grey.

"Castle Creepers"

Palace insiders jokingly label those they consider social climbers trying to make their way into the royal set as "castle creepers". The technique is to buy tickets for such events as the Cartier International Polo Matches, the Henley Regatta and Glyndebourne—which are attended by royalty and the aristocracy—in hopes of being noticed.

Castle of Mey

The Castle of Mey is The Queen Mother's home in the north-west of Scotland. She usually stays there for several weeks during the summer, and is visited by the other royals on their way to Balmoral. She purchased the old property, formerly named Barrogill Castle, shortly after the death of her husband, as a country retreat for herself and Princess Margaret. "I was driving along," she has recalled, "and from the high road saw this old castle; when I heard it was going to be pulled down, I thought it must be saved. The roof was really awful, it took twelve months to rebuild that and put in bathrooms and electric lights." Friends believe that the project of fixing up the old residence helped her to get through the difficult period of adjustment to widowhood.

   From the rooftop, royals have a marvellous view of the rugged red cliffs of Orkney. Yet the beach in front of the castle gardens is quiet enough for royal children to build castles in the sand. When The Queen Mother bought the castle, it had neither electricity nor plumbing. She has succeeded in modernizing the stone building without spoiling its historical features. The interior is painted white and filled with pretty flowers, sparking glass and a collection of delicate china. In The Queen Mother's bedroom is a fireplace of white marble ornamented with a heart medallion that was a birthday gift from the King, who always told guests with a smile, "My wife is very attached to the hearth." Even though cold winds from the Atlantic sweep over the grounds, there are lovely gardens, abundant fruit and vegetables for the table, and flowers in the pinks and blues that The Queen Mother loves.

"Catching Out the Minister"

According to the biography of The Queen by Lady Longford, one of the secret games the royals play is "catching out the minister". It is played by reading state papers so carefully and thoroughly that in meetings with prime ministers, the monarch is able to display a greater familiarity with matters of importance than is the head of government. King George VI used to like to play "catching out the minister"; one of his ministers called it a "friendly contest of knowledge". The Queen continues to play the game with skill. Sir Harold Wilson once confessed that, on a few occasions, The Queen made him feel like an unprepared schoolboy.

Helen Cathcart

Helen Cathcart is the author of nine books about the Royal Family, including *Her Majesty* and *The Queen Mother* and *Anne, The Princess Royal*. She makes a point of keeping a low profile and refuses to make any public appearances herself. "She feels the people she writes about are more interesting than her," says a representative in trying to explain her reclusiveness.

Cats

In the old nursery tale, Dick Whittington and his cat walked to London to visit The Queen. From insider reports, Queen Elizabeth II does not like cats, preferring dogs and horses.

Cecelia Cavendish-Bentinck

Cecelia Cavendish-Bentinck, later the Countess of Strathmore, was the mother of Queen Elizabeth, The Queen Mother. She could trace her ancestry on one side back to the family of the Duke of Wellington, and on the other to William of Orange.

Jackie Chan

Jackie Chan was the beautiful Eurasian star of *The World of Suzie Wong*
who was photographed by Antony Armstrong-Jones and rumoured
to be his fiancée until his engagement to Princess Margaret was
announced.

Chapel Royal Choir

The Chapel Royal Choir augments the Westminster Abbey choir for
ceremonial occasions involving the Royal Family, such as the 1986
royal wedding of Prince Andrew and Sarah Ferguson. An earlier
Chapel Royal Choir sang to give thanks when King Henry V
celebrated his great victory at Agincourt.

The Charles-and-Di Industry

When The Queen announced, on 24 February 1981, that the Prince of
Wales was engaged to Lady Diana Spencer, she inadvertently set off a
frenzy of merchandising. There were mugs with gaudy portraits of
the engaged couple, badges reading, "Don't do it, Di", and—alas for
one manufacturer—medallions bearing a picture of Westminster
Abbey, the traditional site for royal weddings but not the venue
chosen for this one, Prince Charles selecting St. Paul's instead. The

Some examples of royal wedding collector's items.

Courtesy of Josiah Wedgwood & Sons.

Post Office issued two commemorative wedding stamps. Even the Royal Family got in on the act by commissioning a Royal Wedding Souvenir Booklet to raise money for the International Year of the Disabled. Firms such as Wedgwood and Royal Worcester made souvenir plates and plaques. At the other end of the scale, countless plastic plates and cheap cups and saucers with pictures only faintly resembling Charles and Diana made their way on to the market, along with even less tasteful items, such as his-and-hers sets of underwear emblazoned with the royal faces. The souvenirs grew into a multi-million-pound industry.

The whole process was repeated five years later when Prince Andrew married Sarah Ferguson.

Charlie's Aunt

When Prince Charles was born, Princess Margaret joked, "Now I suppose they'll call me Charlie's Aunt."

Charlie's Girls

From the time he went to Cambridge in 1968 until he announced his engagement in 1981, Prince Charles was the world's most eligible bachelor, a status he clearly enjoyed. Among the list of the ladies with whom his name was romantically linked were:

- Lucia Santa Cruz, daughter of the Chilean ambassador, his first love at Cambridge
- Sybilla Dorman, daughter of the Governor-General of Malta
- The Buxton girls, the two daughters of naturalist Aubrey Buxton, an old friend of Prince Philip
- Dale "Kanga" Tryon, an Australian beauty now married to merchant banker Lord Tryon, who remains a cherished friend
- Lady Leonora Grosvenor, daughter of the Duke of Westminster, now married to The Queen's cousin, the Earl of Lichfield
- Lady Jane Grosvenor, Leonora's sister, now the Duchess of Roxburghe
- Lady Victoria Percy, daughter of the Duke of Northumberland, now married to John Cuthbert
- Lady Caroline Percy, Victoria's sister, now married to a Spanish count
- Bettina Lindsay, daughter of a Conservative politician, now married to Peter Drummond-Hay
- Camilla Parker-Bowles, now the wife of an officer in the

Household Cavalry and still a good friend of Charles
- Lady Cecil Kerr, daughter of the Marquess of Midlothian
- Lady Henrietta Fitzroy, daughter of the Duke of Grafton
- Lady Charlotte Manner, daughter of the Duke of Rutland
- Libby Manner, Charlotte's cousin
- Angela Neville, daughter of Prince Philip's private secretary
- Davina Sheffield, a soldier's daughter
- Lady Sarah Spencer, Princess Diana's older sister
- Lady Camilla Fane, daughter of the Earl of Westmoreland
- Caroline Longman, daughter of the wealthy publisher
- Jane Ward, said by some to be the one he loved most
- Louise Astor, who married Jane Ward's brother
- Georgiana Russell, daughter of diplomat Sir John Russell
- Rosie Clifton, now married to Charles's polo-playing friend Mark Vestey
- Sabrina Guinness of the wealthy brewing family
- Anna Wallace, who married Johnny Hesketh
- Lady Jane Wellesley, daughter of the Duke of Wellington, still unmarried and still a friend

Sir Martin Charteris

Martin Charteris was The Queen's private secretary from 1950 until his retirement after her Silver Jubilee in 1977. Ever the perfect gentleman, he is reported to have apologized for being seasick to the men sharing his life raft after their ship was torpedoed during World War II. His hobby is sculpting, and his bronzes are for sale at Asprey, in Bond Street. The Queen knighted him when he left the Palace to become Provost of Eton.

"Chatterbox One"

"Chatterbox One" is the code name given to Sarah, the Duchess of York, by air-traffic controllers. They say she talks as much in the air as she does on the ground.

Chatting with Royals

Royals agree that it can be surprisingly hard to get the conversational ball rolling when they talk to their subjects. Since commoners are not supposed to speak to royals until spoken to, that puts the burden of making the conversation go on the royal shoulders—and sometimes people are so flustered they can't think what to say. For example, The Queen Mother tried to chat with an American Fulbright scholar, saying, "I understand that Arizona is very hot." He answered, "Yes, Your Majesty." She tried to continue: "And I hear that sometimes it is very cold." "Yes, Ma'am," answered the representative of America's best and brightest.

To avoid such stilted conversations, royals generally try to ask open-ended questions that require more than a yes or no, to get the other person talking.

Cheam

Cheam is the preparatory school where Prince Charles first went away to study. Located in Berkshire, Cheam has taught such notables as Lord Randolph Churchill (father of Winston) and Prince Charles's own father, Prince Philip. Explaining how the school was chosen, Prince Charles said, "My father said this is the school to which you ought to go, and here are the advantages and disadvantages. At the age of seven or eight, you were in no position to say, 'I don't want to go.'"

When Charles went to Cheam, The Queen asked that he be treated like any other boy. Alas, in the Prince's first term of two and a half months, the press ran sixty-eight stories about his education. A reporter asked one of the masters whether Charles would be caned if he misbehaved. The master answered, "Yes, in the usual place."

David Checketts

In 1961, Squadron Leader David Checketts of the Royal Air Force became Prince Philip's equerry. Philip then asked him to look after Prince Charles when he was in Australia, which led to a close relationship between the two men. When Charles went to Cambridge, Checketts officially became his personal equerry and then his first private secretary. A smooth public relations man, Checketts helped to steer the Prince through the 1969 investiture and his early years of public duties.

After resigning the post of secretary, due in part to a disagreement with Charles over the proper role of the Prince of Wales, Checketts was knighted. He is still attached to the Prince's household in a minor capacity.

Cheltenham

Cheltenham, site of the hotly contested Gold Cup every spring, is usually attended by The Queen Mother, who presents the Cup. Other royals also like to go if they can fit it into their schedule.

Chevening House

In 1974, when Prince Charles was still the world's most eligible bachelor, it was announced that he would move into his own country house, Chevening House in Kent. The former family home of the Earls of Stanhope, it was given to the British government in 1967 by the last Earl, with the stipulation that it be used as a residence for the Prince of Wales, the Foreign Secretary or the American ambassador. Built in 1625, Chevening has 115 rooms and is set in three thousand acres of woods and parks. But the necessary renovation took so long that eventually the idea was abandoned. Prince Charles had no country house until he bought Highgrove, shortly before his marriage.

Chideock

Chideock was the Dorset house that the new Duke and Duchess of York rented from owner Charles Weld, a publisher. The main reason for their choice was that Chideock (pronounced Chidduck) was only fifteen miles from Prince Andrew's naval base at Portland. The house had thirty acres of grounds, seven bedrooms and a very large kitchen. The Yorks spent their first weekend there in March 1987 and entertained house guests at the same time.

A temporary rented property, the chief drawback of Chideock as a royal home was that a small Catholic church is attached to the house, and a little museum is attached to the church. (Among its treasures are the remains of the hair shirt worn by Sir Thomas More.) The church and museum are open to the public—thus creating real security problems for the royal tenants.

According to one account, the estate itself looks like the one in the opening scenes of the BBC comedy series *To The Manor Born*. It is deep in Dorset, Thomas Hardy country, and built from the mellow golden stone found in the area.

The Yorks are now residing at Castlewood House at Egham, Surrey, while their mock Tudor mansion is being built near Windsor.

Childhood Ambition of The Queen

The Queen as a girl was a passionate lover of animals, especially horses and dogs. To stay near them, she formulated her childhood ambition: marry a farmer, be a lady living in the country, and have lots of cows, horses, and dogs.

China

The Queen first visited China in the autumn of 1986, accompanied by the Duke of Edinburgh. For her first appearance, she wore a coat and hat of dramatic lacquer red, the lucky colour of China, while the band played "God Save The Queen" and "The East Is Red". The Queen visited the Forbidden City of the Chinese Emperors, inspected an army of terracotta warriors rescued from Imperial tombs, and feasted on multi-course Chinese banquets. During an excursion to see the Great Wall of China, she called out to a press photographer, "Please take a picture, someone, or no one will believe I've been here." The success of the trip was marred only by an unguarded remark of Prince Philip's about the slit eyes of the Chinese, which lost its intended joviality when the press repeated it to millions of listeners all over the world.

Chocolate Profiteroles

Chocolate profiteroles are a favourite treat of the Duchess of York. In an interview before her marriage to Prince Andrew, she told a story about how he sabotaged her weight-watching efforts when they had lunch together at Ascot. "He made me eat chocolate profiteroles, which I didn't want to eat at all; I was meant to be on a diet."

Christenings

Royal babies today are christened in the Music Room of Buckingham Palace. The former site of such occasions, the Chapel Royal, was destroyed during the bombing of World War II and later turned into the Queen's Gallery, where she displays her art collection to her subjects. Babies wear a family heirloom gown of Honiton lace. Until quite recently, they were christened with a bottle of water from the Jordan River that had been in the family since the time of Queen Victoria. It has now run out.

Agatha Christie

The mystery novels of the late Agatha Christie are known to be great favourites of The Queen.

Christmas

The royals spend most Christmases at Windsor. Usually more than thirty people gather at the Castle: The Queen and her immediate family, the Kents, the Gloucesters, the Ogilvies, and elderly Princess Alice. Presents are exchanged on Christmas Eve. Favourite choices are appropriate books (especially something on the subject of horses, dogs or hunting) or a sentimental memento. By tradition, The Queen also gives coal to the elderly needy in Windsor (about eight hundred people) and a plum pudding to each of her staff.

On Christmas morning, the entire family attends church at St. George's Chapel. Later that day, the royals gather in front of the TV to watch the national broadcast of The Queen's Christmas Message, which she tapes earlier in the month. They follow this sedentary period with a brisk walk round Windsor Park, perhaps stopping in to see the horses in the stables. On Christmas night, The Queen hosts a joint birthday party for Princess Alice and Princess Alexandra, both of whom were born on Christmas Day and have always shared their special cake.

Christmas Broadcast

In 1932 King George V started a tradition of broadcasting a Christmas message to the nation. He broadcast his last Christmas message in 1935. In 1936, the new King George VI found the live broadcast a heavy burden, because he feared he would stutter on the air. Intimates remember that the coming duty cast a pall over much of the holiday celebration, and no one could relax until the broadcast was finished. Queen Elizabeth II continued the tradition upon her accession to the throne in 1952, and later changed from radio to television. For her, too, the broadcast was an anxiety that muted the family fun of Christmas, until improved technology permitted advance taping. The Queen can now sit with her family at Windsor and watch herself on television on Christmas Day.

The Church of England

The Sovereign must always be a member of the Church of England, and promise to uphold it. Church of England archbishops, bishops and deans are appointed by the Sovereign on the advice of the Prime Minister. All Church of England clergy take an oath of loyalty to the Crown.

The Church has two provinces: Canterbury, comprising thirty dioceses, and York with fourteen dioceses. The Archbishop of Canterbury is Primate of All England; the Archbishop of York is Primate of England. The two archbishops, along with the bishops of London, Durham, Winchester and twenty-one others, sit in the House of Lords. Clergy of the Church of England may not sit in the House of Commons.

Winston Churchill

Winston Churchill was Prime Minister when Princess Elizabeth became Queen. He met her at the airport on her return from Africa after King George VI's death and spoke words of sympathy and support. Privately he worried, "I hope they don't overwork her,"

Courtesy of the British Information Service.

Prime Minister Winston Churchill in his office.

fearing that in her anxiety to do well she would take on too many burdens.

The Queen always treated him as a wise elder statesman, and their mutual admiration continued after his resignation as Prime Minister in 1955, until his death. When asked which of her prime ministers she enjoyed her audiences with the most, The Queen answered, "Winston, of course, because it was always such fun." She enjoyed his impish sense of humour, his fund of amusing stories, and his ability to talk wittily on any subject — including racing, an interest they shared with enthusiasm.

"Cinderella"

Princesses Elizabeth and Margaret and their royal cousins put on a pantomine, "Cinderella", at Windsor Castle in 1943, to entertain the war-weary Royal Family. Princess Margaret argued with her sister over whether they should charge admission. "No one will pay to see us," said Elizabeth; "Nonsense," replied Margaret, "they'll pay anything." In the end, they charged seven shillings and sixpence.

Margaret played Cinderella, and Elizabeth, then seventeen, was Prince Charming in a dashing short jacket and a pair of tights (which her father thought were *too* tight). Cinderella went to the ball in a little coach that had belonged to Queen Victoria when she was a girl, drawn by a tiny white pony. In the final scene of Cinderella's triumph, Princess Margaret sat on a small throne that had also been made for Victoria. Watching all this from the front row of the audience was twenty-two-year-old Prince Philip, whose opinion of his future wife's talent for singing, dancing and impersonating a prince are un-recorded.

Cirencester Park

Ancestral home of the Earls Bathurst, Cirencester Park is where Prince Charles plays polo and the Duke of Edinburgh competes in carriage driving races.

Ciro's

Ciro's was one of the most popular London nightclubs in the 1920s. The future King George VI and Queen Elizabeth often went there during those years. Elizabeth was particularly fond of ballroom dancing and is by all accounts a superb dancer.

Civil List

The Civil List specifies the allowances to be paid by the British Treasury to members of the Royal Family, enabling them to pay their expenses and generally carry on the numerous responsibilities of being royal. The allowances are made against the interest from the Crown Estate, which the Sovereign makes over to the Treasury for the duration of the reign. In 1986, this interest came to nearly £30 million. Historically, the Civil List was always submitted when a monarch took the throne and remained in force throughout the reign. Today, the Civil List is presented to the government annually. In 1986, the Civil List included these allowances:

The Queen	£4,136,800
The Queen Mother	359,100
The Duke of Edinburgh	200,300
Princess Anne	124,800
Prince Andrew	50,000
Prince Edward	25,000
Princess Margaret	121,500
The Duchess of Gloucester	49,200
The Duke of Kent	132,000
Princess Alexandra	125,800

The Prince of Wales receives no money from the Civil List. He supports himself through the incomes of the Duchy of Cornwall. The other royal missing from the Civil List is Prince Michael of Kent, who gave up his right to an income when he married his Roman Catholic wife.

Clarence House

Clarence House is in London, a few steps down The Mall from Buckingham Palace. Actually a part of St. James's Palace, it was first occupied by a Duke of Clarence, who was the third son of King George III and who later became King William IV. The house was completely remodelled around 1825 by Princess Adelaide of Saxe-Coburg-Meiningen when she arrived as a bride of the Duke of Clarence and complained about the "wretched state of dirt" she found there. The plans were drawn up by famed architect John Nash, and the house has an attractive cream-coloured facade punctuated by black window frames and doorways.

The house had been occupied by a younger brother of King Edward

VII until it was turned over to Princess Elizabeth and Prince Philip after their marriage in 1947. Clarence House had suffered from Nazi bombings and the neglect of its former tenant. It hadn't even been wired for electricity! Elizabeth and Philip turned it into a cosy home, which they later gave to The Queen Mother and Princess Margaret when King George VI died and Elizabeth ascended the throne, necessitating a move to Buckingham Palace. Royal brides traditionally stay at Clarence House the night before their wedding.

Clocks

The Royal Family seems to be obsessed with clocks. There are more than 300 in Buckingham Palace, 360 at Windsor, 250 at Balmoral and 160 at Sandringham. It was the habit of King Edward VII to set all of the Sandringham clocks ahead, perhaps in the hope of getting his tardy Consort, Queen Alexandra, to arrive on time. Some of the royal clocks have been running continuously for three hundred years. One of the most famous, in the drawing room at Buckingham Palace, was a purchase of King George IV. The clock is in the shape of the head of a woman. Her rolling eyes tick away the seconds; if you pull on one of her gold earrings, a little pipe organ plays a tune.

Clothes for the Angels

On each side of The Queen Mother's four-poster bed at Clarence House is a pedestal bearing a stone angel who wears a halo and carries a staff. The angels wear frilly white dresses, which each month must be laundered, starched and carefully ironed.

"The Cock, the Mouse and the Little Red Hen"

This children's story tells of the little red hen who keeps saying "Then I'll do it myself" when the other animals refuse to help her with her projects. It was a favourite of Princess Margaret when she was a girl.

Michael Colborne

Prince Charles met Michael Colborne when both were serving aboard the *Norfolk*, where Colborne was a non-commissioned officer, Chief Petty Officer Writer. In 1974, Colborne joined the Prince's household as Secretary of the Prince of Wales Office, handling the Prince's financial affairs, a post he held for ten years. Colborne resigned in 1984 and was awarded a decoration, Lieutenant of the Royal Victorian Order.

Coldstream Guards

The Coldstream Guards is the oldest regiment of the Household Division, and thus they have adopted the motto, "nulli secundus", second to none. Their history as a regiment dates back to 1650. They wear red plumes on the right of their bearskins, and their tunic buttons are lined up in groups of two.

Colherne Court

Colherne Court was the location of Lady Diana Spencer's London flat before she married Prince Charles. With flatmates Carolyn Pride, Virginia Pitman and Ann Bolton, she listened to records by Police, went to an occasional movie, and cooked dinner for friends. Life at Colherne Court was never the same once the news broke about Diana's romance. Shortly after the engagement was announced, she moved into Clarence House and later Buckingham Palace as a protection against the incessant telephone calls and cameras of the press.

Collector's Item "Goof"

The August 1986 issue of *London Illustrated News* has become a collector's item for two reasons. One is its superb coverage of the wedding of Prince Andrew and Sarah Ferguson. The other is the editorial goof that reversed a photograph of Sarah going up the Westminster Abbey aisle. The photo shows her on her father's left instead of his right.

Colours

The Queen's favourite colours for clothes are lime green, pink, aquamarine, peacock blue and red. The Queen Mother favours "sweet pea" colours of blue, pink and lavender. Neither The Queen nor The Queen Mother ever wears black, unless in mourning or calling on the Pope. Princess Diana, however, does wear black. In fact, she created a stir by wearing a strapless black evening dress on her first public appearance as the acknowledged fiancée of Prince Charles. She also likes the sophisticated combinations of black and white or black and red.

All royals wear strong, clear colours so they will stand out in the crowd and photograph well. The Palace claims the royals never consult one another ahead of time to work out their colour coordination, but it does seem oddly fortunate that they never turn up at Royal Ascot or a wedding dressed in the same colour. Once Margaret Thatcher made a public appearance with The Queen, dressed in the same clear blue The Queen had chosen. When Mrs. Thatcher later conveyed her apologies to The Queen for the duplication, she was told by a Palace official, "The Queen never notices what other people are wearing."

John Colville

John Colville (called Jock) was The Queen's first official private secretary, appointed in 1947, when she was still Princess Elizabeth. He served in the post for two years before returning to the Foreign Office. Colville came from a family with a long tradition of royal service. His mother had been a lady-in-waiting, and both his grandfathers had been lords-in-waiting. Jock Colville was considered an up-and-coming young man in the Foreign Office, and he had already been private secretary to three prime ministers: Chamberlain, Churchill and Attlee. At the King's request, he was seconded from the Foreign Office to act as Princess Elizabeth's private secretary. He later married Lady Margaret Egerton, one of the Princess's ladies-in-waiting.

Comfortable Clothes for The Queen

When The Queen's designers create an outfit for her public appearances, one of the chief considerations is The Queen's comfort. Skirts can't be too short or too long, because Her Majesty must climb aboard ships and descend aeroplane steps with assurance. Sleeves mustn't be too tight, as The Queen needs freedom of movement. When one designer forgot this requirement, The Queen had a problem when she was called upon to knight a very tall man. She explained, "I couldn't make him smaller, so I had to reach up with the sword. I heard a ripping noise, and my sleeve got torn. It was hard to know who was the more embarrassed."

The Queen's clothes must also be easy to get into, because she sometimes has only fifteen or twenty minutes in her schedule for changing. She has been known to walk down the hall to her waiting car as she fastens her priceless sapphire necklace and pushes her tiara firmly down into her hair.

Competition Carriage Driving

Considered the best manual on this demanding sport, *Competition*

Carriage Driving was written by the Duke of Edinburgh, a leading enthusiast and former competitor. The book was published by Horse Drawn Carriages Ltd. in 1982.

Complaints About the Royal Family

Playwright John Osborne, author of *Look Back in Anger*, has called the monarchy "a gold filling in a mouth of crumbling teeth".

Labour MP Mrs. Renée Short was appalled when she heard that Prince Charles planned to move into government-owned Chevening House. "A waste of a very beautiful house," she complained. As it turned out, the Prince never occupied Chevening.

The *Daily Express* in 1987 chided the younger generation of royals: "Their world seems to be one of unashamed hedonism. Fun first, extravagance second, showing off third. And duty? Well, that can be conveniently fitted in among the parties, the holidays, the frocks and the champagne."

Lord Altrincham once accused The Queen of relying on "tweedy advisers who are out of touch", and said her voice was "a pain in the neck". He later renounced his title and became plain John Grigg.

Tina Brown, editor of *The Tatler* becoming editor-in-chief of America's *Vanity Fair*, called the Prince and Princess of Wales "glow worms illuminating a black hole in space".

The fashion trade paper *Women's Wear Daily* complained about Princess Anne's looks when she was eighteen: "If I were her mother, the first thing I'd do is slim her down. She has to stop looking like her mother. The frumpy fur stoles, the middle-aged evening gowns. The over-done hair. The under-done hair. The sloppy grooming. It's about time Anne was allowed to bloom on her own."

During a 1969 debate at the Oxford Union as to whether or not "the monarchy should be sacked, Buckingham Palace given to the homeless, and the corgis put to productive work", The Queen was called "a middle-aged housewife with a *pied à-terre* in town and a castle in the suburbs".

When the Prince and Princess of Wales went to the Cannes film festival in late 1986, a French TV critic sniffed at Diana's dress: "It can only be described as English."

In 1973, MP Willie Hamilton, leading critic of the Royal Family, declared that it was "obscene" for the nation to pay £92,000 per year on the Civil List for The Queen Mother, whom he called "the old lady". His motion to cut off her funds was roundly defeated.

Prudence Glynn, the fashion editor of *The Times*, wrote a 1981 article calling Princess Diana "a fashion disaster in her own right".

Malcolm Muggeridge, in 1955, complained, "There are probably quite a lot of people—more than might be supposed—who like myself feel that another photograph of the Royal Family will be more than they can bear... The Queen Mother, Nanny Lightbody, Group-Captain Townsend—the whole show is utterly out of hand."

Confirmation

On 1 March 1942, Princess Elizabeth was confirmed in the Church of England. The ceremony was performed by the Archbishop of Canterbury, Cosmo Gordon Lang, who had been in office during her uncle's abdication crisis. He said he found her intelligent and understanding but "naturally not very communicative". Queen Mary, who had not seen her eldest grandchild for nearly a year, commented that she was much grown and had "very pretty eyes and complexion, pretty figure".

Jasper Conran

Fashion innovator Jasper Conran is a favourite of the Princess of Wales, especially for evening wear. In 1986 he was named British Fashion Designer of the Year, and received his award from the royal patroness in person.

Courtesy of the British Information Service.

Mark Phillips,
contacts in place.

Contact Lenses

Palace insiders like to joke that the polo ground at Windsor is paved with contact lenses. Prince Philip, who is notoriously short-sighted, wore them to play the rough-and-tumble sport and lost lenses constantly.

His son-in-law Mark Phillips is another near-sighted equestrian. In his early days as a show jumper, he always walked the course many times before the event, trying to memorize every jump to compensate for his bad vision. When he started to wear contact lenses, he found they made the ride much easier.

Corgis

The Queen has had a passion for the Welsh corgi since she first owned one in 1933. Her mother advised her to choose the one puppy out of the litter that had a tail: "We must have the one which has something to wag, otherwise, how are we going to know whether he is pleased or not?" As it turned out, the puppy Princess Elizabeth chose was a she, not a he. The Princess named the dog Susan. Shortly thereafter, Princess Margaret, angry that Elizabeth was getting too much attention for winning a lifesaving certificate in swimming class, picked up Susan and pitched her into the lake; then, fully dressed, Margaret jumped in after the dog and rescued her. Susan was apparently none the worse for her adventure.

Since that fateful first meeting, The Queen has never been without at least one corgi-in-waiting, and on her morning walk, three or four are usually happily trotting in her wake. Even on formal occasions, photos often show a corgi or two underfoot. At the time of The Queen's coronation in 1953, her corgis were the first to see her wearing St. Edward's Crown; to learn to balance its heavy weight, she wore it several days in a row while she fed her dogs.

The corgis, by the way, are fed every day promptly at 4.30, with big bowls of chopped liver and dog biscuits spread out on a sheet.

Susan accompanied her mistress on her honeymoon in 1947, and government ministers who meet The Queen report the corgis' presence. Old favourites are buried in a touching little cemetery in the private garden at Sandringham.

None of The Queen's corgis has a dog licence; that is a royal prerogative. She has explained the usefulness of corgis by saying they used to be used for rounding up cattle by biting their legs. Some corgis have coats of white, tan and black, but The Queen breeds hers to eliminate the black and achieve a rich fox-coloured coat. Although many people have tried to interest The Queen in other breeds of dogs, her reply is always, 'Not nearly as nice as corgis".

The Queen and the Duke of Edinburgh at Windsor, with corgi Sugar.

Courtesy of the British Information Service.

Coronation Dates

Elizabeth II	2 June 1953
George VI	12 May 1937
Edward VIII	never crowned
George V	22 June 1911
Edward VII	9 August 1902
Victoria	28 June 1838

Coronation of King George VI

King George VI was crowned on 12 May 1937. The date had actually been chosen by his brother, the former King Edward VIII. When Edward abdicated in December 1936, everyone agreed that there was no need to change the date. As the Prime Minister put it, "Same date, new man".

The whole royal household was roused in the early hours of the morning by a test of the loudspeakers just outside Buckingham Palace, and then again a few hours later by the Royal Marines playing under their bedroom windows. Although it was a rainy day, fifty thousand people were already in The Mall by dawn.

King George and Queen Elizabeth travelled to Westminster Abbey in the golden State Coach. Queen Mary, breaking with the tradition that the widow of a former King never attends the coronation of another, accompanied her grand-daughters, the Princesses Elizabeth and Margaret, in another. Queen Elizabeth wore a white gown lavishly embroidered with Tudor roses and various symbols of the British Empire, high-heeled white satin shoes and the triple-strand pearl necklace she still wears constantly. Her robes were copies of those worn by Queen Alexandra, the Consort of King Edward VII: purple velvet lined with white satin. It took ten needlewomen several weeks to embroider the emblems from every country in the Empire. A new crown was made for her, utilizing the 106-carat Koh-i-Noor diamond, set in platinum. Her maids of honour were dressed by Norman Hartnell; the four duchesses who accompanied her wore gowns from Molyneaux. The King was splendid in velvet and ermine robes, and both Elizabeth and Margaret wore red velvet trains and dainty diadems.

The service was conducted by the Archbishop of Canterbury, Cosmo Lang. The only slight slip-up in the entire ceremony was that the Archbishop put St. Edward's Crown on the King the wrong way round. But since the front and back were virtually indistinguishable, no one noticed the mistake.

Coronation of Queen Elizabeth II

The coronation of Queen Elizabeth II took place on 2 June 1953. It was covered by two thousand journalists and five hundred photographers; television coverage allowed millions of Britons and more than 85 million Americans to watch most of the proceedings. At 10.26 on that rainy London morning, The Queen left Buckingham Palace in the delicately ornamented State Coach that looks like something out of "Cinderella".

She entered Westminster Abbey in the magnificent dress created by Norman Hartnell for the occasion. Its white satin bodice was covered with thousands of seed pearls set in silver; the hem of the skirt was embroidered with emblems of the Commonwealth countries (Scottish thistle, Irish shamrock, Australian wattle, Canadian maple leaf, and so on) interspersed with Tudor roses and set with precious stones. Her twenty-foot-long train was made of crimson velvet and hemmed with ermine. On her head was the Diamond Diadem and around her neck was the Collar of the Garter.

Watching the coronation ceremony from the balcony were the Queen's mother, sister and son Charles; Prince Philip was near her on the floor of the Abbey. After being seated in the Chair of State, The Queen received the recognition of the assembled peers. Then she took her oath, and the religious part of the ceremony began. Her ladies helped her to remove her diadem and heavy robes. Her beautiful gown was then covered by a plain white dress of great simplicity. Thus symbolizing that she put all splendour aside, The Queen was consecrated by being anointed with holy oil. She was then dressed in a cloth-of-gold robe to accept the Royal Spurs and the Sword of State. At last she was covered in the glittering gold Robe Royal, handed the Royal Orb and the two Sceptres, and then crowned by the Archbishop of Canterbury with St. Edward's Crown.

Afterwards, the royals returned to Buckingham Palace, where The Queen rejoined her family, posed for official portraits, and then appeared on the balcony, to the cheers of thousands of loyal subjects filling The Mall.

The Countess of Longford

The wife of the Earl of Longford, Elizabeth Longford has written extensively about the Royal Family. She is the author of *Queen Victoria* (1965), *The House of Windsor* (1974), *The Queen Mother* (1981) and *The Queen* (1983). She also writes occasional magazine articles about the royals. The Countess of Longford is the mother of authors Antonia Fraser and Rachel Billington.

The Countess of Romanones

Like her long-time friend the Duchess of Windsor, Aline, the Countess of Romanones, was born in America and went abroad to seek her fortune. Her best-selling memoirs, *The Spy Wore Red*, recall her adventures as an OSS spy in Franco's Spain during World War II, her marriage to a Spanish aristocrat, and her double life of informing

Photo by Horst, courtesy of Random House.

The Duchess of Windsor's friend, the Countess of Romanones.

on Nazis while moving in the highest international circles. Among her most treasured possessions is the diamond bracelet bequeathed to her in the Duchess of Windsor's will.

The Countess of Rosse

Anne, the Countess of Rosse, is the mother of Antony Armstrong-Jones. After her divorce when Antony was a young boy, she married an Irish peer. Magazines refer to her as "legendarily well-dressed", and her son is said to have inherited her exquisite taste.

Court Circular

The Court Circular is issued daily by Buckingham Palace. It lists all official activities of the royals: visitors received, events attended, new household members. The C.C., as it is nicknamed, first appeared in 1794 to report on a party at the court of King George III. Queen Victoria loved to contribute items about her own activities, such as picnics at Balmoral. Today, the C.C. is prepared by two royal secretaries, who get their information from the press secretaries of each royal household. It is published daily in major British newspapers.

Cousin Halifax

When little Princess Margaret Rose was confronted by her nanny over some piece of childish naughtiness, she always blamed it on her imaginary companion, Cousin Halifax. "It wasn't me, it was Cousin Halifax," she told her nanny virtuously.

Marion Crawford

Marion Crawford, nicknamed "Crawfie", was the governess for Princesses Elizabeth and Margaret in their youth. A Scotswoman with a degree from Edinburgh University, she ruled the two young ladies with a firm but serene hand. She left the Royal Family shortly after the end of World War II, receiving a pension, a grace-and-favour cottage, and a number of royal mementoes.

She married Scots banker Major George Buthley in 1947 and shortly thereafter began writing *The Little Princesses*, the first "below stairs" revelation about the Royal Family, as well as a regular column about the Royal Family for *Woman's Own*. The book was a best-seller, and Crawfie was never mentioned again by any of the royals.

Crisp

Crisp had been valet to the Prince of Wales and went along with him to Buckingham Palace when he became King Edward VIII in 1936. After his abdication at the end of that year, the Duke of Windsor assumed Crisp would accompany him into private life in France. Crisp refused, later saying, "He gave up his job, I gave up mine." Crisp stayed on at the Palace to serve the new King, George VI, and remained with him until the King's death in 1952.

The Crown Estate

The Crown Estate is property that belongs not to the monarch privately but to the British Sovereign as a hereditary part of the

Crown. In 1987 it was revealed that the Crown Estate was worth £1.277million. The income from the Crown Estate goes to the British government, and in return the Royal Family receives the allowances on the Civil List.

The Crown Estate is probably Britain's biggest landlord. It owns more than 170,000 acres of agricultural land in England, nearly 100,000 in Scotland, and about 1,000 acres in Wales. There are slate quarries, clay pits, tin mines, and gold and silver rights. The Crown Estate owns prime property in London, including office buildings in Oxford Street, shops in Regent Street, the architecturally glorious Nash Terraces outside Regent's Park, the Haymarket Theatre and the Strand Palace Hotel. London rents in 1986 totalled more than £27 million.

Prince Charles has announced that it is his hope, when he comes to the throne, to relinquish all Civil List income and live on the income from the Crown Estate. "The Royal Family must have money. If they have to look to the state for everything, they become nothing more than puppets and prisoners in their own countries. That's what happened to the Japanese royal family. They can't even go on holiday without asking Parliament."

The Crown Jewels

The Crown Jewels are kept in the Tower of London, under the guardianship of the Keeper of the Jewel House. They symbolize the continuity of the monarchy and play an important part in the ritual of coronation. Most of the present Crown Jewels date from the time of King Charles II or later, since the earlier ones were all broken up or sold during Cromwell's republic. Among the most significant of the Crown Jewels are the Imperial State Crown, St. Edward's Crown, the Golden Orb, the Sceptre with the Cross, the Coronation Ring, and the Anointing Spoon. The most recent additions to the coronation regalia are the golden bracelets made for Queen Elizabeth II as a gift from the Commonwealth.

Crown Matrimonial

Crown Matrimonial is a play about the romance of King Edward VIII and Wallis Simpson. It ran successfully on the London stage for many months. The Queen Mother attended it one evening, and thereafter amused members of the family with her own imitation of the actress who played her.

Crowned Queen of Scots

Not long after Queen Elizabeth's coronation in Westminster Abbey, she participated in a service at St. Giles Cathedral in Edinburgh, in which she received the Crown of Scotland, an ancient piece of royal regalia that was supposedly made for Robert Bruce.

The Cunard Queens

The Cunard Line has operated three famous ships named after English Queens. The *Queen Mary* was launched on 26 September 1934, and sailed to America on her maiden voyage two years later. She was the first ship to exceed seventy-five thousand tons, and made regularly scheduled trips across the North Atlantic. Her sister ship the *Queen Elizabeth* was launched four years later, the largest ocean liner ever built.

By the time she was fully tested and fitted, Word War II had begun, and both *Queens* were pressed into military service as troop ships. Together, they transported over one and a half million soldiers during the war; Prime Minister Winston Churchill said of them, "The *Queens* helped to win the war in Europe by at least a year." In the 1950s both ships continued to serve as luxury liners for trans-Atlantic crossings,

Courtesy of Cunard.

The Cunard liner *Queen Elizabeth 2*.

and passengers included such royals as Queen Elizabeth (when she was still a Princess), The Queen Mother, and the Duke and Duchess of Windsor. The *Queen Mary* was retired in 1967, and the *Queen Elizabeth* followed a year later.

In 1969 Cunard announced the maiden voyage of the new *Queen Elizabeth 2*, or the *QE2* as she is popularly called. Slightly smaller but more powerful than her sister, she can just make it through the Panama Canal and thus can cruise anywhere in the world. The *QE2* followed the tradition of wartime service, taking British troops to the Falklands in 1982. In 1986, the ship underwent a complete refurbishing designed to take her well into the twenty-first century.

Curtsey

The Queen never curtseys to anyone; sovereigns do not bow to one another. Princes and princesses of royal blood do not curtsey or bow to one another, but they do make the gesture to sovereigns. (Even, it seems, deposed ones; ex-King Constantine of Greece, for example, gets curtseys from English princesses.) To be correct, all royals should curtsey or bow to The Queen when they meet in public, but close relatives often omit that observance. British subjects curtsey or bow when presented to members of the Royal Family. Foreigners may do the same but are not considered disrespectful if they choose not to. The safest rule about curtseying is: when in doubt, do it.

Cyclax

Cyclax is a shop in London that makes skin-care products favoured by The Queen. Based on natural ingredients such as milk, honey and plant extracts, the cosmetics are made according to old Viennese formulas and packaged in elegant purple and silver wrappings. Although Cyclax of course can't take credit for creating The Queen's wonderful creamy complexion, sales of the products used by The Queen are brisk.

Czar Nicholas II

Czar Nicholas II of Russia was a grandchild of Queen Victoria and thus a cousin of King George V. The two men were strikingly similar in appearance and were occasionally confused with one another. "Nicky" married Princess Alix of Hesse, another of Victoria's grandchildren, who became the Czarina Alexandra. King George V was outraged when he heard of the execution of his cousins by the Bolsheviks, and thereafter told his prime minister "how abhorrent it would be to His Majesty to receive any representative of Russia who, directly or indirectly, had been connected with the abominable murder of the Emperor, Empress and their family, the King's own first cousins".

Princes Harry and William watch their father play polo at Cirencester Park, Gloucestershire.

D

D-Day

When a date was set for D-Day, the start of the 1944 invasion of occupied France by combined Allied forces during World War II, George VI let it be known that he thought it would be appropriate for the King to accompany the first wave of invading British troops. Winston Churchill, the Prime Minister, also wanted to go with the first troops. Both planned to go until they realized that if anything were to happen, they would risk leaving the country with a new sovereign and a new prime minister in wartime. In the end they both decided to remain behind. The King did, however, visit troops behind the front lines.

Evelyn Dagley

Evelyn Dagley is Princess Diana's dresser. At home or away, her job is to lay out the Princess's clothes, help her to make a choice, and then make sure the clothes go on without wrinkles or problems. For big evenings, she helps the Princess into her ball gowns and makes sure the right tiara is laid out. When she travels, Diana wears costume jewellery much of the time, considerably reducing the worries of her dresser.

Daily Life of King George V

According to a biography of King George V written by Kenneth Rose in 1985, the daily life of the King was exemplary in its dullness. Alastaire Cooke summed it up in a review:

> He awoke at seven, bathed, trimmed his beard and anointed it
> with lavender water, dressed impeccably in the suit or

uniform that the protocol of the morning required, descended
to tap the barometer, worked on state papers, wrote up his
diary, read through *The Times*, and sat down to breakfast on
the stroke of nine. Thereafter, he received Ambassadors,
Ministers, and such, and walked exactly a mile round the
Palace garden before lunching with the Queen at one-thirty
sharp. Afterward, he slept in an armchair for precisely 15
minutes, fulfilled the afternoon's engagements, and spent an
hour with his stamp collection (which came to be among the
most comprehensive and valuable in the world). In the early
evening, after an hour or more with the dispatch boxes, he
retired to put on his white tie and tails and the Garter star
before dinner with the family. A little reading, a patriotic
tune or two on the gramophone on festive evenings, and at
ten minutes past eleven, he was on his way to bed.

Daily Telegraph Crossword Puzzle

One of The Queen's favourite ways of relaxing is to do the crossword
puzzle in the *Daily Telegraph*.

Richard Dalton

Richard Dalton is the hairdresser who began to tend Princess Diana's
locks in 1984. His first coiffure for the Princess was an upswept style
rolled over her tiara that proved to be unpopular with the public and
was not repeated. Later, he cut her hair shorter, making it easier to
manage and to style, a boon for a busy royal who must make many
public appearances, often with little time in the schedule for
freshening up.

Dancing Lessons

Mrs. Andrée Monzi, nicknamed "Didi", taught The Queen to dance.
One day in 1934, she and Madame Vacani, the owner of the dancing
school in which Mrs. Monzi was employed, were summoned to the
London home of the Duke and Duchess of York and asked to teach a
small dancing class for ten children, including the young Princesses
Elizabeth and Margaret. "We weren't aiming to turn them into
ballerinas," Didi has recalled, "though Margaret would have made a
brilliant tap dancer and mimic. They were lovely children ... so fair-
haired and with such beautiful skin and blue eyes, and such beautiful
manners too. The Queen was not the quiet little mouse some people

seem to think she was. She had a depth of character and the ability to persevere in her studies. She also had quite a temper, you know, although she managed to keep it well under control." Didi says the main point of the dancing lessons was to teach deportment and the social graces. "Elizabeth was the more serious. Margaret learned so quickly and had such style!"

Zita Davisson

The only American ever commissioned to paint a portrait of Princess Diana, Zita Davisson is an internationally acclaimed artist whose subjects have included Gloria Vanderbilt, Princess Grace and Liza

Zita Davisson, with her portrait of the Princess of Wales.

Studio Nine photo courtesy of Zita Davisson.

Minnelli. For her sitting with the Princess of Wales, Zita suggested the regal style that has typified the British Royal Family for centuries. The Princess sits in a classic pose before crimson drapes that frame a coat of arms the artist copied from a portrait of a seventeenth-century Princess of Wales. The painting is now in the American collection of the Daughters of the British Empire.

Lord Dawson

Lord Dawson was the physician in attendance on King George V for the last few weeks of his life. The King suffered from recurrent bronchial trouble, complicated at the end by a weakened heart. On the night of 20 January 1936, Lord Dawson saw that the King was near death; he released a bulletin stating, "The King's life is moving peacefully towards its close."

Over fifty years later, Lord Dawson's private papers revealed that, shortly after writing the bulletin, the King's physician hastened that movement towards the close by injecting the King with fatal doses of cocaine and morphine. A long-time believer in euthanasia, Dawson hastened the King's death to spare him any further suffering and to allow the news to be carried by the morning papers.

Philip Delaney

Philip Delaney is a grocer in Gloucestershire who sells chocolate mints of which The Queen Mother is especially fond. For seventeen years in a row, Her Majesty has stopped off at Delaney's shop on her way to the Cheltenham races to pick up a box of these sweets.

The Diary of The Queen

Since her girlhood, The Queen has kept a diary. One of the early volumes is on public view, turned to the page where she wrote about her parents' coronation day. Nowadays she writes in a leather-bound volume that she keeps by her bedside. The collection of diaries will be a valuable addition to the Royal Archives.

Dinner with Princess Michael

The Tatler ran a feature that asked a number of well-known people, among them Viscount Linley, Princess Margaret's son, what they would give their worst enemy for Christmas. Linley answered without a moment's hesitation, "Dinner with Princess Michael".

Dinner with the Roosevelts

In the spring of 1939, King George VI and Queen Elizabeth paid a visit to America. Their dinner at the White House, at the invitation of President and Mrs. Roosevelt, got off to an odd start when the Roosevelts began to serve tea—at eight o'clock in the evening, before dinner. Catching the King's quizzical expression, the President explained, "My mother doesn't approve of cocktails." The King smiled broadly and replied, "Neither does my mother." Both men then ordered drinks.

The drinks tray was brought by a butler, who lost his footing as he entered the door and then slid across the room on his backside, scattering drinks as he went. Later, a serving table collapsed, and a number of priceless dishes were smashed. The Queen, as usual, was smiling and composed. After the ordeal was over, the butler returned to the kitchen and told the staff about "that honeychile, Mrs. Queen".

Dog Leads

According to one of the favourite stories told by Palace insiders, Prince Charles once took his dog out for a walk at Windsor and came home without the dog's lead. When she learned of the matter, The Queen sent her son back out again to find the missing lead. "Dog leads cost money," she said firmly.

Isley Donald

Isley Donald was an interior designer and a friend of Lady Edwina Mountbatten who undertook the renovation and decoration of Clarence House when it was prepared as a home for Princess Elizabeth and Prince Philip in 1947, after the damage from wartime bombing. Donald did much of the house in the pastel greens and aquamarines that were the choice of Princess Elizabeth. He later revealed that one of his most difficult jobs was to satisfy Philip's demand that the kitchen have the same lighting as the dining room, so the food would look as good when it got to the table as it did when it was being prepared. The redecoration was financed by £50,000 allotted by the House of Commons. It was finished in the summer of 1949, when Princess Elizabeth, Prince Philip and Prince Charles moved in.

Dorgis

Queen Elizabeth has cross-bred her own corgis with a dachshund called Pipkin that belongs to Princess Margaret. The offspring are called dorgis and are even lower to the ground than the sturdy corgis. Several generations of dorgis are now running about the Palace.

Sir Alec Douglas-Home

Sir Alec Douglas-Home was the fourth prime minister of Queen Elizabeth's reign. He was chosen for the post in late 1963, after Harold Macmillan's resignation for reasons of health. (Macmillan later recovered from his prostate operation with no complications and began to regret his decision to resign.) To serve as Prime Minister, Douglas-Home had to renounce his title of Earl of Home to become plain Sir Alec. The Queen and Douglas-Home had in common the fact that they had both been taught by Sir Henry Marten, and Douglas-Home's family was friendly with The Queen Mother's Scottish relations. He remained in office less than a year. In 1974 he was made a life peer, taking the title Lord Home of the Hirsel.

The Drink of Choice

These are the favourite drinks of the Royal Family:

The Queen	barley water; Moselle wine; champagne
Prince Philip	pink gin; beer at lunch
Prince Charles	champagne; dry white wine
Princess Diana	gin with lots of tonic
Duke of York	ginger ale and Perrier
Duchess of York	white wine spritzer
Queen Mother	champagne; Scotch whisky
Princess Margaret	whisky and soda
Princess Anne	Coca-Cola

Drugs in the Palace

In the early 1930s, the Royal Family became unhappily aware that young Prince George, the Duke of Kent, had become addicted to drugs. Apparently he had been depressed over a love affair that ended badly, and he turned to drugs for consolation. When he valiantly tried to break his addiction on his own, the result was a nervous breakdown. At this point his oldest brother, the Prince of Wales, intervened. The future King Edward VIII whisked the Duke of Kent away to his country house, Fort Belvedere, and stayed there with him, supervising his complete withdrawal from all drugs, until he was cured. Only a few months later, George met Princess Marina of Greece, and soon they were engaged. The Duke of Kent had no further problems with drugs.

Duchess Denied "Her Royal Highness"

Only members of the Royal Family may use the title of Her (or His) Royal Highness. It was a style of address that the Duchess of Windsor coveted, and the Duke wanted it for her as well. The Duke, as the son of a King and a former King himself, was of course called HRH the Duke of Windsor. The Duchess, however, had no automatic right by marriage to that title; it would have to be conferred on her by the King, George VI. He chose not to do so, to the lifelong distress of the Windsors. The Duke did his best to compensate for it by himself never failing to refer to his wife as Her Royal Highness.

Her Royal Highness the Duchess of Gloucester

Birgitte Eva van Deurs was born on 20 June 1946, in Odense, Denmark, the younger daughter of a Danish lawyer and his wife. She

Courtesy of the British Information Service.

The Duke and Duchess of Gloucester.

was educated first in Denmark and then at finishing schools in Lausanne and Cambridge. While at Cambridge, she met the younger son of the Duke of Gloucester. Their engagement was announced in early 1972, when she was working as a secretary at the Royal Danish Embassy in London. Shortly after their marriage in July of that year, her husband unexpectedly became heir to the Duke of Gloucester when his older brother was killed in a plane crash.

The Duchess of Gloucester undertakes many official engagements. She is Colonel-in-Chief of the Royal Army Education Corps; Chief Patron of the Women Caring Trust, which helps children in Northern Ireland; President of the Royal Alexandra and Albert School; and patron or president of a host of organizations. She and the Duke have three children: Alexander Patrick Gregers Richard, the Earl of Ulster, born in 1974; Lady Davina Windsor, born in 1977; and Lady Rose Windsor, born in 1980.

The Duchess of Grafton

The Duchess of Grafton is The Queen's Mistress of the Robes. Her duties include supervising all eleven of the ladies-in-waiting and attending The Queen on state occasions, such as the opening of Parliament and visits to foreign heads of state. The Duchess, born Fortune Smith, the daughter of the chairman of Rolls Royce, was appointed a lady of the bedchamber at the time of Elizabeth's coronation in 1953, and she took over as Mistress of the Robes in 1977. For her special services to The Queen, she was made a Dame of the Royal Victorian Order. In addition to carrying out official responsibilities, the Duchess is also one of The Queen's personal friends. She and her husband live at their Norfolk estate, Euston Hall. Three of her children have godparents who are members of the Royal Family.

Her Royal Highness the Duchess of Kent

The Duchess of Kent was born Miss Katherine Worsley, to a family of Yorkshire landowners. In 1961 Miss Worsley (friends call her Kathy) married the Duke, who had succeeded to the title at the age of seven, when his father was killed in a wartime plane crash. The three children of the Kents are George, the Earl of St. Andrews (born in 1962); Lady Helen Windsor (1964); and Lord Nicholas Windsor (1970).

The Duchess has struggled with health problems, such as a slipped disc and gall-bladder surgery, and with psychiatric problems that seem to have started when she had a miscarriage in 1977. Her own difficulties have increased her sympathy for suffering in others, and she serves as Royal Patron of Age Concern, the British Epilepsy Association, the Samaritans, and the Spastics Society. A hardworking royal, she is especially good at meeting children and the elderly.

The Duchess of Windsor

The Duchess of Windsor was born Bessiewallis Warfield, daughter of Mr. and Mrs. Teakle Wallis Warfield of Blue Ridge Summit, Pennsylvania, on 19 July 1896. Her father died of tuberculosis six months later, leaving her and her mother in somewhat straitened circumstances. Detractors like to claim that her mother operated a boarding house, but it was certainly a respectable establishment, and young Wallis, as she had decided to be known, made her debut in exclusive Baltimore society.

In 1916 Wallis married aviator Earl Winfield Spencer Jr., who was described as "the catch of the season", but his heavy drinking soon ended the marriage. Her second husband was an Anglo-American, Ernest Aldrich Simpson, and she moved with him to London, where he worked as a shipping broker. There she met the Prince of Wales in the early 1930s, and the romance that thrilled the world began.

After her marriage to the ex-King in 1937, Wallis became the Duchess of Windsor. She and the Duke travelled constantly, and during World War II lived in the Bahamas, where he served as Governor-General. Eventually they made their permanent home in a charming house in the Bois de Boulogne, leased from the French government for a token payment.

After her husband died in 1972, the Duchess was finally received by The Queen at Buckingham Palace. When the funeral was over, she returned to France and lived on alone for another fourteen years. In the last few years of her life, she was confined to bed and virtually unaware of her surroundings. She died on 24 April 1986, and was laid to rest beside her husband in the Royal Family vault at Windsor.

The Duchess of Windsor's Jewellery

In 1987 Sotheby's held an auction of jewellery that had belonged to the Duchess of Windsor; it was later called "The Sale of the Century". The jewellery had been left, along with most of the rest of the

Duchess's estate, to the Louis Pasteur Institute in Paris. (A few pieces had already been willed away by the Duchess; she gave something to Princess Alexandra, and a few pieces to Princess Michael of Kent, who ingenuously addressed her as "Your Royal Highness" and also called her "Dear Aunt Wallis".) Although the Duke had expressed the wish that his wife's jewellery should be broken up after her death, so that no other woman could wear it, the Pasteur Institute realized it could bring more money intact.

Although the auction was held in Geneva in early April, the jewels were on display in London and New York several weeks earlier. The catalogue of the sale cost £25, and crowds queued for up to five hours to view the exhibition. Some of the jewels were so theatrical that when the Duchess wore them, people assumed they were costume jewellery; many of them were inscribed to suit a romantic occasion or a sentimental feeling.

Among the pieces that drew special attention from the oohing and aahing throngs were:

- The nineteen-carat emerald engagement ring, inscribed "We are ours now", given to Wallis by the King as soon as her divorce from her second husband was final
- Two canary-yellow diamond lapel clips, with earrings to match; the Duchess was especially fond of this colour of diamonds.
- Intertwined ruby and diamond feathers
- Cartier tiger and panther bracelets, so flexible that they bend with each movement of the wearer
- The forty-nine-carat "King of Spain" emerald pendant, meant to hang from a diamond and emerald necklace that one observer called "more minerology than jewellery"
- A ruby and diamond flamingo brooch
- The charm bracelet with jewelled crosses she always wore; she explained, "The crosses are crosses I've had to bear"
- The sapphire and diamond cuff she wore at her wedding, set with forty-five very fine sapphires

The auction was a greater success than anyone had anticipated. The jewels, appraised at nearly £2 million, brought ten times their value, as women all over the world fought to own a memorable piece. Even the insignificant was valuable if it had belonged to the Duchess. A necklace that the auctioneer meticulously pointed out was only imitation pearls and diamonds immediately sold for more than £30,000! After all, the Duchess's jewels were, in their own way, crown jewels—the jewels a King gave to the woman he loved.

Soon after the auction, alert gossip columnists began to spot the
jewels adorning the new owners. Elizabeth Taylor bought a diamond
pin in the shape of Prince of Wales feathers. According to gossip,
Princess Diana had wanted it too but was outbid by the Queen of
Hollywood, who phoned in from beside a swimming pool in California
the winning £384,770 figure. She said she wanted it as a memento of
the friendship she and Richard Burton had had with the Windsors.
Designer Calvin Klein paid over £600,000 for two pearl necklaces for
his new wife Kelly. He considered them a bargain, because Van Cleef
& Arpels had told him it would take at least that much money, plus as
many as ten years of waiting, for them to match up a new necklace of
similarly large pearls. Socialite Mercedes Kellogg got the flamingo
from her new love, oil-rich Sid Bass. The emerald engagement ring
(from Cartier) brought the sum of £1,222,222 from a British jeweller
who bought it as an anniversary present for his wife. The Duchess's
simple platinum wedding band brought nearly £93,000. The thirty-
one-carat McLean diamond was purchased by a Japanese jeweller for
the staggering sum of £1,944,444, motivated by what he said was a
mixture of romance and commerce.

The Duchess of Windsor's Trousseau

According to reports published just weeks before Wallis Simpson
married the Duke of Windsor, her trousseau included one hundred
new summer outfits. News media contrasted this with a total of forty
new outfits ordered for the season by The Queen and twenty-five by
the fashionable Marina, Duchess of Kent. The trousseau contained
fourteen evening gowns ("simple and smart and made along flowing
lines"), including two short-skirted dance frocks; seven afternoon
dresses, mostly in print fabrics with high necks and medium-length
sleeves; five tailored suits of pale tweeds worn with matching crepe
blouses; several short-sleeved linen dresses with simple lines in light
colours for very hot weather; four beach costumes with matching
shorts; an evening coat of white ribbed ottoman silk trimmed with
sable; and a luxurious lamé house gown made with a long-trained
skirt (the train was lined in Wallis blue) buttoning down the front and
worn open to the knees, along with a chic little gold-trimmed jacket.

Her Royal Highness the Duchess of York

Sarah Margaret Ferguson was born on 15 October 1959 at the
Welbeck Nursing Home in London. She was the second child of Major
Ronald Ferguson and his wife Susan; her sister Jane is two years older.

The Duke and Duchess of York leaving the balcony at Buckingham Palace for their wedding breakfast.

Sarah grew up at Dummer Down, the Ferguson family home in the lush Hampshire countryside, riding her pony in gymkhanas and cuddling her favourite toy, Mr. Rabbit. Her father was an avid polo player, who had played with Prince Philip before Sarah was born. Appointed Escort Commander of the Sovereign's Escort of the Household Cavalry, he was jokingly called "The Polo Stick in Waiting". Sarah first met Prince Andrew when she was only four years old, at a polo match in which both their fathers were playing.

When Sarah was thirteen, her mother eloped with Argentinean polo player Hector Barrantes, an event Major Ferguson later reservedly described as "a bit of a fright". Their divorce followed three years later, and thereafter Major Ferguson married a fresh-faced Norfolk farmer's daughter, Susan Deptford. The scandal died down, and Sarah's parents were able to treat one another with distant civility. Sarah began to spend time in Argentina with her mother and stepfather, and seemed to blossom.

Sarah attended Sunninghill, near Ascot, and then Hurst Lodge school. After a brief period at a secretarial school, she worked as a secretary for a public relations firm, Durden Smith Communications; as assistant to an art dealer in Covent Garden; and as executive editor of a printing and publishing firm, BCK Graphic Arts in Hanover Square.

It was when she worked for the art dealer that she got to know Princess Diana, and the two women became friends. Rumour has it that Diana was the matchmaker who reintroduced Sarah to Prince Andrew and subsequently did all she could to encourage the match. Andy and Fergie announced their engagement in the winter of 1986, and were married on 23 July of that year. They divide their time between a suite in Buckingham Palace and their temporary country home, Chideock. Sarah, who became the Duchess of York on her marriage, continued her work at Graphic Arts in addition to assuming her royal duties.

Duchy of Cornwall

The Duchy of Cornwall has traditionally been the source of income for the Sovereign's son, the Prince of Wales, since the time of the first Duke of Cornwall in 1337. Prince Charles is the twenty-fifth Duke, and he has been receiving the Duchy's income since his twenty-first birthday. Unlike his brothers and sister, he receives no income from the Civil List.

The Duchy owns vast acreage in Cornwall, as well as in Devon, Somerset and Dorset. But its most lucrative property is forty-five acres of south London, including The Oval cricket ground. The Duchy's oddest holding is Dartmoor Prison and the surrounding moorland, and its oddest source of income is the right to demand an annual payment of three hundred puffins from the residents of the Scilly Isles. Altogether, the estate produces an annual income of more than a million pounds, of which Prince Charles keeps three-quarters and gives the other quarter to the Treasury as a self-imposed income tax.

Duchy of Lancaster

The Duchy of Lancaster is an estate owned personally by The Queen, from which she derives an annual income in excess of £1.5 million. It includes large pieces of land not only in Lancashire but also Yorkshire, Lincolnshire, Cheshire and Staffordshire. In London, the Duchy owns the ground on which the Savoy Hotel is built. The affairs of the

Duchy are managed for The Queen by a junior cabinet minister, but she makes a ceremonial visit to some part of the estate every year, to be greeted by the toast, "To The Queen, the Duke of Lancaster".

The Duke of Beaufort

For forty-two years, the late Duke of Beaufort was the Royal Master of the Horse. Sir Henry Hugh Arthur Fitzroy Somerset succeeded to the title in 1924, married a niece of Queen Mary, and has been a close friend of the Royal Family for decades. A devoted horseman, the Duke opens the grounds of his elegant Palladian estate, Badminton, every year for the Badminton Trials. Among his hereditary distinctions is the fact that he is the last descendant of the Plantagenet kings.

His Royal Highness the Duke of Gloucester

Richard Alexander Walter George, the current Duke of Gloucester, was born on 26 August 1944, the younger son of the previous Duke, the grandson of King George V. He was educated first at home, then at Eton and Cambridge, where he studied architecture. After receiving his degree, he joined a firm of architectural consultants. When his older brother William died in a plane crash during a 1972 air race, Richard unexpectedly inherited the title. He now spends much of his time managing the family estate at Barnwell, and acts as patron for a number of organizations that preserve and celebrate Britain's architectural heritage. In 1970 he married Birgitte van Deurs, who worked at the London Embassy of her native Denmark. They have three children: Alexander, the Earl of Ulster, born in 1974; Lady Davina Windsor, born in 1977; and Lady Rose Windsor, born in 1980.

The Duke of Gloucester is President of the Society of Architects-Artists, and has published three books on the subject of architecture under the name "Richard Gloucester": *On Public View* (1970); *The Face of London* (1973), and *Oxford and Cambridge* (1980). He is a Fellow of the Royal Society of Arts and Colonel-in-Chief of the Gloucester Regiment.

The Duke of Grafton

The Duke of Grafton, Hugh Euston, was part of the Buckingham Palace set during Princess Elizabeth's girlhood. One of his assignments during World War II was to help guard the heir to the throne at Windsor. Thanks in large part to his rather dashing personality, there were many rumours in the mid 1940s that Hugh was one of the

Princess's suitors. In truth they were really "just friends". The friendship has endured over the years and has extended to Hugh's wife Fortune, who became the Queen's Mistress of the Robes.

His Royal Highness the Duke of Kent

The Duke of Kent is a personal *aide-de-camp* to The Queen, a Colonel in the Scots Guards, and a Major General of nothing (the official label is "supernumerary"). Edward George Nicholas Paul Patrick was born on 9 October 1935, the eldest child of George, Duke of Kent (younger brother of Edward VIII and George VI) and Princess Marina of Greece. When his father was killed in a plane crash during World War II, Edward, usually called Ted, inherited the title at the tender age of seven. He and his sister, Princess Alexandra, and brother, Prince Michael of Kent, were brought up simply and rather spartanly (in royal terms, anyway) by their mother at Coppins, the family home in Buckinghamshire. Edward later went to school at Eton and then Le Rosey in Switzerland. Later he entered the Royal Military College at Sandhurst.

The Duke married Miss Katharine Worsley on 8 June 1961, at York Minster. They have three children: George Philip Nicholas, the Earl of

The Duke and Duchess of Kent in 1985.

Photo by Norman Parkinson, courtesy of the British Information Service.

St. Andrews (born in 1962); Lady Helen Windsor (1964); and Lord Nicholas Windsor (1970). The Duke, who always intended to have a career in the Army, rose to the rank of Lieutenant-Colonel and commanded a unit in Northern Ireland. He left the Army in 1971, after he was relieved of his command for security reasons.

The Duke of Kent is widely regarded as the Royal Family's best soldier. He is still a Lieutenant-Colonel in the Royal Scots Dragoon Guards, Colonel of the Scots Guards, and Colonel-in-Chief of the Royal Regiment of Fusiliers. He usually accompanies his cousin The Queen when she attends the annual ceremony of Trooping the Colour. After the Duke gave up the army as a full-time career, he had to sell the family home because he could no longer afford its upkeep. He and the Duchess now live in Anmer Hall, a residence at Sandringham offered them by The Queen. He serves as Vice-Chairman of the British Overseas Trade Board and President of the Royal National Lifeboat Institution. He is the Chancellor of Surrey University, a Knight of the Garter, and the Patron of the Kent Opera.

His Royal Highness the Duke of York

Prince Andrew Albert Christian Edward is the third child and second son of Queen Elizabeth and the Duke of Edinburgh. Born on 19 February 1960, he was the first of the The Queen's children to be born after she ascended the throne. He and his younger brother Prince Edward had a more relaxed upbringing than Prince Charles and Princess Anne, the older children of the family. Prince Andrew started his education at home, then went to Heatherdown Preparatory School and later Gordonstoun.

As a child, Andrew had something of a reputation for naughty pranks, such as sliding down the Palace stairs on a silver tray, putting bubbles in the swimming pool at Windsor Castle, and tying together the shoelaces of hapless royal servants. As he got older, his naughtiness took on a different character. On the night of the fireworks for The Queen's Silver Jubilee, it was reported that he got so drunk he had to be carried to bed. His escapades with members of the opposite sex were memorialized in his nickname, "Randy Andy".

Prince Andrew joined the Royal Navy in 1979 and fought in the Falklands War two years later. He took photography lessons from Lord Snowdon, and a book of his photographs was published in 1985. He is godfather to Zara Phillips and Prince Harry of Wales, and he acted as his brother Charles's supporter at his wedding to Lady Diana Spencer. Andrew himself married on 23 July 1986 at Westminster Abbey. His bride was the former Miss Sarah Ferguson. Because of his continuing naval career, Prince Andrew undertakes relatively few royal duties.

Philip Dunne

Philip Dunne is a young, rich and handsome investment banker, the godson of Princess Alexandra, whose name was linked in gossip columns with that of Princess Diana during the summer of 1987. Dunne is a friend of the Duchess of York from her skiing days at Verbier, Switzerland, and thus part of the social circle of the younger royals. The rumours started when Princess Diana danced with Dunne and several weeks later was his house guest in the country, without Prince Charles. Dunne vehemently denied all the rumours, as did his girlfriend, Katya Grenfell. The Palace maintained its customary refusal to comment on such subjects.

Dynasty

At a 1987 royal premiere, Joan Collins, who plays the vixenish Alexis in *Dynasty*, was introduced to several royals. Joan wore the pink gown created for Alexis to attend her son Adam's wedding at the end of the 1986-87 season and reported that The Queen Mother said she loved the TV soap. When asked if the Waleses were also fans, Joan said demurely, "That's a secret."

The Prince and Princess of Wales with their children, photographed by Lord Snowdon.

Prince William at his home in Kensington Palace.

E

The Earl of Harewood

The Earl of Harewood, George Lascelles, is the cousin of Queen Elizabeth. Born in 1923, he was the first child of the last Princess Royal, sister of King Edward VIII and King George VI, and her husband, the sixth Earl of Harewood. In a series of events considered somewhat embarrassing for the Royal Family in the mid 1960s, he divorced his first wife, concert pianist Marion Stein, and then had a child by the woman who was yet to become his second wife. He is a patron of the opera and classical music events. He published his memoirs, entitled *The Tongs and the Bones*, in 1981.

The Earl of St. Andrews

George Philip Nicholas, the Earl of St. Andrews, is the first son and oldest child of the Duke and Duchess of Kent, born on 26 June 1962. He attended Eton and Cambridge.

EastEnders

EastEnders is one of Princess Diana's favourite soap operas. In the evening, after the little Princes are tucked up in bed, she likes to relax and watch the machinations of Dirty Den, the scheming landlord. It is an enthusiasm no one else in the family shares. The Queen prefers American soaps, the Prince never watches such lowbrow stuff, and the Duchess of York prefers *Coronation Street*.

Easter

The Royal Family spends Easter at Windsor. They gather throughout the day on Saturday. On Saturday night, The Queen Mother entertains at the Royal Lodge, with drinks in front of a fire in the Octagon Room followed by a buffet in the dining room and dancing. On Easter Sunday there is a service in St. George's Chapel, and afterwards everyone goes to The Queen's private apartments for cocktails. Most of the royals find time for a ride in Windsor Park.

Paul Eddington

Paul Eddington is known to be a favourite actor of The Queen and The Queen Mother. He starred in the BBC comedy series *The Good Life*, which both Queens watched without fail during a recent re-run. He also starred in *Yes, Minister*, which is reputed to be The Queen's favourite TV programme.

Anthony Eden

Anthony Eden was the second prime minister of Queen Elizabeth's reign. A Conservative like his predecessor and father-in-law Winston Churchill, he was already in poor health when he assumed the office in 1956, and he remained there only fifteen months. He was Prime Minister during the Suez Canal crisis, which undermined Great Britain's world prestige and brought about his political downfall. Yet The Queen admired his gallant bearing throughout the difficulties, and when she learned he was to resign, she made the journey from Sandringham to London in order to spare him the trip to see her in person. After his resignation, she conferred on him the title of the Earl of Avon.

Edinburgh University

The ancient Edinburgh University is chancellored by the Duke of Edinburgh, who usually appears at the graduation ceremonies and hands out the honorary degrees.

Courtesy of Josiah Wedgwood & Sons.

A Wedgwood bust of The Queen Mother near the time of her eightieth birthday.

Eightieth Birthday of Queen Elizabeth The Queen Mother

On 4 August 1980, The Queen Mother celebrated her eightieth birthday. Privately, there were many happy celebrations. Publicly, there was the release of a glamorous photo by Norman Parkinson, showing The Queen, The Queen Mother and Princess Margaret all looking positively beautiful and amazingly radiant, with those famous complexions glowing with health and happiness. The official commemoration took place at St. Paul's Cathedral on 15 July and The Queen graciously insisted that her mother should occupy the place of honour and enter the Cathedral last. Escorted by her grandson Prince Charles, The Queen Mother mounted the steps and then waved once to the crowd outside before she entered St. Paul's.

The Archbishop of Canterbury gave an address, saying, "The Queen Mother has shown the human face of royalty." Most touching was the speech given by Prince Charles in tribute to his beloved grandmother: "Ever since I can remember, my grandmother has been the most wonderful example of fun, laughter, warmth, infinite security. For me she has always been one of those extraordinarily rare people whose touch can turn everything to gold."

Dr. Charles Elliott

Dr. Charles Elliott is a homeopathic physician who often treats the Royal Family. For The Queen's sinusitis he prescribes pills said to contain a touch of deadly nightshade. To suppress sneezing during a royal appearance, The Queen drinks Malvern water mixed with a homeopathic tonic that includes arsenic among its ingredients. Prince Charles is also treated by Dr. Elliott.

Elizabeth and David Emanuel

Elizabeth and David Emanuel were the designers, specialists in a romantic yet sensuous look, who created the wedding gown worn by Lady Diana Spencer. The hardest part of the job, they say, was keeping the design a secret until the wedding day. Reporters from all over the world were desperately trying for an advance look. The beleaguered Emanuels had to put all scraps of material from the dress in special bags to keep them away from rubbish-sifting newshounds, and also had to put a shade on the skylight in their workroom at their Brook Street couture salon.

Courtesy of Emanuel.

Elizabeth and David Emanuel.

The Emanuels, whose other clients include Bianca Jagger and actress Susan Hampshire, also made the daring black strapless taffeta dress Lady Diana wore on her first public engagement as the official fiancée of the Prince of Wales. Shortly after the tempest in a teapot about the cleavage of that dress, it was announced that the Emanuels would also make her wedding dress. They continue to design clothes for the Princess of Wales; for example, they created most of her wardrobe for her 1987 Gulf tour. In 1986, the Emanuels opened their first shop, at 10 Beauchamp Place, with a dazzling ready-to-wear collection made in their trademark romantic style.

The Enchanted Isles

The Enchanted Isles was a TV special about the Galapagos Islands, made for American television and later shown in Great Britain as well. It features Prince Philip talking about issues of conservation; reviewers agreed that he—and the film—were less than scintillating.

England II

England II is the polo team on which Prince Charles is a permanent player. The team was originally called "Young England", but as the players aged into their thirties, it was necessary to adopt a more accurate name.

Epiphany Service

Every year on 6 January, an Epiphany Service is held at St. George's Chapel in Windsor. Originally it marked the end of the Court's Christmas festivities; now it is simply ritual. The Queen offers gifts of gold, frankincense and myrrh to commemorate the Adoration of the Magi.

Evacuation

During World War II there was a continual question as to whether or not the Royal Family should be evacuated from the dangers of Great Britain, with the constant bombing and the threat of invasion. It was not only a question of their personal safety, but also of the continuity of the royal line and its symbolic value to the people of the country. Queen Wilhelmina of the Netherlands, for example, left her palace as soon as the German invasion began, taking Crown Princess Juliana to safety in Canada. Why shouldn't the English Royal Family do the same?

King George VI resolutely refused to "desert" his people in their time of danger. Queen Elizabeth would not leave without the King. And as she explained many times about the two Princesses, "The children could not go without me, and I could not possibly leave the King." Thus the entire Royal Family stayed in England for the duration of the war.

Oliver Everett

Oliver Everett was private secretary to the Princess of Wales. He is perhaps best known for the moment when, visiting Nepal, he mounted an elephant for a thunderous game of polo. He is now Assistant Keeper of The Queen's Archives at Windsor Castle.

F

Fabergé

Carl Fabergé was a Russian master craftsman at the Russian court. Queen Alexandra, whose sister Dagmar married the Czar in 1866, was a great collector of Fabergé objects. Once, as a surprise present, her husband, King Edward VII, commissioned Fabergé to make little jewel-encrusted golden sculptures of all the animals at Sandringham, including the Queen's favourite dogs. For some reason, the Fabergé collection is now in the basement of Buckingham Palace. According to one report, it was found there by Princess Michael of Kent when she was looking for discarded furniture from the Palace that she might use in her own home. She told a friend, "If I could just get my hands on one of those eggs, we'd be rich."

Face Lift

According to insider gossip, the Duchess of Windsor had one face lift too many. Although plastic surgeons had warned against another operation at her age because of the effects of anaesthesia on people over seventy, she insisted on going ahead with one last lift—it was, after all, the face of a woman for whom a King gave up his throne. During the surgery, there was rumoured to be some technical difficulty with the anaesthesia, and the air to the Duchess's brain was briefly cut off. This was said to be the cause of the subsequent failure of her mental faculties.

Michael Fagan

In 1982, an intruder named Michael Fagan slipped into the Queen's bedroom in Buckingham Palace. He had climbed over the wall in the early morning and then entered the palace through an unlocked window in the room where King George V's valuable stamp collection is kept. At about 7 a.m., he entered The Queen's bedroom and woke her up. The Queen calmly kept him talking until first a maid, then a young footman, and finally a contingent of policemen came to her rescue. Later, there was an enquiry into the lax security at the Palace that allowed the intruder to get in so easily and that failed to respond to flashing alarm lights and two telephone calls from The Queen asking for help. Fagan himself was released for treatment.

Fainting Spell

In May 1986, as the Prince and Princess of Wales were touring the World's Fair in Vancouver, Diana's knees buckled, and she suddenly fainted. After the first gasps of horror, it was obvious that no serious harm had come to the Princess. Then the rumours immediately started that she was pregnant with a third child. Her press secretary later announced, "She gave no warning to her entourage that she was feeling unwell. It was simply a matter of being too warm. A lot of people were feeling faint. But she's not pregnant." Time proved that statement to be truthful, and the fainting spell must be blamed on the heat, jet lag and a hectic schedule.

Teresa Fairminder

Teresa Fairminder, a professional make-up artist, helped prepare Sarah Ferguson to face the cameras—and her groom—on her wedding day. She used a light coat of foundation to tone down, but not hide, Sarah's freckles, and a light soft lip colour that would not clash with her gorgeous red hair.

False Alarm at Sandringham

In January 1970 it was arranged that The Queen would report a fire to the nearby King's Lynn fire brigade, to provide them with a realistic drill. Once the alarm was raised, seventy firemen on ten engines sped to Sandringham, where they sprayed water on the lawn while the Queen's delighted children watched with glee the result of their mother's false alarm.

Matthew Farrer

Sir Matthew Farrer, knighted in 1985, is the Queen's solicitor. Among the problems he has handled discreetly for the Royal Family were Princess Margaret's divorce, the attempts by the German press to publish transcripts of conversations between Prince Charles and his then-fiancée Lady Diana Spencer, and the prosecution of Michael Fagan, the intruder in the Queen's bedroom.

Fashion for Footmen

At Buckingham Palace, the footmen, always in attendance, wear scarlet uniforms trimmed with gold braid, knee breeches and pink stockings.

"Fat Scotch Cook"

When the Duke of York married Lady Elizabeth Bowes-Lyon in 1923, his brother the Prince of Wales seemed quite fond of his new sister-in-law, and indeed there were rumours that Elizabeth had initially been attracted to him rather than his brother. A pleasant friendship between the in-laws ensued until Edward VIII abdicated in 1936, making his brother the new king. Queen Elizabeth was distressed and angry, deep sentiments that came from her desire to protect her shy and retiring husband. She made some unflattering remarks about the new Duchess of Windsor that got back to the Duke's ears and in turn angered him. Thereafter, he cruelly referred to Queen Elizabeth as "that fat Scotch cook".

Favourite Foods

The Queen is known to prefer simple English food, plainly prepared. Give her a nice Dover sole, some fresh salmon from Scotland or a saddle of lamb, and she is perfectly happy. Her breakfast is usually light, toast and a boiled egg and white coffee with sugar. The chef is instructed never to add garlic to the royal food, and herbs and spices of any kind must be used with a sparing hand. The Queen may drink her favourite Malvern water, a gin and tonic that is almost entirely tonic, or a little pink vermouth with soda. To keep her waistline trim she avoids heavy desserts, but she does like to nibble on chocolate mints that come from Bendick's, a tea shop on Sloane Street.

The Prince and Princess of Wales eat a largely vegetarian diet when they are at home, preferring fresh vegetables, grilled fish, and the occasional egg or piece of cheese. On this spartan regimen, both stay slim and trim. Charles is known to have a taste for champagne, whereas Diana prefers non-alcoholic drinks, especially a tall glass of tonic. She does, however, have a sweet tooth, which she attempts to discipline, and has been known to indulge in Kit-Kat bars and Lindt chocolate.

The Queen Mother serves food that is a treat for the eye as well as the palate: pale pink mousses, bright green vegetables, a creamy glaze of sauce over the meats. Her meals for guests tend to be rich, and there is a special emphasis on desserts. She has the family sweet tooth and likes to nibble chocolates while she reads novels in bed.

According to Palace insiders, Princess Margaret has virtually no interest in what she eats. Never a gourmet, she finds dieting quite easy.

Robert Fellowes

Robert Fellowes is The Queen's assistant private secretary, a tall man who wears pinstriped suits. Son of the The Queen's land agent at Sandringham, he married Princess Diana's sister Jane in 1978, and the Felloweses were responsible for reintroducing Lady Diana to Prince Charles in the summer of 1980. (The couple's first meeting came through Diana's other sister, Sarah.) The Felloweses' young son was an attendant at the wedding of Sarah Ferguson and Prince Andrew. Fellowes was formerly in the Scots Guards and joined The Queen's staff in 1977, the year of her Silver Jubilee. He is quoted as saying, "I love my wife, but I worship my monarch."

The Fergie Bow

The Duchess of York's style of wearing a large flat bow as a fashion accessory to hold back her thick red hair has led to an explosion of "Fergie" bows in all colours and fabrics worn by women all over the globe.

Major Ronald Ferguson

Major Ferguson, father of the Duchess of York, is also Prince Charles's polo manager and the deputy chairman of the Guards Polo Club. He has been managing the Prince of Wales's polo operations since 1972, and always travels with him when he plays polo abroad. "When I travel with him, I go as part of the household, but I'm not employed by him—I do it as an act of friendship," explains the Major.

Ferguson likes to buy all the papers and magazines that have stories about his daughter or pictures of her: "In years to come, in my dotage, when I can't do more than hobble from room to room, I might put them in a book." He is proud of his daughter but also ready to criticize when he disapproves. After his first wife left him for dashing Argentinean Hector Barrantes, he assumed complete responsibility for bringing up Sarah and her sister Jane. He even took them shopping for their clothes and remains interested in what they wear. "They ask me what I think of this and that outfit—Sarah knows I take great interest in what she wears and she also knows that I'm the first to speak truthfully about what I think. When she went out in the evening in a short leather skirt not so long ago, I told her that I don't believe leather should be worn in the evening." He also told her he thought one of her bubble-skirted dresses was quite hideous. But he sympathizes with his daughter's plight in having to look well dressed all the time, on a relatively small income. "Everybody thinks that because you're married to a member of the Royal Family you were rich beforehand and automatically become even richer. Which is ridiculous, farcical... Everybody expects her to wear a new dress every time she does a different engagement."

Lady Ruth Fermoy

Lady Ruth Fermoy is a lady-in-waiting to The Queen Mother and also the grandmother of Princess Diana. Her daughter Frances married Lord Spencer, with whom she had Diana and three other children, and then left him for Peter Shand-Kydd. Lady Fermoy is known to be one of The Queen Mother's confidantes, and Palace insiders report that both The Queen Mother and her lady-in-waiting were pleased when Prince Charles fell in love with Diana Spencer.

Lord Fermoy

Lord Fermoy was the brother of Princess Diana's mother, Frances, and was Diana's favourite uncle. Having threatened suicide several days earlier, Lord Fermoy shot himself in August 1983 while at the stables of his 700-acres estate near Sandringham.

Feuds Between Royals

Princess Anne vs. Princess Diana

Rumour has it that sisters-in-law Anne and Diana are by no means the best of friends. The fact that Anne was not asked to be godmother to either of Diana's two little Princes was widely interpreted as a slap in the face. The fact that Anne and her husband stayed away from Prince Harry's christening was thought to be a retaliation for the snub.

Princesses Anne and Diana seem to have little in common. Anne loves horses and the great outdoors. Diana is interested in fashion and dancing. They don't even see eye to eye on the subject of children. Anne thinks Diana is too "gooey" about hers, and Diana thinks Anne's kids spend too much time romping outdoors. Although Anne's country house, Gatcombe Park, is only a ten-minute drive from Diana's Highgrove, the two families rarely socialize.

Queen Elizabeth vs. Princess Michael

The press has often speculated that The Queen is none too fond of Princess Michael, who has made headlines that are uncomfortable for the Royal Family to read in their morning newspapers. One reason for The Queen's dislike may be Princess Michael's outspokenness. Worst of all, she once said on television that she thought the royal corgis should be shot! It has jokingly been suggested that the general disapproval of Princess Michael by other royals extends even to her choice of pets, her Siamese cats. There are *no* cats at the Palace.

The Duchess of York vs. Princess Michael

Princess Michael, who herself dieted to become stick-thin, reportedly has made a number of critical comments about the Duchess of York's figure, especially her bust line. Sarah is now distinctly cool to her cousin-in-law.

The Queen Mother vs. the Duchess of Windsor

Palace insiders say that The Queen Mother has never forgiven the Duchess of Windsor for causing King Edward VIII to abdicate, thus putting the heavy burden of monarchy on the shoulders of her own husband, King George VI. Her adored "Bertie" had never expected to be King and had not been trained or prepared to handle the job. He often felt himself to be inadequate to the task, and it put him under a severe nervous strain. The Queen Mother always believed that the strain of those years shortened his life, and she puts the blame for the situation squarely on the shoulders of the Duchess of Windsor.

Financial Consequences of the Abdication

The abdication had serious financial consequences for the Windsor family. Without the financial perquisites of kingship, the new Duke of Windsor was financially strapped. Since he had retired into private life, he couldn't be put on the Civil List. So King George VI agreed to pay his brother an annual allowance of £60,000 for the rest of his life. He also bought for £1 million the two estates of Sandringham and Balmoral, royal homes that are privately owned by the Royal Family and had been inherited by the Duke of Windsor on the death of his father. That expenditure made funds tight for the King and his family for some period of time. It took nearly a decade for the royal budget to recover from the strain imposed by King Edward's abdication.

"The Firm"

"The Firm" is the affectionately ironic name given by insiders to the Royal Family and its many enterprises, reputedly first used by King George VI. The Queen, of course, occupies the position of managing director.

First Trip as Queen

Only months after her coronation, Queen Elizabeth II undertook her first state trip abroad. It was a gruelling one: 173 days and 43,618 miles. She visited Canada, Bermuda, Jamaica, Panama, Fiji, Tonga, New Zealand, Australia, the Cocos Islands, Ceylon, Aden, Uganda, Libya, Malta and Gibraltar. She heard "God Save The Queen" sung 508 times and shook 13,213 hands. She made 102 speeches and received 190 official presents. She was accompanied by her husband but Prince Charles and Princess Anne stayed at home. (Near the end of the trip, they came out on the *Britannia* to join their parents for the last few days.) She explained the purpose of her Commonwealth tour in her speech on Christmas Day 1953, broadcast from New Zealand: "I want to show that the Crown is not merely an abstract symbol of our unity but a personal and living bond between you and me."

Fish and Chips

A favourite meal of the Duchess of York is fish and chips.

Five Princes Follow Coffin

At the Westminster Abbey funeral of the murdered Earl Mounbatten of Burma, his coffin was borne on a naval gun carriage followed by five Princes of the realm: Prince Philip, Prince Charles, Prince Michael of Kent, and the Dukes of Gloucester and Kent, who are also royal Princes.

"Flop"

When Prince Philip was a student at Gordonstoun, his classmates nicknamed him "Flop". Referring to a rabbit in a popular children's book, it was a reference to his large, protruding ears.

Florian's

Florian's, the oldest café in the city of Venice, is a favourite of the Prince of Wales.

Floris of London

Purveyors of English flower perfumes and toiletries to the Court of St. James since 1730, Floris is by Royal Warrant perfumer to the The

Courtesy of Floris.

The wonderfully Victorian interior of the Floris shop.

Queen and manufacturer of toilet preparations for the Prince of Wales. Established in London by Juan Flaminius Floris from Majorca, Floris is presently run by the seventh generation of the family and still conducts business at its original location at 89 Jermyn Street in London. Among the famous Floris fragrances are English Violet, Stephanotis, Florissa, and No. 89 for Gentlemen.

Flowers

The Queen is especially fond of white flowers. Prince Philip gives her white carnations every year on their anniversary, and the gardener at Sandringham says her requests for cut flowers for the house are Ice White roses and the old traditional White Provence roses.

The Queen Mother likes her flowers to be in the same colours as her clothes, romantic pinks, mauves and blues, and she prefers big flowers and huge masses of blooms. She also loves flowers with a strong fragrance, such as lilies of the valley and lavender.

Princess Margaret prefers continual variety rather than the same flowers repeatedly, and she doesn't like her bouquets to be too important a part of the room's decor.

Flying Down to Rio

In 1968, The Queen made a state visit to Brazil. The royal equipage included:

- Five aeroplanes
- The royal yacht *Britannia*, with a crew of 251
- Two frigates to accompany the yacht
- Fourteen members of the Royal Household
- Two plain-clothes police officers
- Seven officials
- Twenty-four staff members
- A twenty-two-piece Royal Marine band
- Twenty-four bottles of Liebfraumilch
- Thirty-six bottles of Château Latour
- Three tins of Dundee cake for tea
- Six packets of shortbread biscuits
- Eight boxes of After Eight mints
- Polo mallets
- Two hundred red poppies for lapels on 11 November
- Three bottles of mint sauce for the saddle of lamb
- Twenty-four bottles of Beaujolais

- Three jars of raspberry jam
- Three tiaras
- A turquoise, green and yellow print dress, a tribute to the Brazilian colours
- An aquamarine and diamond necklace given to The Queen by the people of Brazil on the occasion of her coronation
- Hundreds of silver-framed photos of The Queen
- The Queen's monogrammed electric kettle to boil the water for her tea wherever she might be

Fort Belvedere

Fort Belvedere is a small country house, just six miles away from Windsor, that was a favourite retreat of King Edward VIII, both as Prince of Wales and as King. Fort Belvedere was a grace-and-favour residence, originally built by one of the sons of King George II to look something like a child's idea of a castle. The Prince of Wales asked his father to let him have it in 1929, when the previous tenant left, and he fixed up the architectural nonentity to make it a charming residence, complete with all the comforts of central heating, a modern kitchen and even a steam bath. The gardens were filled with delphiniums and alyssum, and a pool was added, with a very bourgeois patio.

During the Prince's courtship of Wallis Simpson, she was a frequent house guest there. As their courtship progressed, she put her own stamp on the hospitality at the Prince of Wales's houses. Reports from other guests were that everything was done "American style", including cocktails served from a shaker and grilled cheese sandwiches. In 1981 Fort Belvedere was purchased by Lord and Lady Abercorn, friends of Queen Elizabeth and Prince Philip.

Freddie Fox

Freddie Fox is the Australian milliner who has made many of The Queen's hats. He has induced her to wear prettier hats than was her wont, and occasionally to try the addition of flowers. When he suggested to The Queen that he might add a bunch of cherries to one of her new hats, she responded jovially, "Mr. Fox, I suppose you will be wearing your fruit-picking gloves in your workroom in future." She gave in to him on the cherries, but stood firmly against a 1930s style little hat he proposed. "Have we been watching too much *Edward and Mrs. Simpson*, do you think, Mr. Fox?" Fox has also made hats for the Princess of Wales.

Dick Francis

Dick Francis, the noted mystery writer, had an earlier career as a steeplechase jockey, in which he frequently rode The Queen Mother's horses. In 1956 he was on Devon Loch and within inches of winning the Grand National, when the horse collapsed and died. The Queen Mother, watching from the stands, immediately went down to comfort him and the stable lads.

The Queen Mother is also a fan of Francis's mysteries and says she has read them all. He always sends her the first copy off the press and says, "I don't think she minds the sexy parts." She has, however, chided him for getting a bit "bloodthirsty".

Freeman of the City of London

In 1987 Princess Diana was made a Freeman of the City of London in a ceremony at London's Guildhall. Among other advantages, it gives her the privilege of driving sheep across London Bridge.

Fiammetta Frescobaldi

In 1987, rumours about the incompatibility of the Prince and Princess of Wales were sparked in part by the fact that Prince Charles dined several times with Contessa Fiammetta Frescobaldi while on a solo trip to Tuscany. He went there to sketch, an interest shared by the attractive twenty-eight-year-old Fiammetta, while Princess Diana remained in England. According to a report in an Italian magazine, "The Contessa is an intellectual who shares the Prince's passionate love for beautiful works of art, whilst Diana can talk only of clothes and babies."

"Frightful Machines"

The Queen is known to have an aversion to helicopters. One day when Prince Charles was learning to pilot the whirlybirds, he decided to stop in and see The Queen at Holyroodhouse on his way back to his base in Scotland. He set the helicopter down on the lawn and headed towards the Palace, hoping to be offered a cup of tea. Instead, he saw The Queen's angry face looking out of the open window. "Go away, Charles," The Queen called, "and take those frightful machines away with you."

Frogmore

Frogmore is a virtual shrine to the love Queen Victoria felt for her husband, Prince Albert. Built in the grounds of Windsor Castle, it is a snug little retreat with beautiful gardens—and Albert's mausoleum. Members of the Royal Family sometimes go there for privacy and quiet while they are at Windsor.

Funeral of King George V

King George V died on 14 February 1936, just before midnight, at his beloved Sandringham. His body first rested in the little church there, then was taken by train to London to lie in state at Westminster Hall. The new King, Edward VIII, decided to hold a "Vigil of the Princes"; he and his three younger brothers stood at the corners of the bier in a long public vigil. Then all four walked behind the coffin to Westminster Abbey for the funeral.

While walking in the funeral procession, King Edward VIII saw "a flash of light dancing along the roadway". It turned out to be the diamond-studded Maltese Cross that tops the Imperial State Crown, which had fallen off the crown while it rested on the old King's coffin. An alert Sergeant-Major scooped it up, and the procession continued. Later, Edward admitted that he thought the incident might have been a bad omen for his reign.

Funeral of King George VI

Official notice of the King's death came to the British public via the BBC on the morning of 6 February 1952: "It is with the greatest regret that we make the following announcement. The King, who retired to rest last night in his usual health, passed peacefully away in his sleep early this morning." The Accession Council announced the accession of Queen Elizabeth II and she responded with a touching Declaration:

> By the sudden death of my father I am called to assume the
> duties and responsibilities of sovereignty. At this time of
> deep sorrow, it is a profound consolation to me to be assured
> of the sympathy which you and all my peoples feel toward
> me, to my mother and my sister, and to the other members
> of my family. My father was our revered and beloved head as
> he was of the wider family of his subjects. The grief which
> his loss brings is shared among us all. My heart is too full for
> me to say more to you today than that I shall always work, as

my father did throughout his reign, to uphold constitutional
government and to advance the happiness and prosperity of
my peoples, spread as they are all over the world. I know that
in my resolve to follow his shining example of service and
devotion, I shall be inspired by the loyalty and affection of
those whose Queen I have been called to be, and by the
counsel of their elected Parliaments. I pray that God will help
me discharge worthily this heavy task which has been laid
upon me so early in life.

For three days, King George lay in state in Westminster Hall. His
coffin, made of oak from his estate at Sandringham, was draped with
the Royal Standard and topped by the Imperial State Crown. After a
brief service attended by three Queens of England—Queen Mary,
Queen Elizabeth The Queen Mother, and Queen Elizabeth II—the
people of Britain filed by in a steady stream to pay their last respects.
His wife said her private farewell just before midnight on the last
night, slipping in the East Door and staying for more than two hours;
her white flowers were on the coffin with a message, "For my dear
husband, a great and noble King". His daughter, the new Queen, sent
a wreath with the message, "To darling Papa from your sorrowing
Lilibet".

As the coffin was carried from Westminster to Paddington Station,
for the train to Windsor, Big Ben tolled fifty-six bells, one for each
year of the King's life. Later there was a private funeral at St.
George's Chapel in Windsor, presided over by the Archbishops of
Canterbury and York, and a long piper's lament, before the King was
laid to rest in the vault there. The King's Lord Chamberlain broke his
white staff of office and threw it on the coffin; the new Queen
Elizabeth threw a handful of rich earth from Windsor contained in a
golden bowl.

Funerals

Following royal tradition, The Queen does not attend funerals except
those for members of her family. The only exception she has made to
date was for Winston Churchill. Her refusal sometimes causes
difficulties in countries unaware of the tradition; for example, there
was some criticism when neither she nor Prince Philip was able to
attend the funeral of former President Dwight D. Eisenhower but
sent Lord Louis Mountbatten instead. However Prince Philip did
attend President Kennedy's funeral.

The Fur Coat Controversy

When the Duke and Duchess of York made a state visit to Canada in 1987, they were both given fur coats; a hip-length leather jacket trimmed with brown fox for the Duchess and a dark grey beaver jacket for the Duke. There was an immediate outcry from animal lovers, demanding that the Yorks return the coats, and there was also a bit of worry from Buckingham Palace over accepting the expensive gifts (which were described as gifts for the couple's first wedding anniversary). Enthusiastic statements from Andy and Fergie about how much they loved the furs seem to have fanned the flames.

Official photograph of the Duke and Duchess of York.

Courtesy of the British Information Service.

Thelma, Lady Furness

Thelma Furness was one of the acknowledged "interests" of King Edward VIII in the 1920s, when he was still the Prince of Wales. Dark-haired Thelma and her twin sister Gloria, who married Reginald Vanderbilt and became the mother of Gloria Vanderbilt, were widely acknowledged to be among the most beautiful women of their day. Thelma married the heir to the Furness Steamship Line fortune, but by 1930 they had publicly agreed to go their separate ways, and Thelma had been taken up by the Prince, although he also continued to see Freda Dudley Ward. The Prince, Thelma and Freda seemed to be a stable triangle for several years, until Wallis Simpson entered the picture.

Thelma, in the autobiography she wrote with her twin sister, claims the honour of introducing Wallis to the Prince of Wales, and it seems that she even had the poor judgement to ask Wallis to "look after" the Prince and keep him entertained while she was away on an extended holiday in the United States. It appears that Wallis took her mission very seriously. When Thelma returned to England, she immediately realized she had been supplanted.

G

Gan-Gan

When Prince Charles was a little boy, he called his great-grandmother Queen Mary "Gan-Gan".

Garden Parties

Every year in June, The Queen gives three or four garden parties in the beautiful grounds of Buckingham Palace. These are not intimate affairs, as each one is attended by seven to eight thousand guests. The lawn is at its best at this time of year, a rich sweep of green grass with a little camomile added for strength during the hot summer days. The lake shimmers in the distance, and pink flamingos gather on one of the islands. The tradition of large garden parties was inaugurated by Queen Victoria, probably around 1865, when Court functions were first held at Buckingham Palace and she could use the parties as an opportunity to meet more of her subjects.

It is not possible to apply for invitations. Guests are recommended by the Palace staff or other officials such as ambassadors or lords-lieutenant. Gentlemen wear morning dress or uniforms, ladies wear afternoon dresses (with hats) or national dress. Two bands play music alternately throughout the party. There is no receiving line. At 4 p.m. The Queen and her family come out on to the terrace as the national anthem is played. Each member of the Family then goes a different route among the guests. The Lord Chamberlain precedes The Queen and introduces people along a roundabout route that eventually reaches the green and white striped royal tent, where the Royal Family and specially selected guests partake of tea, tiny sandwiches, and possibly a dish of fresh strawberries from Windsor covered with

clotted Devonshire cream. Strawberries used to be served to every
guest, but the need to economize took them off the menu for all but
the guests at The Queen's personal tent.

Garrard's

Garrard's of Regent Street has supplied royal jewels for generations.
The company was founded in 1735 under the patronage of the then
Prince of Wales, son of King George II, and was appointed Crown
Jewellers by Queen Victoria in 1843. They recut the Koh-i-Noor
diamond for Queen Victoria, and made the light state crown, or
diadem, that she chose to wear for most royal appearances. They also
made crowns for Queen Alexandra, Queen Mary and The Queen
Mother (whose crown is the present location of the Koh-i-Noor).
They are responsible for maintaining all the crowns, sceptres, and
other regalia that are part of the Crown Jewels. Once a year, a team of
experts from Garrard's visits the Tower of London to check, polish
and tighten up all the jewels.

   The Queen often wears a diamond bow brooch initially made for
Queen Victoria by Garrard's in 1858. Prince Andrew went to
Garrard's for Sarah Ferguson's engagement ring, a large oval ruby
surrounded by ten diamonds that cost about £25,000. Prince Charles
also turned to them for Diana's sapphire; it was circled by fourteen
diamonds and is rumoured to have cost about £30,000.

Courtesy of Garrard's.

The founder, in 1735, of
Garrard's.

Garrard's makes exquisite commemorative silver for numerous royal occasions, and although the pieces are expensive, they are in great demand. At the time of the Queen's Silver Jubilee in 1977, one of Garrard's regular customers rang up the shop to say she was coming to look at the commemorative silver. When she arrived, it had all been sold, and she was so angry she sued them for failing to wait for her!

Photo by Norman Parkinson, courtesy of the British Information Service.

The owners of Gatcombe Park.

Gatcombe Park

Gatcombe Park is the country house of Princess Anne and Mark Phillips. Located within easy commuting distance of London, Gatcombe was a wedding gift to the couple from The Queen, who paid about £500,000 for the estate. It had formerly belonged to the

Master of Trinity College at Cambridge. The Phillips family moved into their new home in November 1977, just a few days after the birth of their son Peter. When Princess Anne's husband decided not to stay on in the army after being given a desk job at the Ministry of Defence, the Royal Family held a conference, and The Queen helped the Phillipses to buy another six hundred acres around Gatcombe to enlarge the estate. It is now a working farm as well as a country retreat, and Mark Phillips spends much of his time supervising the farm work.

The interior of Gatcombe has been characterized as "homelike" rather than royal. Initially, David Hicks, the noted interior designer and husband of The Queen's old friend Pamela Mountbatten, planned an extensive scheme of new decor, but Anne and Mark vetoed it as too expensive and did the house on their own...and within their own budget.

Brian Gearing

Brian Gearing is the editor of *Radio Times*, which began publication in 1923. Gearing feels that bringing the Royal Family into people's homes on the mass media has accelerated the modernization of the monarchy. King Edward VIII's abdication speech on radio was followed a year later by television coverage of the coronation procession of King George VI and his Queen. *Radio Times* issues from July 1937, featuring articles and photos of the Royal Family, have already become valuable collector's items. Since then, the magazine has published many commemorative editions to mark royal occasions.

"The Geese"

"The Geese" is a slightly unkind nickname for ladies-in-waiting to The Queen and The Queen Mother. Like geese, they are said to warn off intruders with loud quacks and hisses.

Bob Geldof

Nominated for a Nobel Peace Prize, knighted by The Queen, dubbed "Saint Bob" by some and "The Mouth" by others, Bob Geldof first found fame with the rock group the Boomtown Rats, which he named after a street gang mentioned in Woody Guthrie's autobiography. In 1985, his modest idea of asking top rock stars to join together in a supergroup called "Band Aid" for a Christmas fund-raising concert started a global fusion of rock fellowship and compassion for the needy. The Band Aid charity has so far raised over $130 million, Live

Bob Geldof
in characteristic pose.

Courtesy of Weidenfeld & Nicolson.

Aid over $80 million. Geldof's passionate commitment to African Famine Relief has taken him to Washington for grain shipments and to Buckingham Palace for meetings with the Prince and Princess of Wales.

Although the demands of his crusade have overshadowed his own career, Geldof avoids public praise. He told *Life* magazine's Cheryl McCall, "I won't let people or myself down by cheapening whatever it is I represent. But at the same time, I don't want to be expected to be saintly. Halos rust very fast." His autobiography, *Is That It?*, was published in 1987.

General Trading Company

This London store, founded in 1920, is a favourite of Fergie's. She chose to be listed on the bridal registry there, so wedding guests in search of the perfect present for the future Duke and Duchess of York could pick something from her list at GTC, which included everything from a circular Georgian dining table seating thirty to fruit-patterned everyday dishes. GTC holds all four Royal Warrants, from The Queen, The Queen Mother, the Duke of Edinburgh and the

Prince of Wales. It is a store also favoured by "Sloane Rangers". It sells everything from garden furniture to dried herbs, and its amenities include a terrace café overlooking a charming small garden. For more information, write to 144 Sloane Street, London SW3.

Gentleman Usher of the Black Rod

One of the lesser known members of The Queen's Household is the Gentleman Usher of the Black Rod. His chief duty comes once a year, at the state opening of Parliament. After The Queen is seated on the throne in the House of Lords, he goes down the corridor to the House of Commons, to invite its members to attend the opening and hear The Queen's speech. By tradition the door is slammed in his face, keeping out The Queen's messenger to show the independence of the Commons. After knocking three times with his Black Rod of office, the door is opened and Black Rod is allowed in to deliver The Queen's message to the Speaker.

George and the Dragon

King George V and his wife Queen Mary were exactly the same height, 5'6", but her fondness for toques (brimless hats with one side raised higher than the other, so that it looked swept up) made her seem to tower over him. Her apparent size, coupled with her unsmiling demeanour, prompted humorists to call the royal couple "George and the Dragon".

George III Christening Cup

At the christening of Prince Charles, his great-grandmother Queen Mary gave him an antique cup that had once been a gift from King George III. She noted, "I gave a present from my great-grandfather to my great-grandson, 168 years later."

The George IV Diadem

The George IV Diadem is one of the Crown Jewels of England and was made for George IV. At the front, the Cross of St. George is picked out in diamonds, and the rest of the circlet contains other emblems of Great Britain. The band of the diadem is set with pearls and diamonds; three large square emblems set with diamonds are interspersed with graceful diamond flowers. Queen Victoria favoured the crown because it is relatively small and light, and Queen Elizabeth wore it to her coronation. She also wears it every year on her way to Parliament for the State opening, changing to the Imperial Crown once she arrives. The Queen is wearing this diadem in portraits on stamps and banknotes.

Ghosts in Royal Residences

According to Joan Forman, author of *Haunted Royal Homes and Castles*, many royal residences possess a ghost or two.

At Windsor, there have been sightings of the ghosts of Elizabeth I, Henry VIII, Charles I (*with* his head) and George III, who sits in the library and mutters "What? What? What?" over again. Keeping company with the royal ghosts is the ghost of a policeman who died at Windsor in the 1940s.

At Kensington Palace, the ghost of George II has frequently been seen peering out of his bedroom window.

Nether Lypiatt, the home of Prince and Princess Michael of Kent, was formerly haunted by the ghost of a young blacksmith hanged by a previous owner for failing to do his work quickly enough. According to rumour, the Prince and Princess had the house exorcized in 1981, and the ghost has not been seen since.

Sandringham has been troubled by the ghost of a small page who goes around snuffing out lighted candles.

At Buckingham Palace, the ghost of a mediaeval monk moves around clanking his chains. A second ghost is that of Major John Gwynne, private secretary to King Edward VII, who committed suicide in his Palace office during his scandalous divorce case.

Princess Diana's childhood home, Althorp, is said to be haunted by her grandfather, who died there in 1975. The next year, Diana's father married her stepmother Raine, and five different members of the Spencer family spotted the ghost of the old Earl attending the reception. Author Forman says, "He seemed quite at ease, and made no acknowledgement to them, although he was smiling."

Giant Pandas

The Duke of Edinburgh is an outspoken supporter of wildlife conservation, and one of his special interests is the plight of the giant panda. In 1985 he made a trip to Wolong Panda Reserve in China to see the animals in their natural habitat. He later commented, "We don't have very much time left if we are to try to save the panda and its habitat, as well as all the other threatened species of wildlife. We'll have to use management and organization, goodwill, enthusiasm and commitment."

Gibbs

Gibbs, a preparatory school in Kensington, London, was the first school for Prince Edward. A fellow student at the time was the Prince's cousin James Ogilvy, the son of Princess Alexandra and Angus Ogilvy.

Gieves & Hawkes Ltd.

The splendid uniforms worn by Prince Charles and Prince Andrew at their weddings, plus those worn by their pages, were made for the occasion by Gieves & Hawkes. By Royal Warrant makers of livery, military and naval uniforms to The Queen and the Duke of Edinburgh, the company opened its doors in 1785. Early customers included Admiral Nelson, the Duke of Wellington, and Captain Bligh of the *Bounty* mutiny fame. When Charles Laughton played Bligh in the 1930s film, he researched the Gieves & Hawkes archives for authenticity. Today, the "Complete Gentleman's Outfitter" provides men's wear from the formal to the casual, exclusive silk ties, shirts, cufflinks, shoes, leather goods and toiletries. For information, write to: 1 Savile Row, London W1.

Photo by Derek Rowe.

Robert Gieve, the Vice-Chairman of Gieves & Hawkes.

Gifts from Royals

When Prince Andrew was six, his parents gave him a miniature Aston-Martin like the one in the James Bond films, with a working smoke screen and non-working machine guns. The licence plate read JB 007.

Prince Charles gave Mark Phillips a pair of leather gun cases as a wedding present.

King George VI made a set of chair covers in needlepoint, at which he was extremely proficient, as a gift for his wife.

Sir Martin Gilliat

Sir Martin Gilliat is private secretary to The Queen Mother. Although he has held the post for nearly thirty years, he likes to joke that he is still waiting to hear whether he will be taken on permanently. A graduate of Eton and Sandhurst, he was formerly the military secretary to Lord Louis Mountbatten. After three decades of royal service, Sir Martin says that in all his years with The Queen Mother he has never once been bored.

Glamis Castle

Glamis Castle is the ancestral home in Scotland of the Earls of Strathmore, The Queen Mother's family. It is here that the young Lady Elizabeth Bowes-Lyon grew up. Glamis (pronounced Glams) is twelve miles north of Dundee, and a pleasant drive away from the royal residence at Balmoral. There is supposed to be a Monster of Glamis, but there have been no recent sightings. The Queen Mother still visits Glamis every summer and sleeps in the pretty, soft-coloured bedroom in which her daughter Princess Margaret was born in 1930. Most of the castle's interior is dark and gloomy, in the Jacobean style, adorned with hunting trophies and filled with legends about the visits of the Stuart family. Although the castle is still in the Strathmore family, parts of it are open to the public during the summer.

The Glass Coach

The Glass Coach is an enclosed carriage with unusually large windows, used when the royals need protection from rain or wind while still remaining visible to their subjects. Since 1910 every royal bride has used the Glass Coach on her wedding day. The sides of the coach are emblazoned with the Royal Arms on the shiny black paint, and like all the royal carriages, the wheels are lacquered a striking red and yellow.

Glassalt Shiel

Glassalt Shiel is the house Queen Victoria built by the side of Loch Muick at Balmoral after Prince Albert died. The Queen went there to grieve in her widowhood, and it has been left very much as it was in her day. One architectural critic describes it as looking exactly like a suburban Victorian house in Wimbledon. The current royals occasionally use it as a place for a picnic or afternoon tea party.

The Glittering Crowns

The Glittering Crowns is a historical documentary that was released on video-cassette in 1981. It contains archival footage of royal coronations and weddings from 1896 to the present.

Gloves

The Queen often wears as many as four pairs of white gloves in a day. They used to be made of white cotton, but her dresser "Bobo" complained about all the work of ironing them. Now they are made of nylon, which can be washed and dried quickly while on tour. In recent years, The Queen has begun to wear coloured gloves for a more stylish look: black shoes, hat and gloves, for example, with a yellow dress. The Queen's gloves are made by Cordelia James.

"Gnashes"

King George VI was a devoted husband and loving father, but he occasionally had fits of temper that the family called his "gnashes". They were usually brought on by world events or bungled arrangements, and his wife learned to cope by soothing him through them. Sometimes she stroked his arm until he calmed down; other times she merely responded with the full force of her sympathetic nature. Once in a gnash in South Africa, the King became infuriated with some political position of the Nationalists and said angrily, "I'd like to shoot them all." Queen Elizabeth replied in earnest support, "But Bertie, you can't shoot them *all*."

God Bless the Prince of Wales

Until he becomes monarch and can listen to his subjects singing "God Save The King", Prince Charles can content himself with listening to that little-known ditty, "God Bless the Prince of Wales", which was sung at his investiture:

Among our ancient mountains
And from our lovely vales,
Oh, let the prayer re-echo,
God bless the Prince of Wales.

"God Save The King" Parody

A popular parody, sung to the tune of Britain's national anthem, joked about the stern manner of Queen Mary:

Queen Mary, so they say,
Had a commanding way
With old King George.
When Georgie had a date
She waited at the gate,
And if he came home late
God Save the King.

"God Save the Queen" from the Sex Pistols

In 1977, in time for The Queen's Silver Jubilee, the Sex Pistols rather patriotically released a record called "God Save the Queen". Needless to say, it was *not* a version of the national anthem.

Golf with Queen Alexandra

Queen Alexandra apparently confused the game of golf with field hockey, and thought that the object of the game was to prevent your opponent's ball from going into the cup. Those who had the experience of golfing with her on the private links at Sandringham said that on every green she enjoyed a good scrimmage to make sure that no rival's ball went into the hole before hers.

The Goon Show

In the early 1960s, BBC radio broadcast the weekly *Goon Show*, featuring the offbeat humour of Spike Milligan, Harry Secombe and

Peter Sellers. The programme was a favourite of Prince Charles. According to insiders, Charles can do creditable imitations of *Goon Show* characters Bluebottle and Neddy Seagoon.

Prince Charles enjoys a regular correspondence with Spike Milligan, who addresses his letters to "Trainee King, Buckingham Palace".

Gordonstoun

Gordonstoun is a public school in Elgin, Scotland, known for encouraging an interest in rugged physical activity more than mere academics. The school's motto is "Plus est en vous", or "There is more in you", and it often seems to be interpreted to mean that you can stand more physical stress and discomfort than you had imagined.

Gordonstoun was founded by Dr. Kurt Hahn, the headmaster of a progressive school in Germany to which the young Prince Philip was sent by his Hesse relatives. In 1934 Hahn fell into disfavour with Hitler and fled to Scotland, where he opened Gordonstoun. Prince Philip continued his education there, and a generation later, all his sons attended. When Philip was a student, Hahn said, "Prince Philip is a born leader but will need the exacting demands of a great service to do justice to himself. His best is outstanding—his second best is not good enough.... His gifts would run to waste if he was condemned to lead a life where neither superior officers nor the routine of the day forced him to tap his hidden resources."

During Prince Charles's years at Gordonstoun, there was one mini-scandal. While on a school cruise, he was hounded by the press and fled into the bar of his hotel to escape. There, in foolhardy fashion, the fourteen-year-old ordered the first drink that came to his mind, cherry brandy. Unfortunately, a reporter was present in the bar, and made the heir to the throne's youthful preference for hard drink a front-page story.

Friends say that Prince Charles has unhappy memories of the school his father adored. The physical layout of Gordonstoun has been described as a collection of crude huts. The dormitories have bare floors, unpainted walls, uncomfortable iron beds. Every student must take a cold shower in the morning, no matter how low the temperature outside.

Grace-and-Favour Residences

Grace-and-favour residences are owned by The Queen personally, or the Crown, and can be conferred by The Queen at will. Although the majority of grace-and-favour residences are small apartments within official royal residences, such as Windsor Castle and Buckingham Palace, a few are magnificent country houses on her estates. The Queen has given these to members of the Royal Family as their country residences.

"The Grand Knockout Tournament"

"The Grand Knockout Tournament" was a 1987 televised event to raise money for four separate charities, including the World Wildlife Fund, a cause dear to the hearts of Prince Philip and Prince Charles. Prince Edward, a member of the organizing committee, is credited with the concept for the event, which he says came from the television series, *It's a Knockout!* A mock mediaeval pageant, the event featured such celebrities as Emlyn Hughes, Cliff Richard, Tom Jones, Pamela Stephenson and John Cleese. The Duke and Duchess of York and Princess Anne appeared with Prince Edward in mediaeval costume and vigorously cheered on their teams in the competitions. The event raised nearly £1 million for charity.

Grand Service

The Grand Service is the array of gold serving pieces in the Ball Room at Buckingham Palace. Most of it was purchased by King George IV in the early nineteenth century.

"Grannie's Chips"

The Royal Family's private name for the valuable diamond brooches originally made for Queen Mary with smaller pieces of the huge Cullinan Diamond (the largest chunk is in the Imperial Crown) is "Grannie's Chips". Grannie's Chips are now owned by The Queen. The largest pin features a pear-shaped diamond of ninety-two carats along with a square one of sixty-two carats.

Cary Grant

Quoted in December 1977, the British-born Cary Grant said, "Prince Charles is a very charming, witty, intelligent, handsome fellow. Something like me."

Graphic Arts

Graphic Arts is the publishing firm for which Sarah Ferguson worked before her marriage to Prince Andrew and where she afterwards continued to perform the duties of an editor. The first book published by Graphic Arts to list her name in the acknowledgements was *The New Painting: Impressionism 1874–1886*. More recently, she has edited and written an introduction for a definitive history of the Palace of Westminster. Sarah's boss at Graphic Arts says of her, "She has tenacity, humour, charm and great professionalism. I know it sounds boring when everybody else says the same thing, but she really is just a wonderful person to know and to work with. She has such enthusiasm."

The Great She Elephant

In 1987 Prince Charles made a visit to Swaziland, where he met young King Mawati III. Although the King was wearing little more than a leopard-skin loincloth at the time, he was in fact educated in England and had a long intimate chat with the Prince about his school days there. Then he introduced his mother under her full ceremonial title, the Great She Elephant. She fastened some beads around the Prince's neck, and he then watched the dancers, row upon row of bare-breasted young women. They sang a song that was translated as, "Prince Charles, why are you so confident? You don't even have a cow."

Later on the same trip, Charles slipped away for a few days in Kenya with his old friend Sir Laurens van der Post. They spent the time in the Kalahari Desert living simply and away from everyone.

Dr. Louis Greig

Dr. Greig was a red-headed, plain-speaking Scot and a friend of the future King George VI since his days at Osborne Naval College. Greig not only oversaw young Bertie's medical treatment (he had to have two operations while he was serving in World War I, one for appendicitis and another to remove a duodenal ulcer) but also encouraged him to assert himself, even to his rather daunting father. Although many people disliked Greig's brash manner and vulgar language, King George V said firmly, "Greig has made a man of my son; he stays." It was not until Bertie married Lady Elizabeth Bowes-Lyon and found domestic happiness that Greig disappeared from the scene.

Grenadier Guards

The Grenadiers form a part of the Household Division charged with the responsibility of guarding the Royal Family. First formed by King Charles II while he was in exile, they have the same motto as the Knights of the Garter: "Honi soit qui mal y pense." They wear white plumes on the left side of their busbies, and their tunics have single buttons, evenly spaced. Prince Philip is their Colonel.

Greyhound Racing

In 1987 Princess Anne entered the world of greyhound racing when she was given a champion, Hardy King, after the death of its owner. She planned to give the dog's winnings to her favourite charity, the Save the Children Fund.

Princess Elizabeth, representing King George VI at the Trooping the Colour ceremony, wears the uniform of a Grenadier Guard.

H

Haemophilia

Geneticists deduce that Queen Victoria inherited the gene for haemophilia, a rare blood disorder that leaves victims without the "clotting factor" that stops bleeding. Women do not actually get the disease, but they can pass the gene along to their sons, who may be stricken, or to their daughters, who can transmit it to the next generation. Although none of Victoria's sons suffered from haemophilia, two of her grand-daughters were carriers. Princess Alix of Hesse, youngest daughter of Victoria's daughter, Princess Alice, brought the gene into the Russian royal family when she married Czar Nicholas II and became Czarina Alexandra; their son Alexei, the young heir to the throne who was executed with the rest of the family by the revolutionaries in 1917, was a haemophiliac. Another grand-daughter of Queen Victoria, Princess Ena of Battenberg, married King Alfonso XIII of Spain. Of their four sons, only one, the father of Juan Carlos, the present King of Spain, escaped haemophilia.

Hair

The musical *Hair*, which featured total nudity, was not staged in England until the early 1970s, after the end of theatre censorship by the Lord Chamberlain. When it did finally reach the London stage, Princess Anne was among those who went to see it. At the joyous finale, she joined other members of the audience in dancing on stage with the cast. Needless to say, her youthful enthusiasm occasioned some complaint from some members of the public.

Halcyon Days Enamels Ltd.

The custom of commemorating great royal occasions with decorative enamel items dates back to the eighteenth century. Halcyon Days Enamels continues the tradition with collector's editions for such events as the royal wedding of Prince Charles and Lady Diana and The Queen and Prince Philip's ruby wedding anniversary. For information, write to: 14 Brook Street, London W1.

Philippe Halsman

Philippe Halsman was the famed portrait photographer whose subjects included everyone from Grace Kelly to Salvador Dali. Commissioned by *Life* to photograph the Duke and Duchess of Windsor for a cover, Halsman later recalled, "They were sitting together rather stiffly, and they looked at my camera with expressions that reminded me of two elderly and hungry hyenas. After taking this picture, I said gaily, 'Don't look at me so carnivorously. You are the most romantic couple in the world—a king who gave up his crown to marry the woman he loved.' The Duke and Duchess smiled, their heads moved closer together, their features relaxed, and suddenly they looked attractive and much younger."

William Hamilton

William Hamilton, who was a Member of Parliament until 1987, has for many years specialized in criticism of the Royal Family. When young Prince William was christened in 1982, Hamilton told the press jovially, "I think it is a very lovely name, and I am sure they had me in mind when they chose it."

Dr. Armand Hammer

Dr. Armand Hammer is the octogenarian head of Occidental Petroleum, and one of Prince Charles's advisors. Hammer contributes heavily to Charles's favourite charities, such as Business in the Community, and he was the organizer of the United World Colleges fund raisers in Palm Beach, at which the Prince and Princess of Wales appeared in 1986. According to Hammer, "Prince Charles is a young man wise beyond his years. In my opinion he will make a great King."

Hampton Court

Hampton Court, located on the Thames between London and Windsor, was built during the reign of King Henry VIII by Cardinal Wolsey, who was the Lord Chancellor at the time. In an effort to ingratiate himself with the King and save his job, Wolsey presented the house and its contents to his sovereign, who immediately began enlarging it. In 1689, Hampton Court was largely rebuilt by Christopher Wren, at the commission of William and Mary.

Although it was a royal residence for centuries, Hampton Court is no longer the home of Britain's monarchs. Part of it is divided into grace-and-favour apartments and the rest is open to the public as a museum. Despite damage from a recent fire, Hampton Court is a popular tourist attraction, featuring a Tudor tennis court and its famed maze of old boxwood hedges in the garden.

Happy Birthday Dear Ma'am

A special documentary filmed to celebrate The Queen's sixtieth birthday, *Happy Birthday, Dear Ma'am* is an affectionate and sentimental tribute. It paints an upbeat portrait of The Queen from her childhood to the present. Photographs and film footage punctuate the royal story of ceremony and hand-shaking. Producer Jenny Barraclough commented, "In the miles of film footage of The Queen, from chatting with President Reagan to inspecting a bore-hole pump in Nepal, she always shows the most enormous kindness. The amazing thing is that she never ever switches off." The documentary contains revealing comments and anecdotes from such diverse figures as Sir Edward Heath and The Queen's jockeys.

Harrods

Harrods, on London's Brompton Road in Knightsbridge, is one of a handful of commercial establishments that has received all four Royal Warrants: from The Queen, The Queen Mother, the Duke of Edinburgh and the Prince of Wales. Founded in 1849 on a site within its present location, Harrods received its first Royal Warrant in 1913, from Queen Mary. With over 230 departments, Harrods can sell to royals, and the rest of us, everything from kippers to a grand piano. An average of thirty thousand customers enter the store every day.

Harrods is Supplier of Provisions and Household Goods to The Queen; Supplier of China, Glass and Fancy Goods to The Queen Mother; Outfitter and Saddler to the Prince of Wales; and Outfitter

Courtesy of Harrods.

Harrods, with the four Royal Warrants displayed over the door.

to the Duke of Edinburgh. Princess Diana is known to pop into Harrods every now and then for a look at the store's irresistible displays of merchandise.

For further information, write to: Harrods, 87/135 Brompton Road, London SW1X 7XL.

Norman Hartnell

Norman Hartnell designed clothes for Queen Elizabeth for more than forty years. When she was just nine years old, he created her bridesmaid's dress—all pink silk and frills—for the 1935 wedding of the Duke of Gloucester. Hartnell later designed The Queen's own wedding dress in 1947, as well as her coronation dress (and the dresses The Queen Mother and Princess Margaret wore to that event). Hartnell's workshop of ninety-five seamstresses specialized in intricate beading, sewing sequins and even semiprecious stones on bodices, sleeves and hems. Most of The Queen's evening gowns were by Hartnell. (Of Hartnell and his colleague and rival Hardy Amies, people used to say, "Norman for the beads, Hardy for the tweeds".)

It was Hartnell's custom to send sketches and fabric samples to Buckingham Palace, where The Queen would then choose the models she wanted. Each one required at least four fittings before it was finally wrapped in many layers of tissue and sent to the Palace in its pristine box. For Hartnell's services, The Queen made him a Knight Commander of the Royal Victorian Order in 1977. When he died in 1979, his design house was taken over by John Tullis. The Queen remained a faithful customer until Tullis retired to Australia in 1981.

The first royal to patronize Hartnell was The Queen Mother, who started buying her own clothes there in 1935. He created for her dresses with floating panels, trimmings of fur and feathers, or rhinestones and pearls. Together they invented a way for her to dress that was flattering to her femininely full figure: blouses and dresses with a crossover neckline, a rather full sleeve (enabling her to wave enthusiastically), the blue and pink "sweet pea" colours that she loves, and always some flirtatious little trimming, such as a ruffle, a big bow or a few beads and sequins. There was usually a pretty scarf and a matching hat, and fabrics were never heavy, never dark.

Courtesy of the British Information Service.

The Queen wearing a typical evening gown designed by Norman Hartnell.

She still dresses exactly the same way, and she still dresses at Hartnell's salon, even though he is no longer there. Sometimes she digs out dresses that are ten or more years old and returns them to the salon, suggesting they add just a bit of sleeve, or some new trimming, and then she begins wearing them all over again. Hartnell made The Queen Mother's dress for the wedding of the Duke and Duchess of York.

Harvard University

When Harvard celebrated its 350th anniversary in 1986, one of the honoured speakers was Prince Charles. He addressed the theme of the school's mission: "We may have forgotten that when all is said and done, a good man, as the Greeks would say, is a nobler work than a good technologist."

Head Scarf

The head scarf is as much a badge of feminine royalty as the tiara. The Queen wears one constantly in the country, as a way of keeping her hair anchored firmly in the breeze. She ties it in the old-fashioned way, securely under her chin, with the sides pulled far forward. The Queen Mother is another scarf wearer, as is Princess Anne; even the

Princess Anne, the Princess Royal, is seen with her son Peter at the Annual Regatta at Littlehampton, Sussex.

Courtesy of the British Information Service.

normally style-conscious Princess Margaret has been known to wear one while in the country. Only Princess Di seems immune to the trend.

Many fashion critics consider the royal scarf to be an unbecoming piece of headgear, likely to flatten out the wearer's hair and make her look rather jowly. In 1978, artist Ruskin Spear painted a portrait of The Queen in a head scarf—a humorous and none-too-flattering portrayal that has made its way to a private collection in Texas.

Prime Minister Edward Heath.

Courtesy of the British Information Service.

Edward Heath

Edward Heath was the Conservative Prime Minister who held office in 1974. He left office when he was unable to form a new government after an election that left his party in the minority by a few seats.

Heatherdown School

Heatherdown is a fashionable prep school located at Ascot, near Windsor. Prince Andrew attended Heatherdown, as did the elder son of the Duke of Kent, the Earl of St. Andrews.

Helicopters

The Queen's Flight includes several helicopters, but The Queen herself almost never flies in them, owing to her dislike of that mode of transport. They are frequently used by the Prince and Princess of Wales as a speedy way to get back from the country or to not-too-distant engagements. The biggest fan of helicopters in the Royal Family, though, is The Queen Mother, who adores them. "The chopper has changed my life as conclusively as that of Anne Boleyn," she once joked.

Henley Royal Regatta

The Henley Royal Regatta takes place every year in the last week of June or the first week of July, at Henley-on-Thames. It is the most prestigious event in rowing competition, and also a chance for the well-dressed spectators to watch one another. The strict dress code prohibits trousers of any sort on women and bans shorts and jeans for men. Prince Albert was the first royal patron of the regatta, in 1851, and the royals still like to view the regatta if their schedule permits.

Major Dick Hern

Major Dick Hern is one of the trainers of The Queen's racehorses, at The Queen's Berkshire stable near Newbury.

Lady Pamela Mountbatten Hicks

Pamela is the younger daughter of Lord Louis Mountbatten and his wife, Edwina. A childhood friend of the young Princess Elizabeth and a cousin of Prince Philip, Pamela was one of The Queen's ladies-in-waiting before her 1961 marriage to famed interior designer David Hicks. She was with the Princess on the trip to Kenya when King George VI died and Elizabeth unexpectedly became Queen. Pamela's daughter, India Hicks, was one of Lady Diana Spencer's bridesmaids; the Hickses also have two older children, Edwina and Ashley.

Sir John Higgs

John Higgs was the secretary of the Duchy of Cornwall until his sudden death after a short illness in 1986. He introduced Prince Charles to the notion that the Duchy should be run like a business concern, and together they turned it into an operation that netted more than £1 million a year. The Prince became very close to Higgs, who was knighted on his deathbed.

Highgrove

Highgrove is the country home of the Prince and Princess of Wales. It is located on 346 acres near the market town of Tetbury, and features a charming Georgian house. With a mere nine bedrooms, Highgrove seems intimate and cosy compared with the palaces in which the family lives the rest of the time. Prince Charles bought Highgrove for £800,000 in 1980, giving rise to increased speculation that he was about to announce his engagement to Lady Diana Spencer. According to contemporary reports, he had asked her to look at it with him one weekend, and she labelled it perfect—he bought it immediately thereafter.

Later, however, Princess Diana decided she much preferred Kensington Palace, at least until she had Highgrove redecorated by Dudley Poplak. It's a little glossier than other royal country houses, but still remains a comfortable family home, with a spot at the bottom of the garden where William and Henry can keep their pet rabbits, and room for them to ride their pony.

At Highgrove, the Prince and Princess can lead a quiet life. It's even quieter now that their neighbours have insisted that they remove the bells from the necks of their cows and sheep. One of them explained crossly, "Bells are used on the hills and in the Alps to locate herds because the farms are so huge. But you can hardly lose a herd in a Cotswold field." Highgrove has a walled swimming pool and a lovely meadow of wild flowers along the drive. One of the features that first attracted the Prince was the large garden, planted with many magnificent trees, including a number of unusual ornamental specimens. Prince Charles has continued to add to the plantings.

Another advantage of Highgrove is its location. Situated near the major road to London, it is convenient for trips to and from the Palace. Racing and polo are nearby, and for those who like to fox hunt, it is right in the middle of Beaufort Hunt country.

Hill House

Hill House Preparatory School for Boys was the first school attended by the young Prince Charles. Located at 17 Hans Place in London, not far from Buckingham Palace, the school publicly proclaims its goal as promoting healthy individual rivalry and the will to win. "A boy's mind is a spark to be kindled, not a vessel to be filled," the school proclaims. One guide describes it as "outdoorsy, for energetic extroverts, with a minimal academic accent". For the slightly shy and possibly overprotected eight-year-old Prince, it must have been quite a change from lessons in the nursery at Buckingham Palace.

Adolf Hitler: Two Reactions

At the onset of World War II, nine-year-old Princess Margaret was
deeply disappointed to be sent to Birkhall, in Scotland, rather than
returning to London in the autumn as usual. "Who," she demanded,
"is this Hitler, spoiling everything?"

   Her uncle, the Duke of Windsor, took a friendlier view of the
German dictator. He and the Duchess called on Hitler when they
visited Germany in 1937, and Hitler supposedly told the Duke that
Wallis would have made a good queen. Perhaps it was those welcome
words that made the Duke say, years later, "I never thought Hitler
was such a bad chap."

Anthony Holden

Anthony Holden is a long-time commentator on the Royal Family. In
addition to scores of articles, he has written a biography of Prince
Charles published in 1979, a biography of The Queen Mother, and a
commemoration of the royal wedding year, *Their Royal Highnesses: The
Prince and Princess of Wales*, published in 1981.

Fiona Holdum

Fiona Holdum was a young blonde receptionist at a resort hotel in the
Bahamas who caught Prince Andrew's eye when his ship, HMS
Invincible, had a three-day layover in Nassau in 1983. They spent days
sightseeing and swimming, and nights dancing and drinking at Club
Med. When the three days were up, the Prince gave her a gold bracelet
and promised to stay in touch.

Holy Oil from Savory & Moore

Savory & Moore are chemists located in Curzon Street in London.
Their head dispenser in 1953, John Jameson, was the man who mixed
(from a formula provided by Buckingham Palace) the holy oil used for
The Queen's coronation. Savory & Moore hold Royal Warrants from
The Queen, The Queen Mother, the Duke of Edinburgh and the
Prince of Wales.

Holy Terror

When Princess Margaret was a girl, she went to a children's party dressed as an angel. Her mother teased her gently as she was leaving by saying, "You don't look very angelic, Margaret." "That's all right," Margaret shot back, "I'll be a holy terror."

Home Video

Among the full-length royal documentaries available on video are:

- *Queen Elizabeth II—60 Glorious Years:* highlights of The Queen's life and achievements in her years on the throne. Colour. Sixty minutes.
- *The Royal Wedding of Prince Andrew and Miss Sarah Ferguson:* the splendour and pageantry of the procession, the wedding ceremony at Westminster Abbey, the Royal Family at Buckingham Palace. Official BBC version. Colour. One hundred minutes.
- *The Prince and Princess of Wales Talking Personally:* the royal couple talking freely about their family life, charity work, and relations with the press; includes delightful sequences playing with the children. Colour. Forty-six minutes.

Homeopathy

Homeopathy is a system of medicine whose practitioners treat illnesses with diluted extracts of plants and mineral compounds. Based on a holistic philosophy, it tries to avoid drastic or intrusive treatment. The Queen and other members of the Royal Family are regularly treated by a homeopath, and Prince Charles has spoken out strongly in favour of the homeopathic view of medicine: "I would suggest that the whole imposing edifice of modern medicine, for all its breathtaking successes, is, like the celebrated Tower of Pisa, slightly off balance. It is frightening how dependent on drugs we are all becoming and how easy it is for doctors to prescribe them as the universal panacea for our ills."

It is unusually strong statements such as this that have earned the Prince the reputation as being a bit of a crank, but he and his mother both continue to take homeopathic treatment with good results. The Queen has even recommended that her racehorses receive homeopathic treatment.

Honey Covers The Queen Mother

Once The Queen Mother was a dinner guest at Hagley Hall, a magnificent building near Stourbridge. It had escaped the notice of her hosts that a swarm of bees had made themselves at home on the rococo ceiling and stored their honey on the gilded chandelier. When the lights were turned on for The Queen Mother's dinner, the warmth melted the honey, which slowly dripped down on the royal guest of honour. Always the well-bred lady, The Queen Mother completely ignored the fact that she was covered with honey.

"Honi Soit Qui Mal Y Pense"

"Honi soit qui mal y pense" is the motto of the Knights of the Garter, as well as of the two cavalry regiments of the Household Division and the Grenadier Guards. Dating back to the Norman kings, it is translated as "Evil be to him who evil thinks."

Honorary Grandfather

Prince Charles always called his great-uncle Lord Louis Mountbatten "Honorary Grandfather", and the nickname was no idle compliment. In fact, Charles was always close to Mountbatten and often sought his advice on everything from the speeches he was to make, to the girls in whom he was interested. The Prince was devastated by his uncle's death from an IRA terrorist bombing in 1979. On Mountbatten's coffin, a large wreath from the Prince of Wales carried a card reading "To HGF from HGS"—To Honorary Grandfather from Honorary Grandson.

Bob Hope

Bob Hope was born in England, although he has since become an American citizen. He is one of The Queen's favourite entertainers. She made him a Commander of the British Empire, and made a special point of dancing with him during her 1976 trip to Washington.

"Hoosh-Mi"

"Hoosh-mi" was a word the young Princess Margaret made up to describe a kind of food she detested, with everything all chopped up and mixed together.

"A Hope for the Newly Born"

When Princess Elizabeth gave birth to her first son and heir, Prince Charles, Poet Laureate John Masefield produced a poem to celebrate the occasion. He entitled it "A Hope for the Newly Born":

> May destiny, allotting what befalls,
> Grant to the newly born this saving grace
> A guard more sure than ships and fortress walls
> The loyal love and service of a race.

Horse and Hounds

Horse and Hounds is the magazine favoured by those who go fox hunting, fishing and shooting. Prince Charles and Princess Anne have been avid readers. In 1986, Mark Phillips began to write a column for the magazine.

Horsted House

Horsted House in Sussex is the former country house of the late Lord Neville, Prince Philip's treasurer. Prince Philip and The Queen spent many weekends there. Now converted into a luxury hotel, Horsted House welcomes visitors with hospitality on a grand scale.

House of Windsor

Members of the Royal Family today are all officially members of the House of Windsor. They took that name in 1917 as a patriotic gesture during World War I. Since the time of Queen Victoria's marriage to Prince Albert, the family name had been the House of Saxe-Coburg and Gotha. But that German name seemed inappropriate at a time when Britain was fighting Germany, and King George V changed it to something more English. All descendants through the male line use Windsor as their last name: for example, the daughters of Prince Charles's cousin, the Duke of Gloucester, are called Lady Davina Windsor and Lady Rose Windsor.

In tribute to her husband, Philip Mountbatten, The Queen announced that the name of the family would in the future be the House of Mountbatten-Windsor. The change of name applies to the next generation of the family, The Queen's grandchildren.

House Guests at Holyroodhouse

According to Andrew Duncan in his book *The Reality of Monarchy*, the following sample list gives The Queen's guests at Holyroodhouse for one week in 1969:

- Mrs. Harold Wilson
- William Ross MP, and Mrs. Ross
- The Duke and Duchess of Hamilton and Brandon
- Sir John and Lady Wheeler-Bennett
- Norwegian Ambassador and Madame Koht
- Earl and Countess of Wemyss and March
- General Sir Richard and Lady O'Connor
- Lt.-Governor of Nova Scotia and Mrs. Oland
- Queen Mother
- The Duchess of Gloucester
- The Dowager Countess of Airlie
- Lord and Lady Reith
- Sir Alec and Lady Douglas-Home
- Sir James and Lady Robertson
- The Earl and Countess of Mansfield
- The Dowager Countess of Elgin and Kincardine
- Baroness Elliot of Harwood
- Lord and Lady Birsay
- Princess Alexandra and Angus Ogilvy

Household Cavalry

The Household Cavalry refers to the two senior cavalry regiments in the British Army, the Life Guards and the Blues and Royals. The Household Cavalry comprises about 350 men, all mounted on black horses. Most of the men serve for three years. They always accompany The Queen in ceremonial processions; an official Sovereign's Escort consists of 116 men. The other duties of the Household Cavalry are mounting The Queen's Life Guard at the Horse Guards Parade in Whitehall; providing the detachment that guards the lines during the annual Garter ceremony at Windsor; and providing a detachment that lines the staircase where appropriate on such occasions as the State opening of Parliament and state visits.

Household Division

The Household Division is the military unit that serves as personal bodyguards to the Sovereign, who is also Colonel-in-Chief of the unit. Prince Philip, a Colonel of the Grenadier Guards who form a part of the Household Brigade, once joked, "What is unique about this regiment? It's the only one in which the Colonel is legally married to the Colonel-in-Chief."

The Division wears the vivid red Guards uniforms, with dark trousers and towering fur busbies. It has seven different parts: the Life Guards, the Blues and Royals, the Grenadiers, the Coldstream Guards, the Scots Guards, the Irish Guards, and the Welsh Guards. Experienced Guards watchers can tell the difference in regiments by the arrangement of their buttons and the colour of the plumes in their bearskins.

"How Good He Is!"

According to the book written by The Queen's former governess Marion Crawford, The Queen was impressed when she first met her third cousin Philip. Prince Philip of Greece was a cadet at the Royal Naval College when the King took his family there for a visit in 1939. Princess Elizabeth was thirteen, and he was eighteen. Miss Crawford records that Elizabeth, watching Philip play tennis, exclaimed, "How good he is, Crawfie! How high he can jump!"

"How Is Your Sister?"

Princess Margaret, although she sometimes enjoys an informal atmosphere, remains a stickler for correct royal etiquette. One of her friends once made the mistake of asking in a friendly way, "How is your sister?" Back came the freezing answer, "Her Majesty The Queen is in perfectly good health, thank you."

How to Bop Like a Prince

According to *The Tatler*, several reporters who have seen Prince Andrew in nightclubs have formulated directions for the princely dancing style:

1. Bounce up and down. Raise left shoulder in the air. Lower right shoulder. Snap fingers of right hand.
2. Continue bouncing. Raise right shoulder. Lower left shoulder. Snap fingers of right hand.
3. Repeat step one.

How to Cheer The Queen

According to the orders issued to the crew of the destroyer *Glamorgan* when they were visited by the royals in 1969, this is the way to cheer The Queen:

> On the command, "Stand by to give three cheers. Off caps", the men drop the left hand to the side and seize the cap at the front with the right-hand fingers on top and together, thumb underneath. On the command "Up", remove the cap and hold up at the full extent of the arm at an angle of 45 degrees directly to the front, crown vertical and outboard. On the command, "Three cheers for Her Majesty The Queen—Hip, hip, hooray", men cheer Hooray synchronizing with the command order at the same time as rotating the arm in a clockwise direction (viewed from the rear) round a diameter extending no lower than the shoulder and returning to the original position after each cheer . . . After the third cheer there is a pause of five seconds, then "On caps"—replace caps, hand remains in position until the order "Down".

How to Entertain a Prince

When Mrs. Wallis Simpson met the Prince of Wales in the early 1930s, she already had the reputation of being a superb hostess. He therefore proposed that she ask him to dinner. Mrs. Simpson quickly complied with the invitation, but after it had been issued, she began to fret over the modest quality of her London flat, so much simpler than anything the Prince was used to. The rooms were small, the furniture ordinary, the paintings by unknown artists. How would it look to the Prince who was used to the splendours of Windsor Castle and Buckingham Palace? Mrs. Simpson solved the problem by going to a florist and renting an enormous mimosa tree, so large it hid the entire contents of the dining room. Then she set the table with her best linens and china, lit the scene with candles, and proceeded to captivate the Prince.

How to Pronounce "Ma'am"

If The Queen is not addressed as "Your Majesty", she is simply called "Ma'am". It it pronounced to rhyme with *jam*.

The Queen, visiting Sri Lanka, demonstrates the proper way to stand.

How to Stand Like a Queen

Being a Queen requires long hours of standing, without ever letting one's subjects see that it is hard on the feet. Queen Elizabeth once explained how it is done: "One plants one's feet apart. Always keep them parallel. Make sure your weight is evenly distributed. That's all there is to it."

Margaret Howell

Margaret Howell designed the mannish cream-coloured formal jacket that Princess Diana wears with black trousers, a wing-collared white shirt and a black bow tie. Apparently, the outfit was Diana's idea; "It will amuse Charles", she explained. The trendy menswear look is becoming to her, and an innovation for the royals.

Helen Hughes

Helen Hughes, a school friend of Sarah Ferguson's, became the Duchess of York's lady-in-waiting after Sarah's marriage.

A portrait of the royal couple.

Husbandly Message to The Queen

Whenever travels or duties separate The Queen and the Duke of Edinburgh, he sends her the same message: "The Lord watch between thee and me".

Lady Susan Hussey

Lady Susan Hussey has been one of The Queen's ladies of the bedchamber since just after the birth of Prince Andrew in 1960. Married to Marmaduke Hussey, a former director of Times Newspapers, and now chairman of the BBC Governors, she was quite close to Princess Anne and Prince Charles before they married. Lady Susan is godmother to Prince William, the first son of Prince Charles and Princess Diana.

Courtesy of the British Information Service.

The Princess of Wales on walkabout outside Ely Cathedral after she had opened the National Flower Clubs flower festival at the cathedral and attended evensong.

Hymns

Queen Mary's favourite hymns were, "Abide with Me" and "Glorious Things of Thee Are Spoken"; both were sung at her funeral. The latter was also sung at the wedding of Princess Anne and Mark Phillips.

Princess Margaret's favourite hymn is "Guide Me O Thou Great Redeemer".

Princess Diana's favourite hymn is "I Vow to Thee My Country", which was sung at her wedding to Prince Charles.

"Lead Us Heavenly Father" was one of King George VI's favourite hymns, and it was sung at his funeral.

I

"I Was Off to Windsor Castle"

"I Was Off to Windsor Castle" is a favourite game of Britain's aristocracy. A version of a familiar childhood game, it requires every player to repeat, "I was off to Windsor Castle, and in my bag I took", and then add another item beginning with the appropriate letter of the alphabet. Originally intended as a test of memory, it becomes instead an arena for witticisms... alas, at the expense of the Royal Family.

"Ich Dien"

The motto on the Prince of Wales's crest is "Ich dien", which means "I serve".

Idea of Heaven

Lady Diana Spencer once told friends that her idea of heaven was shopping at Harrods. The cobalt blue suit that she wore for the official announcement of her engagement to Prince Charles came from Harrods, bought off the rack a few days earlier just for the occasion. The demands of her public appearances as Princess of Wales have led her to have most of her wardrobe made to order, but she still buys some of her casual clothes at Harrods, visiting the store early in the morning, often accompanied by Lady Sarah Armstrong-Jones.

Imperial State Crown

The Imperial State Crown weighs about five pounds and was originally designed for Queen Victoria. After the accession in 1952 of Queen Elizabeth II, the crown was adapted not only to fit her but also to appear more feminine than the high-arched shape for the previous kings. The angle of the cross-pattées and the fleur-de-lys was moved outwards and the arches slightly lengthened and lowered with the monde and the cross on top.

The jewels in this crown are some of the largest and oldest in the royal collection. The sapphire mounted in the cross on the top of the crown is said to have come from Edward the Confessor's hand when his tomb was opened in the twelfth century. He reigned from 1042 to 1066, and if there is truth in this tradition then the sapphire is the oldest jewel in the crown. The Black Prince's ruby is in the front of the crown, in the cross-pattée. Although called a ruby, it is in fact a spinel, and was worn by Henry V at the Battle of Agincourt in 1415. When he was Lord Protector, Oliver Cromwell sold the ruby for £63 (the usual price was £4) and it was bought by a royalist supporter and returned to King Charles II at the restoration of the monarchy in 1660.

Just below the Black Prince's ruby is the second largest diamond in the world, weighing 317 carats. Often known as the Second Star of Africa, it flashes with light every time The Queen moves her head. It was cut from the Cullinan diamond, which was given to King Edward VII in 1907 as a gift from the Transvaal government. (The largest diamond in the world, the Star of Africa, is set in the sceptre with the cross.)

The Stuart sapphire was moved from the front to the back of the crown when the Cullinan was received.

The pearls that hang from the arches are said to have been earrings worn by Queen Elizabeth I. The platinum framework is studded with 2,700 diamonds and hundreds of other precious stones.

Informal Palace Luncheons

Beginning in 1956, The Queen has made a custom of entertaining five or six times a year at informal luncheons at Buckingham Palace. The guests (eight to ten, plus The Queen and Prince Philip) are novelists, figures from the racing world, heads of industry, actors, religious leaders and well-known veterinarians. Conversation is generally light-hearted and surprisingly intimate. These luncheons help The Queen to stay in touch with new ideas and new faces.

Inner City Trust

To facilitate his involvement with problems of unemployment and poor living conditions in Britain's city slums, Prince Charles has set up the Inner City Trust. With the help of architect Rod Hackney and such friends as Lord Scarman, the group sponsors community self-help programmes based on the premise that people are better at shaping their own environments than are outside professionals. Inner City Trust's concept is to raise money to help local voluntary organizations create new businesses and employment, improve housing and attract outside investment.

Investiture

An investiture is a ceremony at which The Queen presents honours to her subjects. Twice a year, a list is published of the individuals to be honoured with a knighthood or an order of some sort. Then, in a series of small ceremonies, The Queen herself makes the presentations. New Year Honours are held in February and March; Birthday Honours in October and November. All told, The Queen presents more than three thousand orders, decorations and medals each year.

The ceremony of investiture at Caernarvon Castle in 1969.

Courtesy of the British Information Service.

Investiture of the Prince of Wales

Although Prince Charles had been created Prince of Wales at the tender age of nine, it was not until he came of age that he was formally invested with the title that has traditionally gone to the Heir Apparent. The Queen had promised that she would send her son to the Welsh when he was old enough to understand the investiture ceremony, and he also spent a term at Aberystwyth University learning the Welsh language. The ceremony itself took place at Caernarvon Castle on 1 July 1969. Princess Margaret's husband, Lord Snowdon, whose titles included that of Constable of Caernarvon Castle, was responsible for designing the setting. He did so with the exigencies of TV cameras in mind, creating a canopied space that was nevertheless open to the lens.

Prince Charles wore naval uniform, and he received from The Queen Welsh robes with a silver-handled sword, an amethyst ring and a crown which had been specially made for the ceremony. The Queen wore a gold silk coat and dress, described as being the same colour as a nugget of Welsh gold. Her matching hat, studded with pearls, was like the head-dress of a thirteenth-century lady, underlining the mediaeval origin of the title "Prince of Wales".

The Prince swore his loyalty to The Queen, and then made a speech in Welsh, complete with Welsh idiom and the quotation of Welsh proverbs. Although there were protests by Welsh nationalists the Welsh people generally agreed the Prince was a good sort.

Afterwards, the Royal Family slipped away for a party aboard the royal yacht *Britannia*, lying at anchor nearby.

Irish Guards

The Irish Guards regiment was formed by Queen Victoria in 1900, the year before her death, because she admired the courage of her Irish troops. They wear blue feathers, and their tunic buttons are grouped in fours. On parade they are always accompanied by a mascot, an Irish wolfhound. Every year, The Queen Mother visits the Irish Guards' Chelsea Barracks on St. Patrick's Day and presents them with shamrocks, which they use to adorn their dress hats.

Irish State Coach

The Irish State Coach was built for Queen Victoria, who first used it to open Parliament in 1852. Her great-great-grand-daughter Queen Elizabeth rides in it every year to the State opening of Parliament. It is also used for other occasions, and was chosen to carry King Fahd of Saudi Arabia during his 1987 state visit to Britain. The coach had to be specially reinforced to accommodate his bulk.

Lady Jacquelin Rufus Isaacs

Lady Jacquelin Rufus Isaacs was the twenty-three-year-old daughter of the Marquis of Reading when she met Lord Snowdon in 1970. Lady Jackie and Lord Snowdon developed a firm friendship that eventually made headlines.

"It's That Man Again" (ITMA)

This was a comedy show on radio during World War II which had top ratings and did much to boost morale during the dark days of the war. The cast was led by Tommy Handley, a comedian from Liverpool, who every week was announced by the words "It's That Man Again".

It was a favourite programme with King George VI and his family, who on one or two occasions joined the studio audience in BBC Broadcasting House to watch the programme going out.

Courtesy of the British Information Service.

Andrew, Duke of York, with his supporters the Duke of Gloucester (left) and the Duke of Kent (right), in the Moses Room at the House of Lords, before entering the Chamber to take his seat at the opening of the House of Lords, a ceremony dating from the reign of King Henry VIII.

J

Marie-Luce Jamagne

Marie-Luce Jamagne is the daughter of a Belgian cigarette manufacturer. She married Peter Townsend in 1959.

James Capel and Rowe Pitman

The firm of James Capel and Rowe Pitman serves as The Queen's
brokers.

Robin Janvrin

Robin Janvrin is a former Foreign Office diplomat who was appointed
The Queen's press secretary in June 1987. He replaced Michael Shea.

Jessica

The luxury three-masted schooner *Jessica* appears to be Princess
Michael's favourite form of travel. Owned by Argentinean weapons
merchant Carlo Perdomo, the *Jessica* is where the Princess hid out
when the press revealed that her father was linked to the Nazi S.S.
and when she was reported to be having an affair with Texan Ward
Hunt. In May 1987 she was again a guest on the ship for a Caribbean
cruise, accompanied by her husband, Prince Michael.

Jigsaw Puzzles

Wherever The Queen is in residence, a jigsaw puzzle is sure to be set
up on a convenient table. At teatime, various members of the family
may put in a piece or two, but the most diligent worker is always The

Queen. The puzzles are one of her favourite forms of relaxation, and she has been known to work on one surreptitiously while listening to conversation.

John Lobb Ltd.

Four generations of Lobbs have shod the rich, famous and royal since John Lobb walked from Cornwall to London in the mid nineteenth century. Clients have included Queen Victoria, Edward VII, George VI and Lord Louis Mountbatten, whose lasts are proudly displayed in a glass case in the shop. John Lobb Ltd. holds Royal Warrants from The Queen, the Duke of Edinburgh and the Prince of Wales.

Situated across the street from St. James's Palace, the shop retains its Victorian atmosphere. Craftsmen, nails in mouth, hammer away at individual lasts. Since every customer must have a unique set, there are between 20,000 and 30,000 of the wooden shapes in the basement. Eric Lobb, grandson of the founder, runs the business from a balcony office lined with books that contain outlines of the world's most illustrious feet, including those of Winston Churchill, Frank Sinatra, Katharine Hepburn, and Her Majesty The Queen, for whom Lobb makes many plain daytime pumps.

The Duke of Edinburgh buys his stout walking brogues there, at a cost of about £750 per pair. Lobb also makes dress shoes, such as the patent leather pumps royals wear on black-tie occasions; they are a bit less expensive, costing only £578.

To get a pair of Lobb shoes requires a lot of patience. On the average, a new pair of shoes take about nine months for a new customer, and two to three for one who already has a last on file at the firm. For a self-measuring form and other information, write to: 9 St. James's Street, London SW1.

Les Jolies Eaux

Les Jolies Eaux is the name of Princess Margaret's villa on the island of Mustique in the Caribbean. The land itself was a wedding present from her wealthy friend the Honourable Colin Tennant, who was developing the island. He also assumed the cost of building a house to her design. Completed in early 1972, the decor of the house, in light colours with lots of wicker furniture, cool shades of green and blue, tropical prints in the fabrics, was done by stage designer Oliver Messel, who is Antony Armstrong-Jones's uncle. The gardens contain palms, hibiscus hedges, and orange and lemon trees.

The villa has always been one of Margaret's favourite places; she says fiercely, "It is the only square inch of the world I own." She goes annually and counts on getting a good tan whenever she stays there. When she is not planning to visit it herself, she sometimes rents it out, at the cost of £750 a week. Although it is a holiday house, it is not particularly informal; even in Mustique, all the pillowcases are embroidered "Her Royal Highness the Princess Margaret".

Ulrika Jonsson

Ulrika Jonsson is an attractive blonde Swede, now living in England, who has been romantically linked with Prince Edward. They met in 1987 at a ball during the Royal Regatta at Henley, and the Prince asked her to the theatre the following week. "The Prince was great company," she later told the press.

Jordan Water

Since the time of Queen Victoria, royal babies have been christened with water from the River Jordan. But when Prince William was christened in the summer of 1982, supplies of Jordan water had run out, and ordinary English water had to be used.

Penny Junor

Penny Junor is the author of a biography of Prince Charles, published in 1987. It is her contention that Charles is unhappy because he lives in his wife's shadow, and that he is still searching for some meaningful role to play within the Royal Family. She calls Charles "one of the saddest people I have ever encountered".

The Prince and Princess of Wales are competent skiers and spend much of their time on the higher slopes away from prying eyes.

The Queen and Prince Philip on their ruby wedding anniversary.

Four generations of royalty on the balcony of Buckingham Palace after
the ceremony of Trooping the Colour.

The Wales family in the garden of Highgrove House.

K

"Kanga" (Lady Tryon)

Dale Tryon's nickname, "Kanga", refers to the kangaroos of her native Australia, where she was romantically linked with Prince Charles in the late 1960s. A rather jolly woman with an outlandish sense of humour, she quite easily became one of the Prince's best friends. She married Lord Anthony Tryon, son of The Queen's treasurer and himself a merchant banker. The couple frequently entertain the Prince for dinner in their London house and as a house guest for hunting and fishing. Kanga now designs clothes under that name, and her frilly, feminine fashions have been very successful. Princess Margaret is one of her customers.

Keeping Busy

The *Illustrated London News* compiled a chart of royal engagements, both at home and abroad, for the period from 1 May 1985 to 30 April 1986. The totals were:

The Queen	653
The Duke of Edinburgh	644
The Queen Mother	146
The Prince of Wales	419
The Princess of Wales	305
Prince Andrew	78
Prince Edward	13
Princess Anne	471
Princess Margaret	124

Courtesy of the British Information Service.

The Queen Mother at work.

"Kei-Deth-Be-Doo"

"Kei-Deth-Be-Doo" was the Indian name given to Princess Margaret during her trip to British Columbia in 1958. It means "Little Princess".

Patrick Kelly

Patrick Kelly is an American designer (from Vicksburg, Mississippi) whose collection was the talk of Paris in 1987. His clothes are skintight and reveal the wearer's curves. One of his most enthusiastic fans is Princess Diana. She tried on a clingy leopard-print dress ornamented with sequins at London department store Harvey Nichols. "It's too tight, isn't it?" she asked her bodyguard. When he agreed, she said, "I'll take it."

Kieran Kenny

Kieran Kenny was a twenty-year-old kitchen assistant at Buckingham Palace in 1983, when he sold a story of life below stairs to the *Sun*. It was advertised the day before with the teaser, "When barefoot Di buttered my toast". As soon as that issue hit the stands, The Queen's deputy treasurer went to court to get an injunction against the publication of the article. In addition, he asked for damages on behalf of the Princess of Wales. The royals won their injunction, the *Sun* paid damages to charity—and Kieran Kenny, who had signed an agreement not to publish anything about the Royal Family, lost his job.

Kensington Palace

Kensington Palace, in London, is the present home of many royals. It originated as Nottingham House, a former country estate purchased by William and Mary in 1689 as a London base to substitute for Westminster, which they didn't care for. They commissioned Christopher Wren to expand and improve the building, and other changes have been made in the centuries since then. Kensington Palace is one of the royal residences owned by the country of Great Britain, and kept up by funds allocated by Parliament; part of the Palace (showing a fascinating collection of Court costumes) is open to the public.

One of its most elegant apartments, in Clock Court, is where Princess Margaret lives. Her first home there was a smaller apartment, now occupied by Prince and Princess Michael of Kent, where the Princess and Lord Snowdon lived immediately after their marriage. They stayed there while renovation went on at the Clock Court apartment, whose last occupant had been Queen Victoria's daughter, Princess Louise. At a cost of just £55,000, Clock Court Number 1A became a beautiful home, thanks in large part to the designs drawn up by Lord Snowdon. The drawing room is decorated with Princess Margaret's collection of exquisite Fabergé pieces, along with the glamorous Norman Parkinson photo of the Princess, The Queen and The Queen Mother taken in 1980. Margaret has added a walled garden for private sunbathing and had it landscaped by Roddy Llewellyn. Clock Court is Princess Margaret's only English home, and she lives there alone now that her two children have grown and found places of their own.

Kensington Palace is also the home of the Prince and Princess of Wales. They can be found in Apartments 8 and 9, which have their own private entrance. Although the Department of the Environment had started a restoration of Kensington Palace in 1975, the apartments were not finished by the time the Waleses were married. The Princess had decorator Dudley Poplak supervise the finishing touches, which include wallpaper with a Prince of Wales feather design. Both the Prince and Princess have private bathrooms and two dressing rooms apiece. Most of Diana's clothes are kept in a special storage area in the basement. Upstairs are the nursery and some guest bedrooms.

At one time, it was thought that Prince Andrew would bring his bride to live at Kensington Palace, in the Clock Court apartment formerly occupied by Princess Alice of Athlone. But they opted instead to occupy his old rooms in Buckingham Palace.

Prince and Princess Michael of Kent use Princess Margaret's old apartment as their London headquarters. Although the rooms are considered small by royal standards, they are attractively decorated. The children usually stay at the Kents' country house.

Kentucky Welcomes The Queen

In 1984 Queen Elizabeth made a private trip to the United States, for the purpose of seeing how American stable owners manage their breeding operations. She was the house guest of Mr. and Mrs. William S. Farish at their farm, Lane's End, in Versailles, Kentucky. Mr. Farish is a vice-president of the Jockey Club in the United States and an acquaintance of the Prince of Wales on the polo fields. In addition to touring Lane's End, The Queen also visited Gainesway, the horse farm owned by John H. Gaines, the dog-food heir; Claiborne, the farm established by the great American breeder Bull Hancock; and Spendthrift, where Seattle Slew stands at stud. Explained a Palace spokesman, "American sires have played an increasingly important part in the breeding of horses racing in Europe, and it will be both interesting and valuable for The Queen to visit the stallion stations and stud farms in Kentucky where she has mares of her own visiting American stallions."

Lavinia Keppel

Lavinia Keppel was the governess to The Queen's children, replacing Miss Peebles, who died in October 1968. A distant relative of Alice Keppel, the last mistress of King Edward VII, Miss Keppel taught Prince Edward at Buckingham Palace before he was sent to Gibbs School. Joining the Prince in his Palace lessons were five other children, including Lady Sarah Armstrong-Jones, daughter of Princess Margaret, and James Ogilvy, son of Princess Alexandra.

Kew Palace

Kew Palace is a small, almost cosy, royal home. It was originally built as a country home for a prosperous Dutch merchant in the 1630s. The Crown purchased the house one hundred years later for use as a country house. (Although Kew is now located in suburban London, it was then still in the countryside.) Apart from the addition of modern conveniences, Kew Palace today is pretty much as King George III left it, during the years when he and his family used it as a summer retreat from the city. It is no longer a royal residence but is open to the public as a museum. One of the featured attractions is the 1772 Queen Charlotte's Cottage, an attractive little picnic house. In 1987 the Prince and Princess of Wales had a small dinner party there.

Kilts

When the Royal Family makes public appearances during their summer holiday in Scotland, they generally wear the kilt, often in their own Balmoral tartan. Prince Philip reveals a well-developed calf and wears his kilt with an air of self-confidence. Prince Andrew, on the other hand, seems ill at ease in his kilt. At the 1986 Braemar Games, he allowed the world to discover that royals *do* wear underwear under their kilts.

King Edward VIII

Edward Albert Christian George Andrew Patrick David was born on 23 June 1894, the first child of King George V and Queen Mary (then the Prince and Princess of Wales). His great-grandmother, Queen Victoria, pronounced him a "pretty baby" and expressed satisfaction

that there were three generations of heirs to her throne. Known as
David to his family, he was sent to naval school at Osborne and
Dartmouth and spent a few months aboard ship. On his sixteenth
birthday he became Prince of Wales, and one year later, on 13 July
1911, he was formally invested with the title at Caernarvon Castle.

Thereafter he studied for two years at Magdalen College, Oxford,
from which he was rescued by the outbreak of World War I. David
was commissioned in the Grenadier Guards and insisted on exposing
himself to dangerous situations. He became a favourite with the men
if not with their officers, who worried about their responsibility for
keeping the heir to the throne safe.

His immense popularity with the people cured the Prince of Wales
of his diffidence. He was widely acknowledged to be an athletic and
handsome young man. He was an expert polo player and won trophies
in steeplechase racing; he also liked to hunt and shoot. During the
1920s and '30s he was the most eligible bachelor in the world, and he
was the darling of the media.

David succeeded to the throne on the death of his father in January
1936 and took the name King Edward VIII. He said he wanted to bring
the monarchy into the twentieth century, and he tried to inject new
life into stuffy Court circles; he protested against the use of red
carpets and tried to avoid wearing uniforms and morning dress on
public occasions. But before he had any chance to make his mark as
King, news of his romance with Wallis Simpson began to hit the
papers. In fact, he had been involved with her before he became King,
and she had obtained her divorce from her second husband in April
1936, four months into the King's reign. By the autumn of 1936 he
was trying to find a way acceptable to the British government and the
Empire by which he might marry the twice-divorced Mrs. Simpson
and still be accepted as King. No way could be found and he decided to
abdicate rather than give up the woman he loved.

Thereafter, he was known as His Royal Highness the Duke of
Windsor. The only official post he was ever offered after his
abdication was the Governorship of the Bahamas during the war, and
the Duke spent most of his time living in France with the Duchess or
travelling for pleasure. The Duke published his memoirs, *A King's
Story*, in 1951. He saw little of his family, who had all disapproved of
his Abdication (he told a friend, "They treated me very shabbily").
However, his niece Queen Elizabeth offered him office space in
Buckingham Palace in the early 1960s, a gesture of reconciliation that
pleased him greatly. It was said of him that although he gave up his
kingship, he never ceased to be royal.

The Queen visited the Duke of Windsor at his Paris home just a few days before his death from throat cancer on 28 May 1972. His body was flown back to England to lie in state at Windsor for three days. On 5 June a funeral service was held in the chapel there, after which the former King was buried in the gardens of Frogmore. As a final token of The Queen's wish to honour the Duke of Windsor, she invited his widow to be her guest at Buckingham Palace for the period of the ceremonies.

King George V's Views

On Parenthood

"My father was frightened of his mother; I was frightened of my father; and I'm damned well going to see to it that my children are frightened of me."

On Travel

"Abroad is awful," said the King firmly. "I know because I've been there."

His Majesty King George VI

Albert Frederick Arthur George was born at Sandringham, in York Cottage, on 14 December 1895, the second son of King George V and Queen Mary. His childhood was clouded by a nervous stomach and a bad stammer, possibly the result of being forced to give up left-handedness. Yet even then he had an unusual persistence, as demonstrated by his eventual skill as a right-handed sportsman.

From January 1907 until the end of 1917, "Bertie", as he was called in the family, was in the Royal Navy. He spent two years at the Naval Training College at Osborne, and two more at the Royal Naval College at Dartmouth. Despite severe bouts of gastritis, an ulcer, and an attack of appendicitis, he managed to serve with the Navy during much of World War I. Afterwards, he attended Trinity College, Cambridge, living in a house with his older brother, the heir to the throne.

Late in 1921, Bertie met Lady Elizabeth Bowes-Lyon, a friend of his sister, Princess Mary. He proposed to his future wife three times before she finally agreed to accept him. They were married on 26 April 1923, at which time he was given the title Duke of York. Their first child, Elizabeth, was born in 1926; the second, Margaret Rose, in 1930.

A formal portrait of King George VI.

The Yorks' quiet life in a rather modest London house at 145 Piccadilly came to an abrupt end when the Duke's older brother abdicated in 1936. "This can't be happening to me!" protested the unhappy King George VI, who took that name in tribute to his father.

World War II was a time of great stress and strain for all the Royal Family, and most especially to the King, who felt he must work as hard, and take as many risks, as any of his subjects. Photographs show how the strain aged him. King George VI began to show obvious signs of illness in the late 1940s. After several operations, the problem was diagnosed as lung cancer; the Royal Family was told, but not the King himself. He died in his sleep on the night of 6 February 1952 at Sandringham, after a day of shooting hare and wood pigeon.

King Hassan of Morocco

In 1980, The Queen and Prince Philip made a state visit to Morocco, at the invitation of King Hassan. Rumour has it that the King, apparently angered by the lengthy and meticulous advance planning of the Household staff, with every minute of the three-day visit accounted for, turned sulky and ended up treating The Queen with surprising rudeness. At a banquet she was supposedly left sitting alone, with no food and no host, for nearly an hour. With delayed meals and erratic transport, The Queen missed many of her appointments with other people, and when she gave a dinner on the *Britannia*, the King was more than an hour late. Apparently, he had never heard the French maxim "punctuality is the politeness of kings". Even The Queen's departure was delayed, because Hassan had suddenly decided he wanted to go to the airport to see her off.

Later, The Queen sent King Hassan a message: "We have been especially touched by the way in which Your Majesty took such a personal interest in our programme." Hassan made a 1987 visit to London that passed off without untoward incident, although The Queen's Household was somewhat puzzled by his insistence on bringing his own bed.

King Hussein of Jordan

There are a number of links of friendship between King Hussein of Jordan and the British Royal Family. His daughter Princess Alia went to school at Benenden with Princess Anne, and he himself was educated at Sandhurst. He recently bought a mansion in Windsor Great Park, and The Queen has leased him a stretch of adjoining property to help with his security arrangements. He and his wife, American-born Queen Noor, have been state guests of The Queen and the Duke of Edinburgh.

King Juan Carlos of Spain

The King of Spain is one of the few men with whom Prince Charles can discuss the "business" of kingship. Carlos took his throne in 1976, at the invitation of the Spanish government. So sceptical were most observers of his ability to stay in power that he was nicknamed "Juan the Brief". But he confounded his critics by demonstrating a real ability to govern, and in 1981 he saved the nation from an attempted coup that would almost surely have started another civil war. Juan Carlos's wife, Queen Sofia, was born a Princess of the Greek royal family and is thus related to Prince Philip.

Juan Carlos and Sofia had to decline their invitations to the wedding of Prince Charles and Lady Diana Spencer, because at that time Spain and Great Britain were at odds over the question of which country should control Gibraltar. But as soon as political conditions permitted, the King and Queen of Spain made a state visit to London. In August 1986 the Prince and Princess of Wales and the two little Princes took a holiday trip to the Spanish island of Majorca. "They have been relaxing and enjoying our beautiful weather," explained Queen Sofia. "The children have never been to the beach before and, just like any other youngsters, it has been a very special time for them. They are such delightful lovable children. . . . I would love to keep them both."

King Peter of Yugoslavia

King Peter of Yugoslavia was born in 1923, the son of King Alexander of Yugoslavia and Princess Marie, a great-grand-daughter of Queen Victoria and daughter of Queen Marie of Romania. King George VI, Duke of York, was the child's godfather and attended his christening.

During World War II, King Peter, whose forces were fighting the Germans, visited his cousin King George VI. The English King, noticing a gold charm King Peter was wearing on his military uniform, told Peter to take it off. "It looks damned silly and damned sloppy," he said. King Peter was deposed in 1945 and died in exile in the United States.

The King's Prayer

In December 1939, King George VI made his usual Christmas broadcast. But that year he especially wanted to find words to console and hearten his people, during this first Christmas of World War II. He and the Queen found a book of poems called *The Desert*, published by Marie Louise Haskins in 1908, which included a passage he adapted for the broadcast. It moved the audience immensely, and was immediately dubbed "The King's Prayer". The words were, "I said to the man who stood at the Gate of the Year, 'Give me a light that I may tread safely into the unknown.' And he replied, 'Go out into the darkness, and put your hand in the hand of God. That shall be to you better than light, and safer than a known way.'"

King's Troop

The King's Troop is a unit of the Royal Horse Artillery and is part of the Household Troops.

It was King George VI's wish after World War II that a troop of Royal Horse Artillery, mounted and dressed in their traditional manner, should once again take part in state occasions. The Troop was reformed under its old name, The Riding Troop, and in 1947 King George inspected them. He was so impressed that as he was signing the Visitor's Book in their headquarters in St. John's Wood, London, he crossed out "Riding" and wrote "The King's", and thus they became the The King's Troop. When The Queen came to the throne she decided that the name should not be changed to The Queen's Troop but should remain in memory of her father's interest in them.

The Troop's duties include firing Royal Salutes in Hyde Park on state occasions, royal anniversaries, Trooping the Colour and Remembrance Sunday.

The Kissing of Hands Ceremony

The Kissing of Hands is an ancient ceremony of greeting or parting. Once an important part of royal etiquette, it is used today only to describe the audience given by The Queen to a new prime minister, or to an ambassador or high commissioner of Great Britain before that person leaves for an overseas post. Information received from Buckingham Palace stresses that "there is no kissing involved". Only the normal courtesy of a handshake is required.

Knight Bachelor

While the Order of Knight Bachelor is conferred by The Queen, the recipients are normally chosen by the government in power. The order is symbolized by a gold medal hanging from a tangerine ribbon. Recipients are asked about two months in advance whether they would be prepared to accept the honour if it were offered, and they are asked to treat the letter as confidential. As they have not received the honour at this point, they usually do!

Private collection.

Telly Savalas, star of *Kojak*, a Royal Family favourite.

Kojak

At The Queen's personal request, actor Telly Savalas was among those invited to the White House dinner given in her honour by President and Mrs. Ford in 1976. He starred in *Kojak*, one of Her Majesty's favourite TV programmes.

Sir Alexander Korda

Sir Alexander Korda, the well-known film magnate, came to The Queen's aid during her coronation in 1953. The Superintendent of the Royal Mews had broken the bad news that the Palace was lacking a large number of carriages for the formal procession. After borrowing as many as could be found from other royals and peers of the realm, The Queen was still short of the necessary total. Gallantly, Sir Alexander Korda offered five broughams and two landaus used in his historical films. It was revealed that he had, in fact, bought them from the Palace in an earlier "deaccessioning".

L

Robert Lacey

Author of *Majesty*, the best-selling biography of The Queen; *Princess*, a pictorial celebration of the Princess of Wales shortly after her 1981 marriage; and *Queen Mother*, an in-depth portrayal of the dowager octogenarian, Robert Lacey was born in Surrey in 1944 and began his writing career on the *Sunday Times*. His other acclaimed biographies include *Robert, the Earl of Sussex; Sir Walter Raleigh; The Kingdom;* and *Ford: The Men and the Machine*. Lacey and his wife Sandi, sons Sasha and Bruno, and daughter Scarlett live in Chelsea, London.

Best-selling author and biographer of The Queen, Robert Lacey.

Ladbroke

Ladbroke is the largest firm of bookmakers in Britain, tracing its origins back more than a century. Until World War II, the firm accepted as clients only those who were listed in *Debrett's Peerage*. Today, it takes bets from the Royal Family.

"The Lady in Red"

Chris de Burgh's hit song "The Lady in Red", which climbed to number one in the British charts, was such a favourite with Andy and Fergie that they took the record with them on their honeymoon. Later, they had a chance to meet the performer when they were special guests at his concert to benefit leukaemia research.

Lucinda Lambton

Self-described fanatical royalty watcher, Lucinda Lambton reports on royal doings for the BBC and has amassed close to one hundred Silver Jubilee mugs on the kitchen dresser in her charming little Gothic rectory at Hedgerley, in Buckinghamshire.

Langley Gage

The Langley Gage is a red, sweet gooseberry that was a favourite of King George VI. The bushes planted in his day still bear fruit. Queen Elizabeth II likes to have the berries served for dessert at Buckingham Palace. They are picked the same morning in the royal gardens at Windsor and sent down to the Palace.

Estée Lauder

Estée Lauder was often hostess to the Windsors during their regular visits to Palm Beach in the 1950s and '60s. The founder of the giant cosmetics conglomerate that bears her name, she is also the mother of Ronald Lauder, the American Ambassador to Australia. Princess Diana is known to use Estée Lauder cosmetics, particularly the eye shadows and mascaras.

Lecture from the Duchess of York

During a public appearance in early 1987, Prince Andrew publicly corrected a slight flaw of royal etiquette he detected in his wife. The newly wed Duchess of York turned to her husband and said, in a voice that all could hear, "Unlike some people, I haven't been doing this for twenty-seven years. I'm going to make mistakes and get things wrong. You might as well accept this and just help me." The outspoken Fergie closed the lecture by pinching her husband on both cheeks and giving him a big kiss.

John Lennon

John Lennon liked to make irreverent comments about the royals. When an American journalist asked him what the Beatles thought of The Queen, Lennon replied cheekily, "She's just like a Mum to us." At the Royal Variety Show concert in 1963, Lennon introduced the Beatles hit "Twist and Shout" by saying, "On this number I want you all to join in. Those in the cheap seats can clap your hands. The rest of you can rattle your jewels."

The Beatles were later honoured by being made Members of the British Empire, but Lennon returned his MBE in 1969. "It was an embarrassment to me," he explained. "It was a humiliation. I don't believe in royalty and titles."

Letters to Her Majesty The Queen

The correct way to write to The Queen is to address her as "Madam". The first formal use of her name should be "Your Majesty", and thereafter the ordinary form "you" should be employed. The correct closing of the letter should be "I am, Madam, Your Majesty's humble and obedient Servant and Subject."

Patrick Lichfield

Patrick Lichfield is a photographer who has taken many pictures, formal and informal, of the Royal Family. Although he prefers to be called plain Patrick when he is working, he bears the title of the Earl of Lichfield and he is The Queen's cousin. His mother, Princess Georg of Denmark, was the daughter of John Bowes-Lyon, The Queen Mother's brother. Lichfield took the official silver wedding portrait of The Queen and Prince Philip, and he was the photographer chosen to document the wedding of Prince Charles and Princess Diana for the Royal Family. A lovely coffee-table book of his photos, called *The Royal Family Today*, was published in 1984.

Helen Lightbody

Helen Lightbody was the nanny engaged by Princess Elizabeth following the birth of Prince Charles in 1948. Lightbody (given the courtesy title "Mrs.") had formerly been with the Duke and Duchess of Gloucester and stayed with them until their younger son, now himself the Duke, was out of the nursery. The Gloucesters then recommended her to Princess Elizabeth, and she joined the staff at Clarence House. Nanny Lightbody accompanied the young Prince to watch The Queen's coronation in 1953.

She retired in 1956 after Prince Charles started school, and lived for many years in a grace-and-favour flat in Kensington, where her former charge often visited her until her death in 1987 at the age of seventy-nine. On one of her last interviews, she said proudly, "I still see the Prince from time to time. He has grown up to be a nice young gentleman." Although Prince Charles was unable to attend her funeral because of a series of previous public engagements, he sent a wreath addressed "To Nana".

"Lilibet"

When the young Princess Margaret Rose first tried to say her sister's name, she always mispronounced it as "Lilibet". Others in the Royal Family picked it up, and the nickname got into the popular press as an appropriate way to refer to the sweet little Princess with blue eyes and blonde curls. Nowadays, only her sister and her mother ever call her Lilibet—and only rarely.

The Little Error

Princess Margaret has long been known as a shrewd and careful manager of her money. In the 1960s she noticed discrepancies in her bank statements and still likes to tease her bank manager about what she called "the little error".

A Little Fun for Queen Mary

Although Queen Mary was widely known for her extreme propriety of manner, she had her own little way of finding moments of fun. For example, when cake was served at teatime, she had the habit of cutting hers into little squares and tossing them into the air to catch in her open mouth.

The Little Lady

One day Queen Mary happened to observe her grand-daughter Princess Elizabeth meeting the Lord Chamberlain in a corridor of Buckingham Palace. "Good morning, little lady," he said kindly. "I'm not a little lady, I'm Princess Elizabeth," she replied—much to her grandmother's dismay. After a royal lecture, the Queen and the Princess went together to see the Lord Chamberlain again. "This is Princess Elizabeth," said the Queen tartly, "who hopes one day to be a lady."

Roddy Llewellyn

Princess Margaret met Roddy Llewellyn in 1973 at a house party hosted by her old friends Anne and Colin Tennant. Fair-haired and funny, he kept her amused at the difficult time that her marriage to Lord Snowdon was breaking up. Roderick Victor Llewellyn was born in 1948, making him eighteen years younger than Her Royal Highness. Although he was the son of a colonel, he lived in a commune and was not considered altogether suitable as an escort for the Princess. Sensitive and emotionally vulnerable, he seemed to need Princess Margaret's attention as much as she needed his, and they helped one another over some difficult times in the 1970s. She visited him at the commune, and seemed happier than she had for some time. Meanwhile, Roddy studied landscape gardening at an agricultural college and launched a short-lived career as a pop singer. In July 1981 Roddy married Tania Soskin and dropped out of the headlines.

James Lock & Co.

Holding Royal Warrants from Prince Philip and Prince Charles, James Lock & Co. are well-known hatters who supply everything from polo caps to the felt slouch hats worn by Princess Diana and the Duchess of York. Founded in the 1660s, the firm obtained its first Royal Warrant in 1719, from King George I.

Lock is most famous for its creation of the bowler hat, made for a wealthy farmer who wanted a hat that would fit tightly and withstand storms and overhanging branches. The customer tested the hat by jumping on it. He was satisfied, and the bowler became the prevailing business (and royal) headgear.

Today the firm numbers among its clients such style setters as Rex Harrison, Tom Selleck, Frank Sinatra, Larry Hagman and Alec

Courtesy of James Lock & Co.

Interior of James Lock & Co, Hatters.

Guinness. For further information, write to: 6 St. James's Street, London SW1.

Lionel Logue

Lionel Logue was the speech therapist who helped King George VI to get over his stutter. When the future monarch was a child, his stutter was so bad he was virtually unintelligible. It was his wife who first heard about Logue, an Australian with an office in London, and she urged her husband to consult him. Logue gave the then Duke of York a number of suitably royal speech exercises, such as "Let's go gathering healthy heather with the gay brigade of grand dragoons." Later, as King George VI, the former Duke was able to make public speeches and radio broadcasts without ever stuttering, although he did frequently pause to gather strength before embarking on such treacherous words as *constitution*.

London Bridge

In 1974 The Queen opened the new London Bridge. It replaced the previous bridge, sold to American entrepreneurs, who had it shipped to Lake Havasu, Arizona, in the mistaken belief that they were acquiring the more famous Tower Bridge.

London Library

The London Library is a members-only library on St. James's Square, with over seven thousand members. The present patron is The Queen Mother, and one of the members is Prince Charles. His selections are sent over by messenger. According to the head librarian, "One's always surprised at what goes out to the Royal Household. Of course, it's mainly factual: research before a trip abroad and so forth. But there has been T.S. Eliot's *Notes Towards the Definition of Culture* borrowed; I suppose it *was* read."

The Long-Running "Royal Family"

A joke in the satirical magazine *Private Eye* that especially amused its readers was printed in 1969: "The long-running show *The Royal Family*, which has for the last thousand years been one of the most popular hits with the British public, has been axed, it was revealed today. The show centres around the person of The Queen, a demure upper-class housewife living mainly in London with her family."

Lookalike to The Queen

The accidental discovery that she resembles Queen Elizabeth II has created a unique career for London-born Jeannette Charles. In July 1972 she sat for a portrait intended as a gift for her husband. The result was so amazingly like The Queen that the artist had it hung in

Royal lookalike Jeannette Charles, in costume, complete with handbag.

Courtesy of Jeannette Charles

A royal fan of the Lucia novels.

the Royal Academy Summer Exhibition. The Trustees, thinking it was indeed a portrait of Her Majesty, contacted the Press Office at Buckingham Palace, which refuted it.

Subsequent media attention has sparked invitations for Mrs. Charles's "royal" participation in TV commercials, talk shows, and series such as *First Among Equals* and *Monty Python*. A year younger than The Queen, Jeannette Charles brings respect, dignity and humour to her impersonations. Her clothes, hairstyle and manner of speech are scrupulously authentic.

The Lucia Novels

The Lucia novels are a set of six novels written by E. F. Benson about life in the mythical English town of Tilling—actually Rye, on the south coast. The novels were dramatized in the BBC series *Mapp and Lucia,* and devotees have established a number of societies, such as the Tilling Society in London, the E. F. Benson Literary Guild in California, and the Miss Mapp Society in New York. Among the current activities of these groups is a petition to have a plaque put up on "Mallards", the house in which so much of the action in the Lucia novels takes place. The house is actually based on Lamb House in Rye, already famous because Henry James lived there when he wrote *The Ambassadors.* One of the signers of the petition is none other than The Queen Mother, an ardent fan of the Lucia novels.

J. Lyons and Company

J. Lyons and Company is the firm of London caterers that supplies the scones, sandwiches and cake for the royal garden parties held every June in the grounds of Buckingham Palace.

Prince William waves goodbye on his first day of school.

M

Pipe Major Alexander MacDonald

Pipe Major Alexander MacDonald, who was once the personal piper to King George VI, went on to teach piping at Eton. He recalls that he started playing for the King at nine in the morning—"he thought that was early enough". In the evening he played a march, a strathspey and a reel of the Royal Family's choice in the dining room.

Harold Macmillan

Harold Macmillan (later Lord Stockton) was the third prime minister of Queen Elizabeth's reign. A leader of the Conservative Party, he was chosen for the post in 1957, after the resignation of Anthony Eden. During the last months of Eden's premiership, Eden was frequently ailing, and the responsibility for governing the nation fell largely on the shoulders of R. A. Butler. Yet when the Cabinet voted on who should be the next prime minister, they overwhelmingly favoured Macmillan. The Queen, aware of that vote and in consultation with various elder statesmen, including Churchill and Eden, sent for Macmillan and asked him to form a new government. Macmillan served for six years, and he and The Queen found one another congenial working partners.

Madame Tussaud's

Madame Tussaud's is the best-known exhibition of wax figures in the world. Located in London on Marylebone Road, the exhibition was established by Marie Tussaud, an art tutor to the sister of King Louis

XVI at the Court of Versailles. From the very beginning, it has concentrated on royal figures. Madame Tussaud moved the exhibition to London in 1802 and added wax figures of English royals to her display. Scenes include the execution of Mary, Queen of Scots; the two little Princes in the Tower of London, imprisoned and later presumed to have been murdered by their uncle King Richard III; and Henry VIII with all six of his wives.

Although Madame Tussaud's was badly damaged by a fire in 1925 and later by the bombing of World War II, it has always been rebuilt quickly and reopened to the public. More than two million visitors a year enjoy the spectacle of Madame Tussaud's, and the figures of the Royal Family remain one of the most popular sights.

Courtesy of Madame Tussaud's.

Young Princess Elizabeth on her pony, a favourite exhibit at Madame Tussaud's.

As part of a planned expansion that will eventually include a theme park, Madame Tussaud's has recently opened a re-creation of the splendours of Queen Victoria's Diamond Jubilee. This is located at Windsor and Eton Station, the original site to which The Queen's guests were brought by train from London.

Magic Circle

The Magic Circle is a British association of magicians, sort of an informal trade union. Prince Charles, who loves magic tricks, is a member.

Maids of Honour

At her coronation in 1953, The Queen was attended by maids of honour, like her great-great-grandmother, Queen Victoria. The six young women selected were all unmarried, ranging in age from seventeen to twenty-three, and were also friends of Princess Margaret. They wore identical dresses designed by Norman Hartnell in white satin with bodices embroidered with pink and green roses. Their names were:

- Lady Moyra Hamilton
- Lady Rosemary Spencer-Churchill
- Lady Anne Coke
- Lady Jane Heathcote-Drummond-Willoughby
- Lady Jane Vane-Tempest-Stewart
- Lady Mary Baillie-Hamilton

Majesty

Majesty is a monthly magazine devoted to the Royal Family. It began publication in May 1980, and features lavishly illustrated articles about the doings of all the royals. *Majesty* carries colour photos of recent royal trips and appearances, plus detailed stories about weddings, births and other royal news. The publishers also print handsome collector's cards and the occasional special issue, such as one devoted to the 1986 royal wedding. Anyone may subscribe to *Majesty* by writing to: *Majesty* Magazine, 80 Highgate Road, London NW5 1PB.

Jane Ferguson Makim

Jane Ferguson Makim is the elder sister of Sarah Ferguson. Jane was born in 1957, two years before Sarah. Jane is slim and dark, resembling her mother, whereas Sarah obviously takes after her father. According to family friends, Jane took the break-up of their parents' marriage even harder than Sarah. When Jane married polo player Alexander Makim, Sarah was a bridesmaid.

Malta

When Princess Elizabeth and Prince Philip were a young married couple, they lived for a time in Malta, where Philip was posted by the Royal Navy. There he was given his first command, the frigate HMS *Magpie*, and for a time, he and Princess Elizabeth lived like the other young naval couples. Well, almost. While Philip was at sea, Elizabeth lived aboard the Commander-in-Chief's ship. She did, however, drive herself around the island in a small car, and she and Philip often went for a swim and a picnic in a secluded cove. They were frequent guests at the Malta villa of the Earl and Countess Mountbatten, Guardamangia.

During the carefree days when the Duke of Edinburgh was still a naval officer, he enjoyed a good game of cricket.

Courtesy of the British Information Service.

Mappin & Webb

Mappin & Webb is a silversmith that holds Royal Warrants from both The Queen and the Prince of Wales. Established in 1774 in the city of Sheffield, the firm received its first Royal Warrant from Queen Victoria a hundred years later. Mappin & Webb silver is used on The Queen's Flight and the royal yacht *Britannia*. Today, from London (170 Regent Street) to Tokyo, from Cannes to Cologne, Mappin & Webb sells silver and jewellery that have pride of place for artistry, quality and beauty.

Marchioness of Abergavenny

The Marchioness of Abergavenny is one of the two extra ladies of the bedchamber to The Queen. She was married to the brother of one of The Queen's closest friends, Lord Rupert Neville, until his recent death. She is a keen sportswoman and a well-known rider to hounds.

The "Margaret Set"

Throughout the 1950s, the press focused much of its attention on Princess Margaret, unmarried and third in line of succession to the throne. Her special friends were called the "Margaret Set". They included Sharman Douglas, the daughter of the American ambassador to Britain; Billy Wallace, the polo-playing heir to a million-pound fortune; Tom Egerton; the Earl of Dalkeith; Mark Bonham-Carter; Lord Patrick Plunkett; and Prince Nicholas of Yugoslavia.

"Margot"

"Margot" is the Royal Family's nickname for Princess Margaret.

Marlborough House

Marlborough House, near Buckingham Palace, was originally built as the home of Queen Victoria's Heir Apparent, the Prince of Wales (later King Edward VII). Queen Mary moved into Marlborough House upon the death of King George V in 1936 and lived there until her death in 1953.

Sir Henry Marten

To improve Princess Elizabeth's knowledge of history, it was arranged in the late 1930s for her to be tutored by the distinguished scholar Sir Henry Marten. He was then Vice-Provost of Eton, and possessed just a hint of eccentricity. According to Lady Longford's biography, he often addressed the Princess as "Gentlemen", as if she were an Eton class.

Master of the Horse

The Master of the Horse is the member of The Queen's Household who is responsible not only for The Queen's carriages and carriage horses but all royal cars as well. He always rides behind The Queen in state processions. Long ago, the Master of the Horse was a powerful man at court; now the position is largely honorary, and the actual duties are carried out by the Crown Equerry. The Master of the Horse is the Earl of Westmorland.

Master of The Queen's Game of Swans

The Master of The Queen's Game of Swans is the member of the Royal Household responsible for managing the royal swans. The origin of the post dates back to the time when swans were a popular item at royal banquets; Henry III, for example, required 125 swans for his Christmas feast in 1251. One of the most serious crimes in the realm used to be "swannage", or the unauthorized consumption of swans by poor people, so a Court post was established to look after the birds along the River Thames. It is still a Crown offence to steal or kill a swan.

Today the swans are never eaten, and the true challenge of the post is trying to maintain the swans in significant numbers. The combination of boat traffic, development of the Thames shoreline, and ingestion of lead weights used by fishermen is killing the swans on the lower Thames, so that their numbers there have fallen to about two hundred.

The ownership of swans is designated by marks cut into their bills in a process analogous to branding cattle. Swans with one notch belong to the Worshipful Company of Dyers; swans with two notches on their bills belong to the Worshipful Company of Vintners. Swans with no bill marks at all—the greatest number—belong to The Queen. Once a year, the Master of the Swans takes a five-day census of the population and reports it to the Palace.

Maternal Views of Queen Victoria

Queen Victoria, the mother of eleven children, summed up her considerable experience with royal babies: "An ugly baby is a very nasty object—and the prettiest is frightful when undressed."

Maundy Service

The tradition of Maundy Service on Holy Thursday dates back to the twelfth century. The Queen distributes specially minted silver pennies enclosed in a white purse to a number of recipients that corresponds to her age. This observance of the tradition of royal charity takes place in various cathedrals around the country.

Denise McAdam

Denise McAdam is the hairdresser who arranges the Duchess of York's long red curly hair for her public appearances. McAdam says of her client, "She's game for all kinds of things", and she has braided, bunned, curled and bowed Sarah's hair, ornamenting it with jewels, feathers, flowers and false hair. McAdam works at the trendy Michaeljohn salon in Mayfair, which has a private room in case Fergie feels like dropping in, but usually McAdam goes to Buckingham Palace to do her work on the spot. She also travels with the Duchess on state visits.

Lady Sarah Spencer McCorquodale

Lady Sarah was the first-born child of the Earl of Spencer and his first wife, Frances, parents of Princess Diana. In the late 1970s Sarah's name was romantically linked with Prince Charles, but she married stockbroker Neil McCorquodale in 1980. In 1978 she gave *Woman's Own* a long interview that was reported to be an annoyance to the Palace. In the interview she said of Prince Charles, "He is fabulous as a person, but I am not in love with him. He is a romantic who falls in love easily . . . Our relationship is totally platonic. I do not believe that Prince Charles wants to marry yet. He still has not met the person he wants to marry. I think of him as the big brother I never had."

It was Sarah who first introduced Charles and Diana (who at that time was somewhat friendly with Prince Andrew, closer to her own age) in November 1977, in the middle of a field where the Prince had come to shoot as a guest of the Spencers. "I remember thinking what fun she was then," Charles admitted later. It was not, however, until he met Diana again a few years later when she visited her other sister, Jane, at Balmoral, that he became seriously interested in her. So Prince Charles turned out to be Sarah's big brother (in-law) after all.

Paddy McNally

Paddy McNally was Sarah Ferguson's boyfriend for three years, before she met Prince Andrew. Although it is generally understood that Sarah and Paddy were close friends after his divorce, he remains chivalrously silent about their relationship. McNally manages racing car teams and raises his two children, with whom Sarah still corresponds regularly.

The Meaning of Monarchy

Writing in 1946, famed British historian G. M. Trevelyan mused on the meaning of the Crown:

> The Crown has high value because it enables every British subject to feel personal loyalty and affection for the State embodied in a person. The State is an abstraction, the King is a man. And he is not a party man, whom half the people hope to turn out at the next election. He belongs equally to all. The King is a man, or the Queen is a woman, like one of ourselves, with an individual character and personality, suffering and rejoicing like us and with us. The King is himself, yet he represents all. I feel a more human and warmer loyalty to him than I could to the abstract idea of a parliament or the clauses of the Constitution. And these feelings are shared by millions all over the world.

Meeting on the Polo Field

When the engagement of Prince Andrew and Sarah Ferguson was announced, it was revealed that they had met on the polo field, first as children and then later as adults. Sarah's mother, who first married polo player Ronald Ferguson and then eloped with another polo player, Hector Barrantes, commented, "I know Sarah met him on the polo field... but then, doesn't everybody?"

Ménage à Trois

Ménage à Trois is a chic London restaurant reputed to be a favourite of Princess Diana.

Yehudi Menuhin

Prince Charles chose to celebrate his coming of age by attending a concert at which Yehudi Menuhin played a Mozart violin concerto.

Kate Menzies

Kate Menzies is often mentioned as a girlfriend of Princess Margaret's son, Viscount Linley. She is also a friend of Princess Diana, and a fellow tennis player at the Vanderbilt Racquet Club.

Sir Peter Miles

Sir Peter Miles is the Keeper of the Privy Purse. He manages The Queen's private fortune, as well as the public royal budget.

Milton's Cottage

The poet John Milton's cottage in Buckinghamshire, where he finished *Paradise Lost* and started *Paradise Regained*, has been under royal patronage since the days of Queen Victoria. The dwelling in Chalfont St. Giles, to which the blind poet fled during the London plague of 1665, has often been visited by The Queen, The Queen Mother and Princess Margaret. The cottage and gardens are both open to the public.

Miracle Cure for Princess Anne

In her youth, Princess Anne was often the victim of bad press. Reporters criticized her for being uncooperative and often surly. They also took jabs at what they termed her matronly clothes and her unprepossessing looks. But as time went by, the press and the British people began to appreciate how hard the Princess works and how devoted she is to the causes she believes in, such as the Save the

Courtesy of the British Information Service.

Princess Anne receiving cheers from the public.

Children Fund. By the mid 1980s, coverage of Princess Anne's activities had become much more approving, as her sense of duty was contrasted favourably with what seemed to be the frivolity of the younger royals. When Princess Anne was asked to comment on the phenomenon, she said dryly, "I had noticed I'd undergone a miracle cure."

Simone Mirman

Madame Mirman is a milliner who works with Norman Hartnell's firm and has supplied many of The Queen's hats. She says that The Queen often likes to watch horse races on television while her hats are being fitted.

"Miss Piggy"

Members of the Royal Family have been known to refer to The Queen in her crosser moments as "Miss Piggy". Her Majesty takes it in the affectionate spirit in which it is intended, and on occasion calls her husband to come and look at her on television "with my Miss Piggy face on".

Montreal Olympics

Princess Anne competed in the 1976 Olympics, held in Montreal, as a member of Great Britain's riding team. The Queen and Prince Philip went to the Games to see her in action. Everyone was concerned when she had a bad fall in one of her early rounds, suffered a mild concussion, and thus lost too many points to be a contender for a medal. Because of the fuss about the use of male hormones by women athletes, all women competitors were given sex tests—with the sole exception of Princess Anne.

Philip Moore

Until his recent retirement, Sir Philip Moore was private secretary to The Queen, taking over after the departure of Sir Martin Charteris. His motto on the job was, "I am going to be ruthless", and he has a reputation for toughness and efficiency. But, of course, he is also an urbane diplomat who smoothed away obstacles in The Queen's path. An Oxford graduate, he was in the Diplomatic Service before taking over the post of private secretary. (On a trendier note, his daughter is married to rock star Peter Gabriel, the founder of Genesis.) Moore was succeeded by William Heseltine, his deputy for a number of years.

Mary Morrison

Mary Morrison, nicknamed "Mossy", is one of The Queen's ladies of the bedchamber. The middle-aged unmarried daughter of Baron Margadale, she drives a car with the licence plate "MAM" (the proper way to address The Queen). She went to school at Heathfield with Princess Alexandra.

Ann Morrow, biographer of royals.

Photo by G. Fenn-Smith.

Ann Morrow

Ann Morrow is that rare breed of royal biographer who has travelled thousands of miles with the Royal Family for over a decade as a Fleet Street correspondent. Thus able to observe royal circles first-hand and in both formal and casual situations, Morrow enlivens her work with wry anecdotes and a keen eye for detail. Her first two books were *The Queen* and *The Queen Mother*, both best-sellers in Britain, and future royal biographies are in development. Her other books include *Highness*, an exotic report on the Maharajahs of India. Born in Dublin, the daughter of a prominent Irish newspaperman, Ann Morrow lives in London with her husband and they spend their weekends at their 300-year-old cottage in Gloucestershire.

Mother's Race

Princess Diana competed in a race against other mothers at Prince William's school sports day in June 1987—and won. In the fathers' race, Prince Charles was defeated. The traditional annual event of Wetherby School was held at the Richmond Athletic Ground in Surrey.

René Moulard

René was for many years Princess Margaret's favourite hair stylist. He accompanied her on several of her state visits abroad to ensure that her coiffure always looked perfect.

Lord Louis Mountbatten

Lord Louis Mountbatten was born in 1900, the son of Queen Victoria's grand-daughter Princess Victoria and her husband Prince Louis of Battenberg. Prince Louis, his father, served Britain as the Admiral of the Fleet during World War I and found it advisable at the time to change his Germanic surname to something more English; Mountbatten is the anglicization of Battenberg.

Lord Louis himself had a distinguished military career throughout World War II, and capped his public service by acting as the last Viceroy of India, with the specific mandate of making India independent. In 1922 he married the Honourable Edwina Ashley, daughter of the first Lord Mount Temple, and they had two daughters, Patricia and Pamela. Lord Louis was created the First Earl Mountbatten and made a Knight of the Garter in recognition of his many services to his country. The uncle of Prince Philip, he was also a close advisor to Prince Charles.

Earl Mountbatten was killed in 1979 by a terrorist bomb on his yacht. His funeral service (which he had already planned years in advance) was held in Westminster Abbey, where Prince Charles read the lesson. Prince Philip, Prince Charles, the Duke of Gloucester, the Duke of Kent and Prince Michael of Kent all walked on foot in the funeral procession.

The Mousetrap

The Mousetrap, a play by the doyenne of mystery writers, Agatha Christie, has the distinction of being the longest-running play on the London stage. It opened the year of Queen Elizabeth's accession to the throne; it was still playing twenty-five years later at the time of her Silver Jubilee. The author, incidentally, is a favourite with both The Queen and The Queen Mother.

Mouton Cadet

Mouton Cadet is the claret that is always The Queen Mother's first choice for a meal. It is a low-priced offering from the famed vineyards of Baron Philippe Rothschild. It is robust enough to offset The Queen Mother's favoured sauces, which are heavy with cream, butter and herbs.

"Mr. Puniverse"

According to published reports at the time Prince Edward left the Royal Marines, his fellow cadets had nicknamed him "Mr. Puniverse".

"Mrs. Gwin"

When The Queen travelled to Tuvalu, her loyal subjects there greeted her as "Mrs. Gwin".

Sally Muir

Sally Muir was the creator of one of Princess Diana's favourite jumpers, the red one decorated with white sheep. After the Princess was widely photographed in that version, she appeared in a subtle variant: the same jumper in which one of the sheep had become black. The press scrutinized the jumper for a message, and one newspaper held a competition—"Who do you think is the black sheep of the Royal Family?"—and gave out similar jumpers as prizes. Meanwhile, Sally Muir quietly sold twenty-five hundred of them in her Chelsea shop, "Warm and Wonderful."

Lawrence Mynott

Lawrence Mynott is an English painter whom The Queen Mother commissioned to paint a portrait of the Princess of Wales for her collection. Mynott explains why royals (and other aristocrats) prefer paintings to photographs: "Well, a photo by Lichfield or Beaton is all right for the piano, but they don't do on the walls, do they really?"

The Mystery of Queen Alexandra's Emeralds

Queen Alexandra owned a wonderful set of emeralds, believed to have been a gift from her husband, King Edward VII, after his state visit to India, where they were presumably given to him by one Maharajah or another. Some people believed that those emeralds were part of the Crown Jewels, rather than private property, and there was a great to-do when the Duchess of Windsor was spotted wearing something that looked suspiciously like Queen Alexandra's emeralds. Other authorities say the emeralds were private property, that Alexandra left them to one of her daughters, who sold them to Garrard's, who sold them to Cartier's, who sold them to the Duke of Windsor. Yet the emeralds were not found among the jewels of the Duchess when they went up for auction after her death.

The explanation for the mystery may lie in the theft of a trunk from under the bed of the Duke and Duchess when they were visiting the Earl and Countess of Dudley in England in 1947. The contents of that stolen trunk were never publicized, but the Windsors made a claim against their insurance company for "miscellaneous" jewellery. (The Duke did not want to itemize his gifts to the Duchess, since presumably many of them had been purchased by the allowance he received through the generosity of his brother the King.) Since the final insurance settlement was in the vicinity of £2 million, some very valuable pieces must have been in that trunk.

Myths About the Royal Family

The Queen never wears the same clothes twice. In fact, The Queen gets good wear out of her wardrobe, appearing in several different countries and on several different occasions in each of her outfits. Evening gowns may remain in her wardrobe for as long as five or six years, since styles in evening dress change slowly.

The Queen is the ruler of Great Britain. The truth is that The Queen reigns over Great Britain, but she does not rule it. Her functions are symbolic; she has only the right to be consulted, the right to encourage, and the right to warn the country's government.

The Queen used to call her grandfather King George V "Grandpapa England". Princess Margaret told the Queen's biographer Lady Longford that they were much too awed by their grandfather's stentorian manner to call him anything but just plain "Grandpapa".

The Queen is very shy. Those who know her well assure us that The Queen is anything but shy. She is, however, reserved and somewhat isolated because of her unusual destiny. She is not normally assertive, since in her position, her slightest wish is someone else's command.

The Queen sends £4 to the parents of quadruplets born in Great Britain. Alas, this quaint custom was discontinued in 1957.

The Duchess of York boards a Red Arrows' Bulldog training aircraft at
RAF Scampton. During her hour-long flight over the countryside,
under instruction, the newest royal aviator looped the loop and
performed a barrel roll.

N

The Nahlin

The large white yacht *Nahlin* belonged to King Edward VIII's friend Lady Yule, and the King chartered it in the summer of 1936 for a cruise along the coast of Greece. His guests included Wallis Simpson and other friends such as Diana and Duff Cooper. Even the King's most loyal friends later said they were shocked when they heard Mrs. Simpson imperiously order David to go and fetch her a nail file. The press printed pictures of the King in his shorts, standing on his head, while Wallis looked haughtily in the other direction; these were the first photos of the couple together to appear in print in Great Britain.

After watching the couple together, Diana Cooper wrongly predicted that the affair wouldn't last. "The truth is she's bored stiff by him, and her picking on him and her coldness towards him, far from policy, are irritation and boredom."

Names of Monarchs

British monarchs have sometimes chosen to reign under a name different from the one by which they were known to their families. Thus King Edward VIII was known to his intimates as David, and King George VI was always called Bertie by his parents and wife. When Elizabeth II was told on that February morning in 1952 that her father had died and she was the new monarch, she was asked what name she would use as Queen. "My own, of course," she replied firmly.

National Apple Week

When the Beatles launched their Apple label in 1965, they proclaimed 11 to 18 August "National Apple Week". Presentation boxes of "Our

First Four" releases were ceremoniously delivered to The Queen, The Queen Mother and Princess Margaret. The Queen Mother sent a thank-you note saying she was "greatly touched by this kind thought from the Beatles" and "much enjoyed listening to these recordings".

Nether Lypiatt

Nether Lypiatt is the Gloucestershire country home of Prince and Princess Michael of Kent. The Princess, who was an interior designer before her marriage, decorated the house herself. Its handsome Georgian architecture is enhanced by light colours and comfortable furniture. The Princess has a cluttered study, in which she keeps her Radio Shack word processor and writes her books. Outside there are thirty acres of trees and parkland, where the family rides and romps with assorted dogs and cats.

Never Princess Andrew

When Sarah Ferguson married Prince Andrew, she did not become Princess Andrew. The reason is that on the morning of his wedding Prince Andrew was created Duke of York, and therefore when he married a few hours later, his wife became the Duchess.

Lord Rupert Neville

Lord Rupert Neville was for many years Prince Philip's private secretary and a trusted friend of both The Queen and her husband. The royal couple often stayed at Neville's country house, Horsted House in Sussex, which is now an exclusive small hotel.

New York Church Pays Back Rent

During the royal visit to New York in 1976, Her Majesty was given 279 peppercorns in a Steuben glass container as payment of 279 years of "back rent" from Trinity Church. In 1697 the church received its original charter from King William III, stipulating a nominal yearly rent of one peppercorn. Until July 1976, the rent had never been paid.

Graham Newbould

Graham Newbould was chef for the household of the Prince and Princess of Wales until his resignation in 1987. Despite many pleas for some of their favourite recipes, the chef maintains rigid secrecy on the subject. "I've signed the Official Secrets Act, and anything to do with the Royal Family is taboo." He left to take the position of head chef at Inverlochy Castle in Scotland, one of Britain's premier country hotels.

David Nicholson

David Nicholson is the owner of a racing stable at Stow-on-the-Wold, in the Cotswolds. From 1986, one of his regular jockeys has been none other than Princess Anne. Although she started out racing on the flat, she moved on to the more challenging (and dangerous) steeplechase. A horse she frequently rode in races was Cnoc Na Cuille, on loan to Nicholson from its owner. The Princess had just ridden past the winning post on this favourite mount at Warwick on Saturday 21 May 1988, when Nicholson advised her to dismount quickly. She did so as the ten-year-old steeplechaser collapsed and died of a heart attack. David Nicholson has said of the Princess, "She's a brave and skilful rider, but you still worry." The Princess Royal often drives over to Nicholson's stables to help exercise the horses in the early morning.

John Camden Nield

John Camden Nield was an elderly miser and a great admirer of Queen Victoria. So thankful was he for the blessings of her prosperous reign that when he died he left the Queen his entire fortune, which amounted to about £250,000. That nest egg augmented the savings that Queen Victoria had made from Parliament's allowances and helped to start the fortune in property and financial instruments owned by today's Royal Family.

David Niven

During his filming of *The Prisoner of Zenda* in Hollywood in 1937, David Niven was among the British performers asked to make a special radio broadcast that would coincide with a hot-dog picnic that President and Mrs Roosevelt were giving for King George VI and Queen Elizabeth during their visit to Hyde Park on the Hudson River. Laurence Olivier delivered the "Into the breach" speech from *Henry V*. Brian Aherne recited Rupert Brooke's "The Soldier". Vivien Leigh, Errol Flynn, Ronald Colman, Madeleine Carroll, Cary Grant and Niven himself all took part.

A few years later David Niven was presented to The Queen, and he asked her how the guests at the picnic had enjoyed the broadcast. "Oh, wasn't it awful," Her Majesty replied. "The President's battery ran down just before it came on."

Tricia Nixon

At one time, the press carried many stories about a putative romance between Tricia, daughter of President Richard Nixon, and Prince Charles. Although the rumours might have represented the hopes of some Americans, who liked to imagine Richard Nixon as an in-law of

Prince Charles greets President Nixon at Buckingham Palace

Courtesy of the British Information Service.

The Queen, there was no truth to the story. The Prince subsequently confessed that he had an uneasy feeling that President Nixon was trying to throw him together with Tricia; for example, she was chosen to represent the presidential family at Prince Charles's investiture as the Prince of Wales in 1969. Apparently, he simply wasn't interested.

HMS Norfolk

HMS *Norfolk* was the first ship on which Prince Charles served after he joined the Royal Navy. The ship carried thirty-three officers, so Sub-Lieutenant HRH the Prince of Wales was only one cog in the machinery. Yet it was an exciting time for him, as aboard the *Norfolk* was the first time in Charles's life that he was free of the presence of a detective to watch over him.

O

Oak Grove

Oak Grove was the first home of Princess Anne after she married Mark Phillips. Located on the grounds of the Royal Military Academy at Sandhurst, it is normally occupied by senior staff members. With five bedrooms and stabling for six horses, it met the young couple's needs perfectly during the time that Mark was an instructor at Sandhurst. They stayed at Oak Grove for a little over two years, until they finally found Gatcombe Park.

An Officer and a Gentleman

The film *An Officer and a Gentleman*, starring Richard Gere as a naval officer candidate and Debra Winger as the factory worker with whom he falls in love, is said to be the Duchess of York's favourite.

Angus Ogilvy

Angus Ogilvy is a Scottish businessman married to Princess Alexandra. Himself the younger son of a Scottish earl (the Earl of Airlie), he bears the title Honourable. It is said that he declined the offer of a further title at the time of the marriage in 1963, claiming he was just a simple businessman. His decision meant that the two Ogilvy children also carry no titles. Although Angus Ogilvy joins the Royal Family for private social occasions, such as birthdays and holiday celebrations, he rarely attends public functions, although he accompanies his wife on occasions.

James Ogilvy

James Robert Bruce Ogilvy, the first of the children of Princess Alexandra and Angus Ogilvy, was born on 29 February 1964. He attended Eton and St Andrew's University in Scotland. In July 1988 he married Julia Rawlinson, the daughter of the vice-chairman of the Morgan Grenfell Group. James Ogilvy works in an investment bank.

Marina Ogilvy

Marina Victoria Alexandra Ogilvy is the second child of Princess Alexandra and Angus Ogilvy. Born in 1966, Marina went to school at St Mary's, in Wantage, took a secretarial course in order to look for a job in London, and teaches Outward Bound classes to inner-city kids in the summer. The man who hired her for that job says, "Marina is a lady of some personality, understanding, a considerable presence and a terrific sense of humour. She became a qualified instructor in rock climbing and canoeing. She is also a competent sailor. She has been living in very basic circumstances in a bungalow with other instructors. Everyone knows her as 'Mo'. Nobody has any idea who she is."

Genasio Okriror

Genasio Okriror was a young Ugandan boy, suffering from leprosy, who was adopted by Princess Margaret in 1967. She kept a framed picture of him in her home at Kensington Palace.

Old Clothes

What happens to The Queen's old clothes? Does she give them to a thrift shop? Hand them down to poor relatives? Palace insiders answer the question firmly: "She *wears* them."

"Old Man of Lochnagar"

This was the name of a story written by Prince Charles to entertain his two younger brothers when they were children. Subsequently published as a children's book, the story is about a reclusive old man who decides he wants to visit London but fails to get there... somewhat to his secret pleasure. A few sentences give the flavour of what Charles now calls "my idiotic book": "The door was made of deer skin, and the doorknob consisted of a stag's antler which, when pressed, prodded a tame grouse and made it cry out, 'Go back, go back!' That way the Old Man succeeded in remaining totally alone for years and years and years."

Bruce Oldfield

Bruce Oldfield is one of Princess Diana's favourite fashion designers. The son of a West Indian boxer and an English woman, Oldfield's life story is one of triumph over adversity. His glamorous and sexy clothes are worn not only by Diana but also by such stars as Joan Collins and Barbra Streisand. Diana's favourite Oldfield creation is said to be a blue-dotted one-shoulder evening dress with a ruffle around the top.

145 Piccadilly

In 1927 the then Duke and Duchess of York moved, with their little daughter, the future Queen Elizabeth, from the house at 17 Bruton Street they had borrowed from the Duchess's parents into their own home at 145 Piccadilly. The new house was near Hyde Park and near a typical small London garden of shrubs and grass called Hamilton Gardens. The house had four storeys and was built of stone; there were always daffodils or hydrangeas in the window boxes. The house suffered a direct hit in the bombing during World War II, and the ruins were later torn down to make room for the widened Park Lane.

"One Hip Chick"

Jazz great Louis Armstrong's description of Princess Margaret after meeting her was "one hip chick".

Opera

Insiders joke that The Queen will go to an opera only if it has a horse in it. She does, however, enjoy an evening of Gilbert and Sullivan. Prince Charles loves opera and sometimes slips into the royal box in an ordinary suit to sit in the shadows at the rear, wanting to see the performance without the usual fuss. The biggest opera buff in the Royal Family is The Queen's cousin Lord Harewood, who became the managing director of the English National Opera.

Classical music lover Prince Charles also plays the cello.

Order of Succession to the Throne

1. Prince of Wales
2. Prince William of Wales
3. Prince Henry of Wales
4. Prince Andrew
5. Princess Beatrice of York
6. Prince Edward
7. Princess Anne
8. Peter Phillips
9. Zara Phillips
10. Princess Margaret
11. Viscount Linley
12. Lady Sarah Armstrong-Jones
13. The Duke of Gloucester
14. The Earl of Ulster
15. Lady Davina Windsor
16. Lady Rose Windsor
17. The Duke of Kent
18. Lord Nicholas Windsor
19. Lady Helen Windsor
20. Lord Frederick Windsor
21. Lady Gabriella Windsor
22. Princess Alexandra
23. Mr. James Ogilvy
24. Miss Marina Ogilvy

Courtesy of the British Information Service.

The Princess of Wales, representing Queen Elizabeth II, is asked to inspect newly commissioned Women's Royal Army Corps (WRAC) officers on the 93rd Sovereign's Parade at the Royal Military Academy, Sandhurst.

Order of the Garter

The Order of the Garter is the oldest and most desirable of all the honours The Queen can bestow on her subjects. It dates back to an endearing moment in royal history. It was the night of 23 April 1349, when King Edward III (father of the Black Prince, whose ruby decorates St. Edward's Crown) was dancing with the attractive Countess of Salisbury. Accidentally or on purpose, her blue garter slipped from her leg to the floor. The King picked it up for her and then noticed the leers of the other dancers. "Honi soit qui mal y pense," he said (at that time, the Norman-descended kings spoke French), meaning, "Shame on anyone who thinks bad thoughts". The motto is often translated as "Evil be to him who evil thinks".

From this light moment, the Order of the Garter was born. Originally, it was limited to twenty-five members, but the number was increased in the nineteenth century by removing all British and foreign royals from the head count. However, it is still an honour not lightly bestowed, and the ancient ceremony is impressive. It takes place in the Throne Room of Windsor Castle and is presided over by The Queen, who also selects the recipients of the honour. She buckles a blue and gold garter on the new Knight's left leg, while the Bishop of Winchester says, "To the honour of God Omnipotent and in Memorial of the Blessed Martyr, St. George, tie about thy leg, for thy Renown, this Most Noble Garter." Afterwards, all the Knights of the Garter, wearing blue velvet robes, plumed hats, and the big gold and blue Garter insignia on the left breast, lunch together at Windsor, and then walk in an informal procession down from the private apartments of Windsor Castle to St. George's Chapel for a special Service. The Order of the Garter takes precedence over all other Orders.

The Order of the Thistle

The Order of the Thistle is an ancient order of knights that is often called the Scottish equivalent of the Order of the Garter. Of course, after Scotland was joined with England at the time of the reign of King James I, the order was no longer exclusively Scottish. Throughout the nineteenth and early twentieth centuries, the Order of the Thistle was bestowed by the prime minister, primarily for political service to the prime minister's party. King George VI succeeded in changing that in 1946, when he persuaded Clement

A 1960 photo of The Queen and Prince Philip, taken by Antony Armstrong-Jones. The Queen is wearing the Collar of the Order of the Garter.

Attlee to allow him to choose the recipients of both the Orders of the Garter and Thistle.

Throughout history, there has been only one Lady of the Thistle, and that is The Queen Mother. King George VI gave her a glittering Badge and Star, the emblem of the Order, made of diamonds, sapphires and emeralds, at the end of the day of their coronation—his way of thanking her for all her support and love.

Orders of the British Empire

The Queen bestows six types of Orders of the British Empire as honours to subjects who have served their country well. In order of importance, they are Knight or Dame Grand Cross of the British Empire (GBE), Knight Commander of the British Empire (KBE), Dame Commander of the British Empire (DBE), Commander of the British Empire (CBE), Officer of the British Empire (OBE), and Member of the British Empire (MBE).

Bryan Organ

Bryan Organ is a portrait painter whose royal portraits have often been criticized as too sweet and sentimental, more suitable for greeting cards than posterity. He is one of the godfathers of the second son of the Prince and Princess of Wales, Prince Harry.

Original Turkey Mill Kent

The special thick paper used for The Queen's correspondence is called "Original Turkey Mill Kent". Letters from The Queen bear no stamp, but only her cipher ER in the corner. So much mail goes in and out of Buckingham Palace that it has its own post office.

James Orr

James Orr was the Duke of Edinburgh's private secretary. Like the Duke, Orr attended Gordonstoun school. He later went to the military academy at Sandhurst. Observers have commented that training for war could be helpful experience for the post of Prince Philip's secretary.

Osborne House

Osborne was a seaside residence on the Isle of Wight built by Queen Victoria at her personal expense, and of course with the help and advice of her beloved Prince Albert. It was completed in 1846. After her husband's death, the Queen spent as much time as possible at Osborne and made it a virtual shrine to Albert's memory, keeping everything just as it was when he was alive. Victoria died there in 1901, and Osborne is no longer used as a royal residence. It is now open to the public, remaining just as it was in Prince Albert's day.

Lady Angela Oswald

Lady Angela Oswald is lady-in-waiting to The Queen Mother. One suspects that Lady Angela and The Queen Mother spend much of their time together chatting about horses: Lady Angela is the wife of Michael Oswald, who manages the royal stud.

Michael Oswald

Michael Oswald is the manager of The Queen's racing stud. The Queen keeps about fifteen horses for breeding and racing and remains devoted to the sport. According to Oswald, "She is incredibly knowledgeable about horses, their form and conditions, but she never bets at the racecourse. That I can guarantee."

"Over the Moon"

Prince Charles's reaction to the birth of his first child, Prince William, was, "I'm over the moon!"

Owen the Groom

Owen, a groom employed by the Royal Family, was the first person to give The Queen riding lessons. She had been given a pony when she was just three and a half. She looked up to Owen and quoted his opinion constantly. Once, when she asked King George VI some question about horses, he answered jokingly, "Don't ask me, ask Owen."

Catherine Oxenberg

Making her acting debut in the 1982 TV film *The Royal Romance of Charles and Diana* was Catherine Oxenberg, playing the role of Lady Diana Spencer. Herself related to the Royal Family, she is the daughter of Princess Elizabeth of Yugoslavia and the great-niece of the late Princess Marina, Duchess of Kent.

The Royal Family are very popular in America. This cover of *People Weekly* magazine from 4 August 1986 was one of the best-selling issues ever.

P

Palace

Palace was a magazine about the Royal Family. In addition to good photographic coverage of events in the lives of the royals, there were royal trivia competitions, prizes for readers' photos of the royals, and other participatory features. The publishers also issued books commemorating royal events, such as the thirty-fifth anniversary of The Queen's accession to the throne.

Palace of Holyroodhouse

Every year, The Queen spends a full six days at this official residence in Edinburgh, Scotland. The time is primarily devoted to entertaining some of her Scottish subjects; there are garden parties and always a full complement of house guests. Built on the site of an old abbey, Holyroodhouse was once the home of Mary Queen of Scots and the site of her two weddings, the murder of her secretary Rizzio, and the setting for her fabulous court masques.

Most of the present palace dates from the seventeenth century, at the time of the restoration of the monarchy under Charles II. It is oddly Italianate from the outside, while the interior features Dutch details, such as Delft tiles. The present Queen's grandmother, Queen Mary, gave Holyroodhouse some much-needed restoration in the 1930s, but it has never been a favourite of any member of the Royal Family. The Queen's contribution to its decor is a collection of modern paintings by distinguished Scottish artists.

The Palace of Westminster

The Palace of Westminster stands on the bank of the Thames, not far from Westminster Abbey. A palace occupied the site as early as the year 1000, in the reign of King Canute. It burned shortly after his death and was rebuilt by Edward the Confessor. The adjoining hall we see today was largely the work of King Richard II, in the fourteenth century. The palace itself was totally rebuilt after the huge fire of 1834. Westminster ceased to be a royal residence during the reign of King Henry VIII, who moved his court to Whitehall, but by that time Westminster was already associated with the seat of government, and it has remained the home of Parliament ever since.

Norman Parkinson

Norman Parkinson is known for his glamorous pictures of the Royal Family, the women in particular. A fashion photographer, he was known for "taking photography out of the embalming tank". After many years of living on a farm in Wiltshire, Parkinson moved to a stylish house on the Caribbean island of Trinidad.

Patriot Games

Patriot Games, Tom Clancy's best-selling novel of 1987 published by William Collins Sons & Co. Ltd., opens in London with a terrorist plot to kidnap the Prince and Princess of Wales. The plot is thwarted by American CIA analyst Jack Ryan. When, months later, the young heir to the throne and his pregnant wife visit Ryan's family during a

Courtesy of G. P. Putnam.

Tom Clancy,
author of *Patriot Games*.

goodwill tour of America, the stage is set for a harrowing, suspense-filled showdown when the terrorists strike again.

Paxton & Whitfield Ltd.

Cheesemongers to Queen Elizabeth The Queen Mother, Paxton & Whitfield began business in 1740 in Clare Market, now the Aldwych, in London. By 1853 the growing business had moved to 93 Jermyn Street, where today a Victorian atmosphere still prevails. Along the walls are shelves laden with huge wheels of cheese, and hundreds more are stored in temperature-controlled conditions in vast cellars below.

Catherine Peebles

Catherine Peebles (known as "Mispy") was the governess who taught Prince Charles and Princess Anne when they were children, before they went away to school. She was recommended to The Queen by Princess Marina, Duchess of Kent, because she had educated the two younger Kent children, Princess Alexandra and Prince Michael. The Queen and Prince Philip gave Miss Peebles only one instruction: "No forcing".

Albert Perkins

Albert Perkins was The Queen's detective from the time she came to the throne until the early 1970s, when he retired and his position was filled by Michael Trestrail. A former policeman, he had been detective to King George VI for just a few months before his death. Nicknamed "Admirable Perkins", he rode with The Queen, donned morning dress to accompany her to Royal Ascot, and tried to keep the photographers from bothering her.

Personal Standard of the Duke of Edinburgh

The Duke's personal standard has the emblem of Denmark—three blue lions on a gold field surrounded with hearts—in the first quarter; the Greek white cross on a blue field in the second quarter; the Mountbatten arms—two vertical black bars on a white field—in the third quarter; and the symbol of Edinburgh—a black castle on a hill—in the fourth quarter.

Personal Standard of The Queen Mother

The Queen Mother's personal standard bears the Royal Standard on the left half and her own arms on the right. Her arms are rampant lions of Scotland, in blue on a silver field, in the first and fourth quarters, and three red longbows on a white field in the second and third quarters. Her arms are a pun on her maiden name, Bowes-Lyon.

Personal Standard of Other Royals

All The Queen's children use the Royal Standard topped with a white stripe, or "label", that has three points. Her grandchildren use a label with five points.

Prince Charles flies a three-label Royal Standard on which the central point is covered by a shield bearing the Welsh arms and a Prince's coronet.

Princess Margaret flies the Royal Standard with the three-point label that indicates the child of a king. The central point has a Scottish thistle; the two outer points Tudor roses.

The Duke of Kent, as a royal grandson, flies the Royal Standard with a five-point label. Three of the points bear a blue anchor, two a red cross.

The Phantom of the Opera

The Phantom of the Opera is a musical written by Andrew Lloyd Webber, of *Cats* fame. Princess Diana loves the musical so much that she has seen it several times. Prince Charles, an opera lover, has yet to accompany her.

"Philip's House"

At Balmoral, The Queen has found a small getaway house for her husband, tucked away in the woods by a winding river. There Elizabeth and Philip enjoy simple domesticity, occasionally cooking a meal for themselves and cleaning up the kitchen afterwards. Sir Harold Wilson remembers being invited there for tea when he was a guest at Balmoral during his tenure as Prime Minister. After tea, he reported, The Queen and Mrs. Wilson did the dishes, one washing the cups and the other drying them with a tea towel.

Captain Mark Phillips

Captain Mark Phillips, the husband of Princess Anne, was born on 22

A family photo, at Sandringham, of Princess Anne, her fiancé Captain Mark Phillips, and their parents.

September 1948. His father is a farmer and businessman. He was educated at Stouts Hill Preparatory School and Marlborough College. He joined the army in 1967 and attended Sandhurst Military College, being commissioned into The Queen's Dragoon Guards in 1969.

A distinguished horseman and Olympic gold medallist in riding, Captain Phillips met Princess Anne on the competitive riding circuit. They were married in Westminster Abbey on 14 November 1973. They have two children: Peter, born in 1977, and Zara, born in 1981. He retired from the army in 1978 to take up full-time farming on their estate at Gatcombe Park. Although his wife carries out a number of official duties, Mark Phillips rarely appears in public with the Royal Family.

Peter Phillips

Peter Phillips, born in 1977, is the first child of Princess Anne and Captain Mark Phillips, and was the first grandchild of the Queen. One of his godfathers is the Right Reverend Geoffrey Tiarks.

Sarah Phillips

Sarah Phillips is the younger sister of Captain Mark Phillips, the

Courtesy of the British Information Service.

Peter Phillips with his parents and sister, Zara.

husband of Princess Anne. When Sarah married a broker, Francis Staples, in 1981, one of the pages at her wedding was nephew Peter Phillips, then aged three.

Zara Phillips

Zara Phillips was born on 15 May 1981, just three months before Princess Anne's thirtieth birthday. The second child of Princess Anne and Captain Mark Phillips was christened Zara Anne Elizabeth, the name suggested by Prince Charles.

Picnics

When the royals are at Balmoral, they love to have picnics. One day it may be a small family affair, with Prince Philip presiding at the barbecue; the next it will be for twenty-five or thirty guests. One of those guests described a Balmoral picnic for the *Sunday Mirror* in 1980:

> Picnics are among the highlights of The Queen's holiday and she plans them down to the last detail. She chooses one of her favourite places in the hills or lower mountains on the estate. All the food, crockery and cutlery are packed in hampers and taken there by Landrover. Everyone wears very casual clothes, and some of them really do look as though they had seen better days. But The Queen *always* wears her pearls.
>
> She takes charge of everything—there are no servants on the picnics—and she opens the hampers and serves everyone herself. You eat off your knees sitting on rugs. The Queen gives huge helpings and no sooner is your plate empty than she comes up and says, "And now for a second helping". There are magnificent game pies, pork pies and mutton puddies, all kinds of cold meats, and every sort of pickle imaginable. Then there is a special sweet which the royals love, rather like cold Christmas pudding but made with beer. The Queen is meticulous about tidying up and personally puts everything back into the hampers.

Pilot Royal

Pilot Royal is the name of a film made in 1975 and aired on the BBC on 14 November, the date of Prince Charles's twenty-seventh birthday. The film shows the Prince in action, piloting military planes and landing a helicopter in a constricted area. It also gives the Prince a forum for some of his thoughts about the need for Great Britain to set a good example for the rest of the world: "Other countries I have visited do look to Britain for an example and a lead in so many different things."

George Pinker

George Pinker is the royal gynaecologist who has presided over the births of the two Wales children. Princess Diana opted for natural childbirth, her only aid being the ice cubes she sucked on to prevent dehydration. Prince Charles was present for both births.

Pinkle Ponkle

Pinkle Ponkle was an imaginary creature invented by little Princess Margaret. Pinkle Ponkle's chief activity was hovering in the air over large cities.

Pitkin Pictorials

Famous for distinctive, inexpensive paperback books on the Royal Family and historic buildings, Pitkin Pictorials was founded in 1941 and offers a large range of heavily illustrated books. Subjects include the various royal palaces, Queen Mary's dolls' house, Royal Ascot, royal weddings, and The Queen's Silver Jubilee, which sold over a million copies. For information, write to: North Way, Andover, Hampshire SP10 5BE.

Playing the Piano

The Queen took piano lessons as a girl, from Miss Mabel Lander, known as "Goosey". She learned to play Beethoven, Chopin and Debussy. The royal who is most likely to be found tinkling the ivories is Princess Margaret, who enjoys playing tunes from Broadway shows and singing the lyrics.

Poet Laureate

The Queen appoints the Poet Laureate, whose only formal duty is to officiate over a committee that awards The Queen's Medal for Poetry. Unofficially, it is considered desirable for the Poet Laureate to pen a few lyrics about great royal occasions. The pay for Poet Laureates has been the same for the past three hundred years: £70 a year, plus an additional £27 today (instead of the bottles of wine formerly allotted), along with the privilege of being buried in Westminster Abbey. Former Poet Laureates in the reign of Queen Elizabeth have been John Masefield and Cecil Day Lewis. In 1986, Ted Hughes was appointed to the largely honorary post.

Polo

Polo has long been one of the favourite sports of the Royal Family. The Duke of Windsor was well known to be an enthusiast, and Prince Philip was introduced to the game by his uncle Lord Mountbatten, who not only was a superb player but also wrote an authoritative book on the subject. Philip in turn introduced his son Charles to the

Prince Philip playing polo in 1957.

Courtesy of the British Information Service.

pleasures of falling off a horse at a gallop. Prince Andrew is not a polo player, but he does go to watch Charles on the field, which is how he frequently bumped into Sarah Ferguson, the daughter of Charles's polo manager. Although Diana has never particularly cared for polo, she has attended many matches for her husband's sake. Charles is a four-goal player; Prince Philip was a five-goal man. (The higher the number, the better the player.)

Dudley Poplak

Dudley Poplak is Princess Diana's favourite interior designer. He has spruced up the Waleses' apartment at Kensington Palace, as well as their country house at Highgrove.

Lord Porchester

Lord Porchester manages The Queen's racing stables, although she personally supervises the breeding programme of the royal stud at Wolferton. The son of Lord Caernarvon, he took over as her manager in the 1960s and helped make her stables businesslike. He and his American wife, Anne, sometimes have The Queen and Prince Philip as house guests in their country house in Hampshire. He reports, "The Queen is a wonderful person who enjoys her brief visits with friends, away from state problems, when she can see her studs and look at her racehorses."

Cole Porter

The American lyricist-composer Cole Porter was an intimate friend of the Duke of Windsor dating back to their halycon days in the 1920s. Porter enjoyed discussing music with the Duke, but in a moment of candour was heard to say, "They had to get rid of him as King. He's simple."

Sir Laurens van der Post

The elderly Laurens van der Post has been a major influence on Prince Charles. A writer, film-maker and philosopher, van der Post is a South African who has spent many years of his life trying to understand the culture and lifestyle of the bushmen of the Kalahari Desert. He is lyrical, even mystical, on the subject of the bushmen's communion with nature and their concept of the harmony of the universe.

He has taught the Prince his own philosophy and counselled him on how to interpret his dreams. Prince Charles's speeches often show the effect of van der Post's philosophy: "I rather feel that deep in the soul of mankind there is a reflection of the beauty and harmony of the universe," he told a bemused Canadian audience in 1986. Van der Post is godfather to Charles's first son, Prince William.

Postcards for Collectors

Britain's largest publisher of Royal Family postcards is Whiteway Publications. For information, write to: Unit 14, Victoria Industrial Estate, Wales Farm Road, London W3 6UE.

Pranks of the Royals

When Princess Margaret was a girl, she used to put acorns in boots left inside the porch.

Prince Charles handed out exploding cigars one night after dinner at the Royal Naval College at Dartmouth.

Prince Philip once donned Dracula fangs as he chased The Queen around the royal train.

Prince Michael of Kent poured invisible ink all over the carpet of his childhood home. Alas, once on the carpet, it was all too visible.

On the night of Prince Andrew's stag party, his fiancée Sarah Ferguson and her sister-in-law-to-be Princess Diana dressed up as policewomen and went to a nightclub, where they sat sipping champagne.

The Queen and her ladies-in-waiting put on false beards to receive Prince Philip when he returned from a trip on which he had grown a real beard.

As children, King Edward VIII and King George VI used to put salt and pepper in their grandmother's glass of water. Queen Alexandra always humoured them by taking a sip, even though she knew what they had done.

Prince Andrew once put bubble bath in the swimming pool at Windsor.

Present from Gandhi

For Princess Elizabeth's wedding, Mahatma Gandhi gave her a tray cloth for which he had personally woven the thread. Queen Mary mistook it for one of Gandhi's loincloths and remarked loudly, "How indelicate".

Presents Received on 1969 Trip to Austria

According to a list published in Andrew Duncan's book *The Reality of Monarchy*, the Royal Family received the following official presents while on a state visit to Austria in 1969:

- Two Haflinger ponies
- Book about Haflinger horses
- Stamp album
- Two books of sketches
- Four leaflets entitled "Sights of Austria"
- Four copies of *Masterpieces of Kunsthistorisches Museum*
- Book of prints from the Albertina Collection
- Three copies of book on Crown Jewels of Austria
- Silver reproduction of the Cellini salt cellar
- Records of music from Vienna
- Copy of piano score by Johann Strauss
- Records of *Die Fledermaus*
- Books from Abbey of Klosterneuburg
- Large painted wooden chest
- Bronze cauldron
- Two gold medallions
- Cut-glass urn
- Album of prints of Salzburg
- Sketches of St. Stephen's Cathedral
- Large gold medallion
- Book entitled *Austria and the Anglo-Saxons*
- Umbrella with picture of Spanish Riding School
- Record of Austrian music
- Two books on Piber horse stud
- Austrian cloth
- Book entitled *Romantic Danube*
- Mannlicher rifle and case
- Bronze statue
- Hunting dagger
- Eumig camera
- Book of prints of military uniforms
- Case of pipes
- Book entitled *Count Bernadotte*
- Gold medal
- Skis, boots and poles
- Tablecloth
- Austrian coat for Princess Anne

Press Coverage of Prince Charles

In 1987 Prince Charles commented on the trend of his portrayal in the popular press: "As far as I can make out, I'm about to become a Buddhist monk, or live halfway up a mountain, or only eat grass. I'm not quite as bad as that. Or quite as extreme."

"A Pretty Girl Is Like a Melody"

In 1919 the Prince of Wales (later King Edward VIII) made his first trip to the United States. During his stay in New York, he was taken to a special performance of the Ziegfeld Follies, where he heard the hit song "A Pretty Girl Is Like a Melody". For months afterwards, the Prince went around whistling the song, until his father, King George V, protested that he couldn't stand the annoyance of hearing the "damned tune" one more time.

Prime Ministers of Queen Elizabeth II's Reign

- Winston Churchill
- Anthony Eden
- Harold Macmillan
- Sir Alec Douglas-Home
- Edward Heath
- Harold Wilson
- James Callaghan
- Margaret Thatcher

The Prince and the Towel

In the summer of 1987, Buckingham Palace was quite put out to notice the publication of a photograph of Prince Philip, wearing nothing but a towel wrapped around his middle, with his arm around the attractive Duchess of Abercorn. Her husband is on his other side, and a young friend of the Abercorns, blonde model Hilary Frayne, is also in the picture—also wearing only a towel. The picture was apparently taken at Fort Belvedere, bought by the Abercorns in 1981. How it got into the hands of the newspapers is unknown.

Prince Andrew of Greece

Prince Andrew of Greece was the father of Prince Philip. Andrew was the younger son of King George I of Greece, whose sister Alexandra married King Edward VII, and the grandson of King Christian IX of

Denmark. In 1903, he married the daughter of Prince Louis of Battenberg, who renounced his German title during World War I and became the Marquess of Milford Haven. Prince Andrew and his wife had five children: Margarita, Theodora, Sophie, Cecelie and Philip.

Andrew's father was assassinated by a madman in 1913 and was succeeded by his older son, King Constantine I, who was deposed in 1917. The whole Greek royal family was exiled; they fled first to Switzerland and then to France. Prince Andrew drifted away from his family and ended up on the French Riviera, hobnobbing with various other former royals. He died there at Menton in 1944, leaving his son nothing but two suits and an ivory-handled shaving brush.

His Royal Highness the Prince Charles, Prince of Wales

HRH Prince Charles Philip Arthur George is the eldest son of Queen Elizabeth and Prince Philip. He was born at Buckingham Palace on a bleak Sunday evening, 14 November 1948. His roster of godparents included the King and Queen of England (his grandparents), the King of Norway, his uncle Prince George of Greece, the Queen's brother David Bowes-Lyon, his great-grandmother the Dowager Marchioness of Milford Haven, Princess Margaret, and Lord Louis Mountbatten's daughter Patricia. The young Charles spent his first three years at Clarence House. When his grandfather, King George VI, died in 1952, his mother became Queen, and the family moved to Buckingham Palace.

Charles was tutored at home until he was eight, and he has commented that he thinks the isolation from other children made him awkward and shy. Still, he was the first heir to the throne to go to public school. He attended a day school, Hill House in London, and then boarded at Cheam, where his father had once been a student. When he was fourteen, he went to another of his father's old schools, Gordonstoun in Scotland, known for its spartan rigour. In 1966 he spent two terms at Timbertop, an Australian school. On his return to England, he entered Trinity College at Cambridge, where he studied anthropology and archaeology, in addition to British constitutional history. He spent one term at the University College of Wales at Aberystwyth.

When he left school, Prince Charles, like his father, grandfather and great-grandfather before him, entered the Royal Navy. He was a student at the Royal Naval College at Dartmouth, where he obtained his wings as a jet pilot and learned to fly helicopters. He served with the Royal Navy for five years, leaving in 1977, when he had achieved

Photo by Snowdon, courtesy of the British Information Service.

the rank of Commander and gained experience in commanding a coastal mine-hunter.

Charles was officially invested Prince of Wales in 1969. When he left the Royal Navy, he took up the nebulous duties of heir to the throne. That seemed to mean travel to far-flung parts of the Commonwealth, plenty of "photo opportunities", and choosing a wife to share the burden of monarchy when he takes the throne. On 29 June 1981, Charles married Lady Diana Spencer, now the Princess of Wales, and they have two children: Prince William (1982), the heir to the heir to the throne, and Prince Henry (1984).

In addition to his public duties, Prince Charles enjoys playing polo and the cello, painting, gardening, fishing and flying. He has been a Privy Councillor since 1977; he is also the Chancellor of the University of Wales and President of the International Council of the United World Colleges. He serves as Chairman of the Royal Jubilee Trusts and is a trustee of the National Gallery.

Prince Charles on Cambridge

Shortly after his arrival at Trinity College in Cambridge, Prince Charles wrote a short article about his experience (*Varsity*, 9 March 1968):

> I arrived not without trepidation. I was wedged into a mini, which is a form of travel not normally employed when there are people to meet upon disembarkation. First impressions took on a distorted aspect because all that could be seen in front of Trinity Great Gate were serried ranks of variously trousered legs, from which I had to distinguish those of the Master and the Senior Tutor before meeting them. If you have ever tried to get out of a mini, you will know through what contortions you have to go. Having performed these in front of quite a large number of people, I was taken through the gate and into Great Court.
>
> After the antics outside, Great Court was rewardingly silent, except for the everlasting splashing of the fountain and the sound of photographers' hob-nailed boots, or their equivalent, on the ringing cobbles, together with the click of shutter in lens.
>
> In contrast to the almost detached innocence and beauty of the surroundings, you have the ordinary everyday and every night activities going on, as in my case, directly under your detached and innocently beautiful window. This is something

I find hard to accustom myself to, particularly the ringing
note of a dust lorry's engine rising and falling in spasmodic
bursts of agonized energy at 7 o'clock in the morning,
accompanied by the monotonous, jovial dustman's refrain of
"O come, all ye faithful", and the head-splitting clang of the
dustbins.

Prince Charles's Watercolour

A watercolour by Prince Charles submitted anonymously to the
prestigious Royal Academy was chosen for the 1987 summer show in
a selection process that rejected some 90 per cent of the entries.
Entitled "Farm Building in Norfolk", the $3\frac{1}{2}$-inch square painting is
signed "C" and is attributed in the catalogue to Arthur G. Carrick.
Arthur and George are among the Prince's Christian names, and Earl
of Carrick is among his titles. The summer exhibition consisted of
1320 works by established and unknown artists.

His Royal Highness the Prince Edward

Edward Anthony Richard Louis is the youngest of the four children of
Queen Elizabeth and Prince Philip. He was born on 10 March 1964;
soon afterwards, there was a momentary scandal when the press
printed pictures allegedly stolen from the royal photo album. The
photos showed The Queen sitting up in a bed-jacket cuddling the new
arrival.

Edward, whose godmother is Princess Alexandra, was always
known as the quietest of the royal children. He started his education
with private lessons at the Palace, then moved on to Heatherdown
Preparatory School. Like his father and brothers, he later attended
Gordonstoun School in Scotland. He acted as junior master at the
Collegiate School in Wanganui, New Zealand in 1982 and the
following year was admitted to Jesus College, Cambridge, although
some of his fellow students were upset that he got a place after his
reported low A-level results were leaked to the press. He studied
anthropology, acted in student productions, and played rugby for the
B team. Prince Edward shared a twenty-first birthday party at
Windsor Castle with his cousins Lady Sarah Armstrong-Jones, Lady
Helen Windsor and James Ogilvy.

Prince Edward has taken part in both the recent royal weddings as
supporter for both brothers. But his biggest publicity to date came in
1987, when he decided to leave the Royal Marines, which he had
joined in 1983 and to which he had just been accepted as a full-time

Prince Edward as a schoolboy.

officer. He made a good initial impression; one of the drill sergeants remembered him as "a friendly young man with a pleasant personality. He was a good mixer—the sort of fellow you can take to. He certainly wasn't a clever sod"—apparently meant to be a compliment. Edward survived fourteen weeks of gruelling training at Lympstone, soldiering on through a twisted ankle, bloody nose and damaged knee, and then decided that he simply didn't like it well enough to go on. Many people criticized him for being a wimp and sissy; others applauded him for being his own man and choosing what he wanted to do. It is said that Prince Philip is still angry at his son over what he views as a failure and is deeply disappointed over the end of his military career.

By the end of 1987 Prince Edward began to shoulder the responsibility of royal appearances. As the sole remaining bachelor he is likely to be the focus of much media coverage as the public waits for the next royal romance.

Prince Edward loved the theatre from his days at Cambridge University, and he has joined Andrew Lloyd-Webber's company to learn the craft.

His Royal Highness Prince Henry of Wales

Prince Henry Charles Albert David is the second son of the Prince and Princess of Wales. He was born in London at St. Mary's Hospital on 15 September 1984. Called "Harry" by his family, he is still too young to have made much of an impression on royal watchers.

His Royal Highness the Prince John

Prince John was the youngest child of King George V and Queen Mary. Born in 1905, he was never strong. He suffered from childhood epilepsy, which in those days was more or less untreatable. The Royal Family did its best to keep Prince John's problems out of the public eye. He lived at Sandringham all his life with his valet and nurse and the King and Queen visited him very frequently. He died while still a boy, aged thirteen, in 1919.

His Royal Highness Prince Michael of Kent

Prince Michael George Charles Franklin (after his godfather, President Franklin Roosevelt) is the youngest child of the late Duke of Kent and Princess Marina of Greece. He was born in 1942, only a few weeks before his father was killed in a plane crash while on active duty in World War II, and raised in quiet circumstances at the family home in Buckinghamshire. At the age of five, he acted as a page at the wedding of Princess Elizabeth and Prince Philip. He was educated at Sunningdale Preparatory School and Eton. It was clear from the beginning that he was one royal who would have to earn his own living, as what was left of the family estate would all go to his elder brother. Prince Michael entered the army and went to Sandhurst, the

A Wedgwood Jasper portrait medallion of Prince Michael of Kent.

Courtesy of Josiah Wedgwood & Sons.

Royal Military Academy. Eventually he attained the rank of Major in the Royal Hussars. He left the army in 1981.

Prince Michael became a subject of controversy when he announced his intention in 1978 to marry Baroness Marie Christine von Reibnitz, who was both divorced and a Catholic. She had divorced her first husband, the English banker Thomas Troubridge, the year before. The marriage, although finally approved by The Queen, required him to give up his right of succession to the throne, and at first it was not recognized by the Catholic Church because of Princess Michael's divorce.

Prince and Princess Michael were married in Vienna on 30 June 1978. It was a civil ceremony at Vienna's Town Hall. Attending the wedding in a demonstration of royal support were Princess Anne, Princess Alexandra and her husband, the Duke of Kent and his daughter Lady Helen Windsor, and Earl Mountbatten.

Prince and Princess Michael have no official engagements and are not on the Civil List. The couple have two children: Lord Frederick Michael George David Louis Windsor, born in 1979, and Lady Gabriella Marina Alexandra Ophelia Windsor, born in 1981. At the time of Frederick's birth, his mother said of him, "Look at his lovely big hands. He should make an excellent plumber." The family lives at Kensington Palace and Nether Lypiatt, a country house in Gloucestershire. Prince Michael is interested in racing cars, horses, yachting and even ballooning. He holds directorships in a number of business organizations.

Prince of Wales Feathers

The symbol traditionally associated with the Prince of Wales is a plume of three ostrich feathers. When King Edward VIII acceded to the throne in 1936, after twenty years as the Prince of Wales, he made his first public appearance as King at a British Industries trade fair, and was seen to linger by the booth that displayed ostrich feathers. "I would like to see them come back," he told the press, "but I don't know if I can move the fashions." As it turned out, he could. Hundreds of women immediately stampeded the booth, clamouring to buy a Prince of Wales feather for their hats.

His Royal Highness the Prince Philip, Duke of Edinburgh

Prince Philip was born on 10 June 1921 in an odd location—atop the dining table at his family's home on the Greek island of Corfu. His father was Prince Andrew of Greece, and his mother, Princess Alice of Battenberg, was a great-grand-daughter of Queen Victoria. Although Philip was a Greek prince, he didn't have a drop of Greek blood; his father's family were Danes who had been invited to take over the Greek throne in 1863.

After a peripatetic childhood, during which his family lost the Greek throne and had to go into exile, Philip was educated at Cheam, Gordonstoun, and then the Royal Naval College at Dartmouth. He served at sea in World War II, achieving the rank of Lieutenant. He was second in command on the destroyer *Wallace* and took part in the invasion of Sicily. Later he fought in the Pacific War and was present at the surrender of Japan at Tokyo Bay. A major influence on his choice of the Navy was his uncle Lord Louis Mountbatten.

Philip had known Princess Elizabeth since childhood, and they began exchanging letters when he was at sea. Before his engagement to Princess Elizabeth was announced, Prince Philip renounced his Greek title and became a naturalized British subject, adopting his uncle's name, Mountbatten. On 19 November 1947, on the eve of his wedding in Westminster Abbey, King George VI installed Lieutenant Philip Mountbatten as Knight Commander of the Most Noble Order of the Garter, and created him Duke of Edinburgh, Earl of Merioneth and Baron Greenwich. King George wrote to Queen Mary, "It is a great deal to give a man all at once, but I know that Philip understands his new responsibilities in his marriage to Lilibet."

The Duke of Edinburgh ended his naval career abruptly with the death of King George VI in February 1952, when he shouldered

Courtesy of the British Information Service.

The sixtieth-birthday portrait of Prince Philip, the Duke of Edinburgh.

official engagements and the running the of the estates held by The Queen.

When asked to explain his role in the monarchy, Prince Philip once joked, "Constitutionally, I don't exist." He is not in the line of succession to the throne, and he has no official duties as the husband of The Queen. Nevertheless, he has been a big influence on the Royal Family and the way they conduct the "family business" of being royal. Philip is the one who has pushed the Royal Family into the twentieth century, embracing television, travel by helicopter (which he often flies himself), and more normal lives for the royal Princes and Princesses. At the same time that he urges The Queen to try new things, he also does his best to protect her. Sometimes his temper flares when he sees that she is being bothered by protestors or photographers or simply too many people eager to get a glimpse of her royal self.

Early in her reign, The Queen used to start so many speeches with the words *my husband and I* that it became a standing joke. That turn of phrase does indicate something of her willingness to depend on her husband, as does her attempt to honour him publicly, as when she decreed in 1960 that, although she and her children would continue to belong to the House of Windsor, her grandchildren would henceforth be members of the House of Mountbatten-Windsor.

The Duke is an active patron of hundreds of organizations. He serves as chancellor of Cambridge and Edinburgh Universities; a Privy Councillor; the colonel-in-chief of a number of regiments; President of the World Wildlife Fund; and the founder and sponsor of the Duke of Edinburgh's Award Scheme for young people.

Courtesy of the British Information Service.

Prince Philip relaxes with his paint set.

Prince Philip on the Monarchy

While on a tour of Canada during a time when French-speaking separatists were making a fuss over the outdated institution of the monarchy, Prince Philip told a gathering in Ottawa, "The answer to this question of monarchy is very simple. If the people don't want it, they should change it. But let us end it on amicable terms and not have a row. The monarchy exists not for its own benefit, but for the country. We don't come here for our health. We can think of better ways of enjoying ourselves."

His Royal Highness Prince William of Wales

Prince William Arthur Philip Louis is the first son of Prince Charles and Princess Diana. He was the first heir to the throne to be born in a hospital (St Mary's in Paddington), delivered in his mother's private room with his father in attendance—another royal first—on 21 June 1982. Afterwards, Prince Charles told the waiting crowd, "It's rather a grown-up thing, I find, rather a shock to my system." Only twenty-four hours later, Prince William and his mother went home to Kensington Palace. His godparents include Princess Alexandra, ex-King Constantine of Greece, and Sir Laurens van der Post.

Often called "Wills" by the Royal Family, the young Prince is full of energy and, occasionally, mischief as well. "William's very enthusiastic about things," says his mother tactfully. "He pushes himself right into it." There have been a few problems with the princely temperament: in his first year at nursery school, he froze when he had to deliver his lines in the Christmas pageant, and more than once he has been sent home when he got too rambunctious on an outing. Yet he acquitted himself well of his first royal responsibility when at age four he acted as a page at his Uncle Andrew's wedding. Insiders say he has "amazing aplomb" when he meets the public.

A Prince's Concerns

In a 1985 speech, Prince Charles expressed his personal concern over the problem of Britain's decaying inner cities: "We have very little time to waste. The problem is too pressing, and too many people's lives are being wasted through such intolerable inertia to allow it to continue." The speech was widely interpreted as a criticism of Prime Minister Margaret Thatcher's policies on such matters.

Prince William in his trend-setting snowsuit.

Prince's Trust

In 1972 Prince Charles adopted the idea of helping individual young people who needed some sort of assistance with their lives, so that they could make a contribution to society. At first the plan was handled informally, and amounted to little more than Prince Charles giving his naval salary to deserving youngsters. But in 1976 he formalized the idea as a charitable trust called the Prince's Trust. Since then he has done an excellent job of fund-raising for the Trust. In 1986 he joined it to The Queen's Silver Jubilee Trust, of which he was President, so that the monies the trust can give away amount to over half a million pounds per year.

The Prince's Trust All-Star Rock Concert

Two generations of rock stars joined together on 20 June 1986 for the Prince's Trust All-Star Rock Concert at Wembley Arena, to celebrate the tenth anniversary of one of Prince Charles's favourite charities, the Prince's Trust. The "royalty" of rock artists included Bryan Adams, Eric Clapton, Phil Collins, Elton John, George Michael, Rod Stewart, Sting and Tina Turner. A historic repertoire of rock hits ranged from Paul McCartney singing the sixties Beatles classic "I Saw Her Standing There" to Paul Young's eighties ballad "Every Time You Go Away". The Prince and Princess of Wales presided over the event from their royal box, clapping and dancing to the beat. The event was such a success that it has since become an annual event.

Princes of Wales Through History

Although the sovereign's eldest son is the Prince of Wales, the title was not used for many reigns until King George V revived it and devised an investiture ceremony in 1911 for his son, later the Duke of Windsor. The eldest son of George III was called the Prince Regent until he came to the throne as George IV.

Edward (later Edward II)	1301
Edward the Black Prince	1343
Richard (later Richard II)	1377
Henry (later Henry V)	1399
Edward (son of Henry VI)	1454
Edward (later Edward V)	1472
Edward (son of Richard III)	1483
Arthur Tudor	1489
Henry Tudor (later Henry VIII)	1503
Henry Stuart (son of James I)	1610
Charles (later Charles I)	1616
Charles (later Charles II)	1630
George (later George II)	1711
Frederick (son of George II)	1727

George (later George III)	1751
George (later George IV)	1762
Edward (later Edward VII)	1841
George (later George V)	1901
Edward (later Edward VIII)	1911
Charles	1958

Her Royal Highness Princess Alexandra

Princess Alexandra Helen Olga Christabel was a "Christmas baby", born on 25 December 1936. Her father was Prince George, Duke of Kent, a younger brother of King George VI, and her mother was Princess Marina of Kent, a favourite of the Royal Family. Alexandra has an older brother, now the Duke of Kent, and a younger brother, Prince Michael of Kent. Her father was killed in a wartime plane crash in 1942, and she was brought up simply by her impecunious mother at the family home, Coppins, in Buckinghamshire. Later she attended a girls' school at Heathfield—the first English princess to be sent away to boarding school. She finished her education in Paris while living with the family of the Count of Paris for a year.

Princess Alexandra.

Courtesy of the British Information Service.

In the late 1950s and early 1960s, the press coverage of Princess Alexandra's social life rivalled that of Princess Margaret's. She was a jazz fan and had her own "signature tune", Fats Waller's "Ain't Misbehavin". Alexandra was married in Westminster Abbey on 24 April 1963 to the Scottish businessman Angus Ogilvy. They have two children: James Robert Bruce Ogilvy, born in 1964, and Marina Victoria Alexandra Ogilvy, born in 1966.

Princess Alexandra and her family live at Thatched House Lodge in Richmond Park, a grace-and-favour residence given to them by The Queen. (It had formerly been the home of The Queen's parents when they were the Duke and Duchess of York.) She represents the Crown on many state occasions, and serves as Patron of the British Red Cross Society, Chancellor of the University of Lancaster, and President of the Alexandra Rose Day, founded by Queen Alexandra to raise money for hospitals through the sale of roses. Princess Alexandra is godmother to young Prince William. A close family friend said of the unpretentiously elegant Princess, "She is never happier than when she is eating chocolate cake in the kitchen after everyone has gone home."

Her Royal Highness the Princess Alice, the Duchess of Gloucester

Princess Alice is the widow of the late Duke of Gloucester and the mother of the present Duke. Born Lady Alice Montagu Douglas Scott in 1901, she was daughter of the Duke and Duchess of Buccleuch, and a young woman of musical and artistic tastes. She married Henry, Duke of Gloucester, in 1935, in a wedding that was quiet because it took place not long after her father died. Because of her mourning, the wedding was transferred from Westminster Abbey to the chapel at Buckingham Palace. Princesses Elizabeth and Margaret were her bridesmaids, identically dressed in dainty dresses covered with sprigs of rosebuds.

Alice and her husband had two children: Prince William, born in 1941, and Richard, born in 1944. William was killed in a plane crash in 1972, and Princess Alice's husband, who had been in failing health for several years, died in 1974. She continues to be patron of various organizations and carries out engagements with them and with her regiments.

Princess Andrew

Prince Philip's mother, who was born Princess Alice, the daughter of

Queen Victoria's grand-daughter Princess Victoria and Prince Louis of Battenberg (later the first Marquess of Milford Haven), took the name Princess Andrew when she married into the royal family of Greece. In fact, the Greek royal family are not Greeks, but Danes who were invited to take over the throne in 1863. When her husband's brother, King Constantine, lost the throne in 1917, the whole family went to Paris to live. There Princess Andrew ran a shop that sold old jewellery and objets d'art. Later in her life she and her husband drifted apart, and Princess Andrew started her own order of nuns, the Christian Sisterhood of Martha and Mary. She devoted herself to doing good works on the Greek island of Tinos while wearing a plain grey nun's habit.

Princess Andrew, who was deaf from birth but taught herself to be an expert lip-reader, was an outspoken woman with strong opinions about everything, and she passed some of that stubborn character on to her son. The Queen's engagement ring was made from stones that had belonged to Princess Andrew. She attended her son Philip's wedding to Princess Elizabeth in 1947, but claimed to be too busy to go to King George VI's funeral several years later; she told reporters her work must come first. Princess Andrew spent her last years in poor health at Buckingham Palace and died there in 1969.

Her Royal Highness the Princess Anne

Her Royal Highness the Princess Anne Elizabeth Alice Louise is the second child of Queen Elizabeth and the Duke of Edinburgh. She was born at Clarence House on 15 August 1950, the same day her father was promoted to Lieutenant-Commander in the Royal Navy; he immediately described her to the press as "the sweetest girl". Anne's mother became Queen in 1952, and the family moved into Buckingham Palace.

Anne was first educated at home in the Palace, and at the age of thirteen she was sent to a girls' school, Benenden in Kent. There she continued with the riding lessons that had begun in her early childhood, and started to compete in show jumping and dressage events. She has won a number of trophies for her skill as a horsewoman, including the Individual Women's European Championship in 1971, and she competed in the 1976 Olympics on Great Britain's riding team.

In May 1973, Princess Anne's engagement to Captain Mark Phillips of The Queen's Dragoon Guards was announced, and the couple was married on 14 November of that year. Four years later they moved to their present home in Gatcombe Park, purchased with the help of The

Princess Anne and Captain Mark Phillips at the time of their engagement.

Queen. Anne and Mark's first child, Peter Phillips, was also the Queen's first grandchild, born in 1977, the year of her Silver Jubilee. When The Queen learned that her horse-loving daughter was pregnant she said dryly, "We might well expect it to have four feet." After the birth, Anne wearily remarked that "three-day eventing at Burghley is a doddle compared to this". The Phillips' second child, Zara, was born in 1981.

Princess Anne is President of the Save the Children Fund, as well as Chancellor of London University, and she carries out a heavy schedule of public appearances. In 1987 The Queen honoured Princess Anne by giving her the title of Princess Royal.

Her Royal Highness the Princess Margaret

Her Royal Highness Princess Margaret Rose was born on 21 August 1930 at her mother's ancestral home in Scotland, Glamis Castle. She was the second child of the then Duke and Duchess of York. In 1936, when King Edward VIII abdicated, Princess Margaret's father became King George VI and the family moved into Buckingham Palace. Margaret was a lively and talented girl, and was always considered to be the beauty of the family. In the 1950s she was the subject of extensive press coverage. Her friends, her clothes (she was named on the best-dressed list several times), and most especially her romances

The young Princess Margaret with her sister, Princess Elizabeth.

Courtesy of the British Information Service.

were favourite topics of gossip throughout Britain. When she announced she would not marry Group-Captain Peter Townsend, she was rewarded by the heartfelt sympathy of the entire world.

On 6 May 1960 Princess Margaret married the photographer Antony Armstrong-Jones, who was later given the title Earl of Snowdon. They had two children: David, Viscount Linley, in 1961; and Lady Sarah Armstrong-Jones in 1964. In 1976, Princess Margaret and her husband separated, and two years later they were divorced. She remains the subject of much gossip and speculation about her romances, her sometimes erratic public behaviour, and her health. In 1987 the Palace confirmed that the Princess had undergone surgery but made no comment on the rumours that the surgery was to treat cancer.

Princess Margaret carries out many royal duties. She is Colonel-in-Chief of Queen Alexandra's Royal Army Nursing Corps, Chancellor of the University of Keele, and President of the Royal Ballet. She enjoys holidays at her Caribbean home on the island of Mustique, and she continues to see her large circle of friends, including many show-business luminaries.

The Princess Margaret Look

Princess Margaret has definite preferences about her clothes. She hates rough fabrics of any kind: tweeds, crepes, mohairs. She never wears trousers, she loathes the colour brown, and she has customarily preferred fitted styles that show off her small waist. She

The Princess Margaret look.

Courtesy of the British Information Service.

clings to open-toed platform shoes that make her look taller, and now that she is older, she chooses evening gowns that don't expose too much skin. She wears hats when necessary for her public duties but admits, "I am convinced I look ridiculous in a hat."

Princess Marie Astrid

Princess Marie Astrid is the daughter of the Grand Duke and Grand Duchess of Luxembourg. During the 1970s she was widely believed to be a likely candidate to marry Prince Charles. But Charles met Lady Diana Spencer, and Marie Astrid married Archduke Carl Christian, grandson of the last Emperor of Austria, in 1982. Her wedding was attended by Prince Andrew.

Princess Marina, Duchess of Kent

One of the most popular royals of the twentieth century was Marina, Duchess of Kent. Born a Princess of the Greek royal family (and first cousin to Prince Philip), the young Marina had flawless features and beautiful wavy chestnut hair. One story, possibly apocryphal, about her childhood is that she was punished by having to eat her porridge in a plain china bowl instead of her favourite silver one.

When King George V discovered that his son George, the Duke of Kent, was planning to marry Marina, he said, "George has chosen the most beautiful princess in Europe—and the poorest!" Queen Mary commented approvingly, "No bread-and-butter miss would be of any help to my son, but that girl is sophisticated as well as charming; theirs will be a happy marriage." Their wedding, in 1934 at Westminster Abbey, was a lavish spectacle, and all agreed that Marina made a beautiful bride. The Kents had three children: Edward, the current Duke of Kent; Princess Alexandra; and Prince Michael.

The Duke was killed in a plane crash over Scotland while in the RAF during World War II. His widow was left both grief-stricken and impoverished, since the Duke's income from the Civil List died with him. She received the normal pension for an air commodore's widow with three children, and a small income from the Kent estate (most of which was held in trust for the heir). Marina found herself constrained to sell family antiques and pieces of jewellery to make ends meet, but she continued to hold a reputation as the best-dressed and most elegant royal. She even started a fad for her favourite style of hat, which became known as the Marina hat. Marina numbered

Princess Marina and her husband, the Duke of Kent.

among her friends such celebrities as Noel Coward, Laurence Olivier and his then wife Vivien Leigh, and Danny Kaye. Princess Elizabeth and Prince Philip did much of their courting at Marina's house, Coppins. She died in 1968.

Princess Michael of Kent

Easily the most controversial member of the Royal Family today, Princess Michael is the wife of Prince Michael of Kent, the brother of the present Duke. At the time of her wedding to the Prince, The Queen was quoted as having said, "She sounds much too grand for us." Yet when her cousin fell in love with the divorced Baroness Marie Christine von Reibnitz, The Queen was quick to grant permission for them to marry—on the necessary condition that Prince Michael remove himself from the line of succession to the British throne.

Princess Michael's engagement ring was a lovely sapphire surrounded by diamonds that had belonged to her fiancé's mother, Princess Marina.

Tall (six feet without tiara) and blonde with classic features, Princess Michael is nicknamed MC (for Marie Christine) by her old friends. She has done her part to improve the family fortunes by writing a book, *Crowned in a Far Country*, about historic royal women who married foreign kings and became queens of other countries. The book sold well, but then distinguished authors Harold Kurtz and Daphne Bennett stepped forward to charge Princess Michael with plagiarizing their works.

This development cast something of a shadow over Princess Michael's literary career, although her agent says she is at work on a new opus. The Princess herself said, "People think it's a miracle that a princess can ever read or write, let alone publish a book." She did, however, weep over the accusations and say that since she was left on her own to do the book, she couldn't help making mistakes. She paid a settlement to the outraged authors and included their names in a revised bibliography at the end of her book. Before that scandal had died down, reports arose that Princess Michael's German father had been a devout Nazi with links to the SS.

Her Royal Highness the Princess of Wales

Lady Diana Spencer was born on 1 July 1961, the daughter of the Eighth Earl of Spencer and his first wife, Frances Roche. The third of four children of that marriage, Diana grew up at Park House, an estate in the park at Sandringham that her father rented from The Queen. When Diana was only six, her mother left her father to marry millionaire Peter Shand-Kydd. That caused more than a little scandal. Diana's mother was named co-respondent in the Shand-Kydd divorce, and at the same time was engaged in a lengthy and bitter custody battle for her own children. She lost the custody fight, and did not see her children for a number of years. They continued to live with their father and his new wife, Raine, Countess of Dartmouth, whose mother is best-selling novelist Barbara Cartland. It was not until Diana was in her teens that she once again began to see her mother, visiting her at the Shand-Kydd estate in Scotland.

Diana went to a boarding school called Riddlesworth Hall, and then to West Heath, where she was captain of the hockey team. At sixteen

The Prince and Princess of Wales with their first-born, Prince William.

she was sent to a Swiss finishing school, the Institut Alpin Videmanette, where she learned to cook, speak French, ski and dress well. On her return to England she stayed close to home for a time because her father had suffered a massive stroke. It was he who bought her a large three-bedroom flat in South Kensington, which she shared with one girlfriend who was studying music and another who was a Cordon Bleu chef. Rather than devoting herself to the endless round of deb parties, Diana chose to work at the Young England Kindergarten.

In the summer of 1980 Lady Diana went to visit her sister Jane, whose husband, Robert Fellowes, is The Queen's assistant private secretary. The Felloweses had gone to Balmoral with the Royal Family. Diana was familiar with the royal circle, as her maternal grandmother, Lady Ruth Fermoy, was lady-in-waiting to The Queen Mother, and her other sister, Sarah, had previously been romantically linked with Prince Charles. In fact, Sarah had once introduced her younger sister Diana to the Prince, as they stood in a field at Sandringham. At Balmoral, Prince Charles met Lady Diana again . . . and the rest, as they say, is history.

The Prince and Princess of Wales have two children: Prince William Arthur Philip Louis, born in 1982, and Prince Henry Charles Albert David, born in 1984. The Princess is Colonel-in-Chief of the Royal Hampshire Regiment and patron of a number of organizations connected with Wales.

The Princess's Knee

The comedian Spike Milligan is a favourite of many members of the Royal Family, including Prince Charles and Princess Margaret. Her Royal Highness once spent an evening at a nightclub with Milligan's friend and former colleague on *The Goon Show*, Peter Sellers. Suddenly Milligan turned up on stage to address a poem to the Princess and her escort:

> Wherever you are,
> Wherever you be,
> Please take your hand
> Off the Princess's knee.

Privy Council

About twelve times a year The Queen meets with her Privy Council. Cabinet ministers, who must be Privy Councillors, are sworn in when they take office and they form the active Privy Council while they are in power. Membership is retained for life. The prime minister recommends eminent people to The Queen from other walks of life. When The Queen is away from Buckingham Palace, the Privy Councillors follow her to whichever palace she is presently occupying. Thus some of the council meetings have something of a holiday atmosphere, as the councillors are invited to play golf on The Queen's private course, or go fishing, riding or walking on one of her estates. Councillors say the only drawback to an otherwise enjoyable visit is the continual presence of the corgis sniffing their trouser legs.

Problems of Being a Prince

Shortly before Prince Charles announced his engagement to Lady Diana Spencer, he was chatting with reporters during a visit to India. "It's all right for you chaps," he told them. "You can live with a girl before you marry her. But I can't. I've got to get it right from the word go."

Protest

In 1982, when The Queen visited poverty-stricken Merseyside, a group of protestors waved banners reading "Reality Not Royalty".

In the course of a 1969 visit to Stirling University in Glasgow, The Queen was greeted by beer-drinking students shouting, "Queen Out".

On a visit to Adelaide, Australia, The Queen was greeted by a small group of demonstrators shouting, "Royalty pounces on the poor."

When The Queen visited Belfast in 1966, a seventeen-year-old threw a block of concrete at The Queen's car to protest against Britain's Irish policy. He missed.

When The Queen and Prince Philip visited Oslo, Norway in 1981, IRA supporters tried to throw ketchup on them as The Queen inspected the King's Guards along with King Olaf. Luckily she was wearing bright red that day, so if a drop or two did spatter on her, it wasn't at all noticeable. The Queen never lost her composure.

In 1973, after Britain joined the Common Market, The Queen and Prince Philip were booed by a group of British demonstrators when they appeared at the Covent Garden Opera. The crowd shouted "Sieg heil", in an apparent criticism of links between Britain and Germany, England's wartime enemy.

The Queen Mother was riding in her car through Windsor Park when some teenage boys began to throw stones at her car and others. She asked the driver to halt the car, then got out and spoke to the boys. "What on earth," she asked reasonably, "Will the American tourists think of us?" That was the end of the boys' bad behaviour.

Putting the Royals at Ease

Social psychologist Dr Maryon Tysoe gives advice about putting the royals at ease during conversation: "If you ask them questions that make royals feel uncomfortable, or which they don't want to answer, then that effectively ends the conversation and they will move on. Whilst they may want you to feel that you can talk to them *naturally*, that does not mean that you can talk to them *intimately*."

The Prince and Princess of Wales.

Courtesy of the British Embassy.

Q

Queen Alexandra of Yugoslavia

Queen Alexandra, the wife of King Peter II of Yugoslavia, was a cousin of Prince Philip. Her grandfather was the elder brother of his father, Prince Andrew. In 1959, long after the royals had lost the throne of Yugoslavia, the ex-Queen wrote a biography of her cousin Philip.

The Queen and the Deserter

One evening during World War II, Queen Elizabeth went to her bedroom in Windsor Castle as usual to change for dinner. Suddenly she felt a hand grab her round the ankle. It was a young deserter, who had got into the castle by posing as a worker who had come to replace some light bulbs and then hidden behind a curtain in her room. Apparently the war and the death of most of his family in an air raid had unhinged his mind. The Queen talked to him soothingly until she was able to reach the bell and ring for help; like her daughter forty years later, she remained calm despite the intruder in her bedroom. Later she spoke of him sympathetically: "Poor man, I was so sorry for him."

Her Majesty Queen Elizabeth II

Princess Elizabeth Alexandra Mary was born on 2 April 1926 at the London home of her maternal grandparents, 17 Bruton Street, Mayfair. Her parents were then the Duke and Duchess of York. Along with her younger sister Margaret Rose (born in 1930), Princess Elizabeth was educated at home. In 1936, when Elizabeth was just ten years old, her uncle, King Edward VIII, abdicated and her father became King George VI. Princess Elizabeth was then the Heiress

Her Majesty The Queen.

Presumptive to the throne. She began her public duties early in life, making her first radio broadcast at the age of fourteen and handling her first public engagement at sixteen, when she inspected the Grenadier Guards, of which she was Colonel. Shortly after her eighteenth birthday, she was appointed a Councillor of State while the King was out of the country, touring World War II battlefields.

On 27 November 1947 Princess Elizabeth married His Royal Highness the Prince Philip, Duke of Edinburgh. Their first child, Prince Charles, was born in 1948; Princess Anne was born in 1950; Prince Andrew in 1960; and Prince Edward in 1964. In February 1952, while the Princess and her husband were on tour in Kenya, she received the news that King George VI had died. She became Queen Elizabeth II, and her coronation was held at Westminster Abbey on 2 June 1953.

Since her accession to the throne, Queen Elizabeth has travelled extensively throughout the Commonwealth. Her work as Sovereign includes close contact with the prime minister and others in the Cabinet; hosting heads of state and notable visitors to Great Britain; officially opening Parliament; giving out honours at investiture ceremonies; and undertaking other symbolic activities of a monarch who reigns but does not rule. In 1977 Her Majesty celebrated her Silver Jubilee of twenty-five years as Queen, and in 1986, ceremonies marked her sixtieth birthday. An active horsewoman and horse breeder, The Queen is also a devoted grandmother and family woman.

Her Majesty Queen Elizabeth The Queen Mother

The Queen Mother was born Lady Elizabeth Angela Marguerite Bowes-Lyon on 4 August 1900. Her father was the fourteenth Earl of Strathmore, whose home was Glamis Castle in Scotland, and her mother was the former Nina Cecelia Cavendish-Bentinck. Elizabeth was the ninth child in the family. The oldest had died in a typhoid epidemic, and a younger brother and last child was born two years later. She was educated at home and then served as a nursing assistant when Glamis Castle was turned into a hospital during World War I.

A lively and popular young woman, Elizabeth was acquainted with the Royal Family and acted as bridesmaid to Princess Mary, the Princess Royal (daughter of King George V and Queen Mary), when she married the Earl of Harewood in 1922. Months later, Elizabeth's own engagement was announced, to the second son of the King and Queen. On 26 April 1923 she married the then Duke of York. He had proposed to her twice before, but she had turned him down. Years later, she said of her eventual acceptance, "I'm not sure my reply wasn't more of a surprise to me than it was to him."

The Duke and Duchess of York had two children: Elizabeth, born in 1926, and Margaret, born in 1930. They enjoyed a number of carefree years of family life, until the day in 1936 when the Duke's older brother, King Edward VIII, abdicated and the Duke became King. The new King and Queen's coronation took place on 12 May 1937, the date originally set for the coronation of King Edward VIII.

The Queen Mother has always been popular with the public thanks in large part to her personal warmth, charm and courage. During the World War II bombing she and the King remained in London, sharing the dangers and privations of air raids and shortages. Afterwards she continued to be one of the most accessible of royals. She and King George celebrated twenty-five years of happy married life in 1948, but shortly thereafter his health began to fail. When the King died in early 1952, she became The Queen Mother, doing all she could to support her daughter, the new Queen Elizabeth II.

The Queen Mother continues to carry out a heavy schedule of public appearances even as she approaches ninety. She is a Fellow of the Royal Society and President of the Royal College of Music; for many years she was Chancellor of the University of London. She is the only British Lady of the Order of the Garter and the only Lady of the Order of the Thistle. Her enthusiasm for touring the Commonwealth remains unabated. The Queen Mother's eightieth birthday in 1980 was an occasion of great celebration, both for her own family and for the nation at large.

Queen Margrethe of Denmark

The Queen of Denmark is a distant cousin of The Queen of England; both had the same great-great-grandfather, King Christian IX of Denmark. One of his daughters married King Edward VII of England; another married Czar Alexander III of Russia; a son was invited to become King of Norway. Queen Margrethe was educated in England, first at a public school and then at Cambridge and the London School of Economics. She is married to a Frenchman, a former diplomat. She and her cousin The Queen are great friends and frequently write to each other. In the course of their duties they have exchanged state visits.

The Royal Family at Buckingham Palace in 1947, shortly before the marriage of Princess Elizabeth.

Courtesy of the British Information Service.

Queen Mary

Princess Victoria Mary Augusta Louis Olga Pauline Claudine Agnes was born in 1867, the daughter of the Duke and Duchess of Teck, minor German royalty. She was known as Princess May of Teck; after her marriage, her parents moved to England. Queen Victoria chose the moral and dutiful Princess May as the ideal fiancée for her dissolute grandson Eddy, the Duke of Clarence, who was the heir to the throne.

When the Duke of Clarence died not long before their wedding, Queen Victoria insisted that Princess May should still marry into the Royal Family, and much to her embarrassment the Princess became engaged to the new heir to the throne, Prince George. But the marriage that they embarked upon out of duty became a genuine love match, and in later years King George V was unable even to mention his wife's name in public without displaying tears of emotion. The King desired to have his Queen near him at all times, a dictate that Queen Mary followed faithfully, even though it circumscribed her existence.

George V became King in 1910, on the death of his father, King Edward VII. King George's and Queen Mary's coronation ceremonies took place the following year. When her husband died in 1936, Queen Mary became The Queen Mother, although she never used the title officially. She lived to see the Abdication of her son Edward VIII, the reign of her son George VI, and the accession of her grand-daughter Queen Elizabeth.

Queen Mary died on 24 March 1953, only a few months before Elizabeth's coronation. Putting the duties of royalty above personal gratification to the very end of her life, Queen Mary had insisted that there should be no prolonged mourning for her death to spoil the joy of her grand-daughter's crowning, and her wish was observed. After a procession through the London streets, Queen Mary was buried at Windsor Chapel, beside King George V.

Queen Mary's Dolls' House

Queen Mary's dolls' house, now on display at Windsor Castle, is one of the most charming and complete miniatures ever created. It is so meticulously detailed that it even includes a special Sherlock Holmes story, written as a gift by Sir Arthur Conan Doyle, in a tiny binding.

Queen Mary's Secret Ambition

Near the end of her life, the ever-so-regal Queen Mary confided to her daughter-in-law Queen Elizabeth (The Queen Mother) one of her unfulfilled ambitions: "Do you know there is one thing I never did and I wish I had done: climbed over a fence."

Queen Mary's Views of Royal Education

At the time that the Royal Family began to suspect that King Edward VIII might abdicate, Queen Mary suddenly focused her attention on the education of her grand-daughter Elizabeth, who seemed more likely than ever to ascend the throne one day. She felt there was no point in belabouring the subject of arithmetic, since Princess Elizabeth was never going to have to work out change. She encouraged more Bible reading, and the memorization of poetry for its training value. She considered old-fashioned geography "hopelessly out of date" but thought it would be valuable for Elizabeth to have some knowledge of India and the Dominions. History she considered the most valuable of all subjects for the young girl who might be Queen, and she thought a good way to learn history was through the genealogies of the Royal Family.

Queen Mary's Views on Submarine Travel

When King George V was still merely the Prince of Wales, he was taken for a ride in a submarine by Admiral Sir John Fisher. The future Queen Mary came to the dock to bid him goodbye and told the Admiral calmly, "I shall be very disappointed if George doesn't come up again."

Queen Noor Takes Precedence

American-born Queen Noor of Jordan, as the wife of reigning monarch King Hussein, took precedence over Princess Anne at the 1987 Ascot Ball, which aids the St. John Ambulance Brigade. Princess Anne's mother owns the Ascot racecourse. Princess Anne was quoted as saying, "I'm not sure I'll enjoy giving precedence."

Queen Elizabeth II with the Duke of Edinburgh.

Courtesy of the British Information Service.

The Queen Vic

The Queen Vic is the name of the pub owned by "Dirty Den", the hero (or antihero) of the soap opera *EastEnders*. In 1987 The Queen spent £250,000 to build a pub for her staff at Balmoral, to give them a place of their own to relax in the isolation of the Scottish countryside; they instantly named it the Queen Vic. The royal most likely to appreciate the allusion is Princess Diana, known to be a fan of the programme.

Queen Victoria in Heaven

An artist who was working on miniatures at Osborne once heard young David (later to be King Edward VIII) ask, "Are there kings and queens in heaven? Is everybody equal?" When he was told that heaven was an extremely democratic place, he thought immediately of his great-grandmother, Queen Victoria. "Great-Granny won't like that," he opined.

Queen Wilhelmina

Queen Wilhelmina of the Netherlands is one of the few women monarchs, other than Queen Victoria, to whom The Queen might have looked as a role model. Although the Dutch court is not connected by marriage to the British court, the two have always had a good relationship. During World War II, the British offered the Dutch Queen a safe home in Canada when the Nazi invasion forced her to flee her own country. It was then that The Queen Mother learned to be an excellent shot with a rifle and a pistol; she was determined that if she faced the same situation, she would not go quietly. Forty years later, The Queen Mother was still horrified that Queen Wilhelmina had to leave her country with nothing more than a small handbag.

The Queen's Coming of Age

Elizabeth came of age while on a royal tour of South Africa with her parents and sister. She was the first heir to the throne to celebrate her twenty-first birthday in the Commonwealth, and she marked the occasion with a speech broadcast from Cape Town. "I declare before you that my whole life, whether it be long or short, shall be devoted to your service and the service of our great Imperial Commonwealth to which we all belong." She continued humbly, "But I shall not have strength to carry out this resolution unless you join in with me, as I now invite you to do; I know that your support will be unfailingly given. God bless all of you who are willing to share it."

Queen's Desk

At Buckingham Palace The Queen works at a desk that had been used by her mother, Queen Elizabeth, and her grandmother, Queen Mary. There is always a vase of fresh flowers, and a silver-framed picture of The Queen's father, King George VI, with Prince Charles when he was a boy.

The Queen, working at her desk, with Prince Charles looking on.

Central Office of Information, Crown Copyright Reserved.

The Queen's Flight

The Queen's Flight is the air transport provided for The Queen and the immediate Royal Family by the Royal Air Force. It was established in 1936 by King Edward VIII, as part of his programme to bring the monarchy into the twentieth century. Based in Oxfordshire and piloted by RAF officers, The Queen's Flight today consists of two

somewhat outdated twin-turboprop Hawker Siddeley Andover CC
Mk 2 passengers planes (used for trips within the British Isles or to
the Continent), two British Aerospace 146 jets for longer trips (they
have a range of sixteen hundred miles and cost £16 million), and two
Westland Wessex HCC 4 helicopters to whiz the royals around
London and environs. The Queen Mother is the most frequent of the
royal helicopter passengers, but The Queen herself hates helicopters.

The total cost of The Queen's Flight is about £5 million per year,
which is paid by the British government. Maintenance of The
Queen's Flight has been called "cautious to a neurotic degree".
Engines are constantly being stripped down and rebuilt, and all parts
are replaced long before they are in any danger of failing.

The Queen's Gallery

Queen Elizabeth wanted to share the vast art collection of the Crown
with her people. So in 1960 she announced that she would build a
gallery at Buckingham Palace, called The Queen's Gallery, where the
Royal Chapel had been before it was destroyed by a direct bombing hit
in 1940, and where The Queen herself had been christened. The
gallery opened on 18 July 1962. The Palace explained, "Her Majesty
had always wished to make it possible for the works of art which
belong to her family, and which have in the main already been shown
on a considerable scale, to be even more widely seen by the public."
Exhibitions of art owned by the Royal Family change periodically, and
there is a steady stream of visitors.

Queen's Household

The total Household staff numbers approximately 350 people. All fall
under the supervision of the Lord Chamberlain.

The Queen's Luggage

When The Queen travels, her belongings are packed in blue trunks
labelled "The Queen" in gold. They contain all her clothes (including a
set of mourning), her personal necessities such as a hot water bottle
and her own pillow, and all the gifts she will present to her hosts
during the trip.

The Queen's Messengers

A corps of thirty-four gentlemen between the ages of forty and sixty
make up The Queen's Messengers. Established in the reign of King

Henry VIII, the Messengers carry confidential documents on behalf of the monarch and the monarch's government. Although today many documents are transmitted electronically, certain papers still need to be hand-carried to British embassies all over the world.

The Queen's Messengers are usually former military officers, who travel unarmed; according to one report, their greatest danger is not hold-up at gunpoint but physical fatigue and boredom.

Queen's Personal Flag

On occasions when the Royal Standard would be inappropriate, The Queen may choose to fly her personal flag. Adopted in 1960, it is royal blue with a gold fringe and carries in the centre a large E topped by a crown, enclosed by a circle of Tudor roses.

The Queen's Handbag

One of the most asked questions about The Queen is, "What's in her handbag?" The fact that she *always* carries a bag, even when she is wearing an evening gown and a crown, has not escaped public notice, nor has the fact that her handbags are uniformly old-fashioned and boxy. (Hardy Amies once gave The Queen a dashing white shoulder bag for Christmas, hoping to wean her away from the sturdy lunch-box style she favours; The Queen said "How kind", but has never been seen with it since.)

One assumes The Queen doesn't need to carry money or credit cards, doesn't need the keys to the Rolls or the front door of the Palace—so what is in there? An authoritative source says The Queen always carries a hanky and her trademark bright red lipstick. Although she concedes it is not flattering to her close up, the strong colour photographs well and shows up at great distances, so The Queen frequently applies a fresh coat of lipstick, and can even do it deftly and discreetly right out in public at the end of a banquet before the mingling afterwards.

As to why she feels she always has to carry a handbag, dressmaker Hardy Amies once explained, "With her handbag and gloves, she is equipped, ready to face the world." Or we might consider the notion of Dr. Freud that a handbag is a symbol of female sexuality. The Queen is a woman in what is often a man's occupation, so perhaps she has reason to show the world her badge of femininity.

Queen's Robing Room

The Royal Robing Room in the Palace of Westminster opens off the Norman Porch at the head of the staircase. It is so large that for ten years from 1941 it served as the chamber for the House of Lords after the Palace of Westminster had been bombed.

There is hardly a square inch which is without decoration; even the great double doors through which The Queen leaves to begin her procession have Tudor roses in fine metal all over them. Prince Albert, who took a great interest in the rebuilding of this Palace after a disastrous fire in 1834, was the Chairman of a Fine Art Commission set up to oversee the decoration. He revived the mediaeval style and encouraged William Dyce to reintroduce frescoes to England. They are painted round the walls of the Robing Room on the theme of the chivalry of King Arthur and his Knights.

The Queen is in the Robing Room for only a few minutes each year as she puts on her parliamentary robe and the Imperial State Crown, surrounded by mirrors so that she can see that all is well. She then begins her procession to the House of Lords.

Queen's Sixtieth Birthday

On her sixtieth birthday in 1986, The Queen started the day by attending a service of thanksgiving with her husband and children at St. George's Chapel in Windsor. Later she received greetings and bouquets from schoolchildren in front of Buckingham Palace. That evening, accompanied by Prince Philip, she went to a special performance at the Royal Opera House in Covent Garden.

The Queen's Titles

Her Most Excellent Majesty ELIZABETH THE SECOND (Elizabeth Alexandra Mary of Windsor) by the Grace of God of the United Kingdom of Great Britain and Northern Ireland and of Her other Realms and Territories Queen, Head of the Commonwealth, Defender of the Faith, Sovereign of the British Orders of Knighthood and Sovereign Head of the Order of St. John, Lord High Admiral of the United Kingdom, Colonel-in-Chief of The Life Guards, The Blues and Royals (Royal Horse Guards and 1st Dragoons), The Royal Scots Dragoon Guards (Carabiniers and Greys) 16th/5th The Queen's Lancers, Royal Tank Regiment, Corps of Royal Engineers, Grenadier Guards, Coldstream Guards, Scots Guards, Irish Guards, Welsh

Guards, The Royal Welch Fusiliers, The Queen's Lancashire
Regiment, The Argyll and Sutherland Highlanders (Princess Louise's),
The Royal Green Jackets, Royal Army Ordnance Corps, Corps of
Royal Military Police, The Queen's Own Mercian Yeomanry, The
Duke of Lancaster's Own Yeomanry, Canadian Forces Military
Engineers Branch, The King's Own Calgary Regiment, Royal 22e
Regiment, Governor-General's Foot Guards, The Canadian Grenadier
Guards, Le Régiment de la Chaudière, 2nd Bn. Royal New Brunswick
Regt. (North Shore), The 48th Highlanders of Canada, The Argyll
and Sutherland Highlanders of Canada (Princess Louise's), The
Calgary Highlanders, Royal Australian Engineers, Royal Australian
Infantry Corps, Royal Australian Army Ordnance Corps, Royal
Australian Army Nursing Corps, The Corps of Royal New Zealand
Engineers, Royal New Zealand Infantry Regiment, Royal New
Zealand Army Ordnance Corps, Royal Malta Artillery, Malawi Rifles,
Captain-General of Royal Regiment of Artillery, The Honourable
Artillery Company, Combined Cadet Force, Royal Regiment of
Canadian Artillery, Royal Regiment of Australian Artillery, Royal
Regiment of New Zealand Artillery, Royal New Zealand Armoured
Corps, Air-Commodore-in-Chief, Royal Australian Air Force, RAF
Regiment, Royal Observer Corps, Air Reserve (of Canada), Australian
Citizen Air Force, Commandant-in-Chief, Royal Air Force College,
Cranwell, Hon. Air Commodore, RAF Marham, Hon. Commissioner,
Royal Canadian Mounted Police, Master of the Merchant Navy and
Fishing Fleets, Head of the Civil Defence Corps.

"Queenyboppers"

In the 1980s a set of young royals began to attract press attention.
Tagged the "Queenyboppers", these royal cousins, who have
virtually grown up together, include The Queen's son Prince Edward;
the daughter of the Duke and Duchess of Kent, Lady Helen Windsor;
Princess Alexandra's children James and Marina; and Princess
Margaret's son and daughter, Viscount Linley and Sarah Armstrong-
Jones. These young people are freer of the constraints of royalty than
those closer to the throne, and they seem to be able to enjoy
themselves like ordinary mortals.

R

Racing Camels

On Princess Anne's 1987 trip to Qatar, one of the Arab kingdoms in the Middle East, her host the Amir asked her if she would like to try riding a camel. Anne, always game, said yes, and quickly changed into makeshift riding attire of blue jeans, pumps and the ever-present head scarf. But her mount was no ordinary camel. It was a six-year-old racing camel in its prime, with a ferocious temper and a headstrong attitude. The Princess proved herself equal to the challenge. Within a short time she had mastered the camel, and she was riding around the desert letting out joyous shouts, looking as comfortable on her swaying mount as any Bedouin.

Racing Colours

The Queen's racing colours are purple with gold braid, scarlet sleeves, and a black cap with gold tassle.

Racing Pigeons

The Queen breeds and races pigeons, an interest she inherited from The Queen Mother, another pigeon fancier. The Queen's racing pigeons live in the royal lofts in the racing manager's home. The Queen visits the royal lofts at least once every year, to say hello to their trainer and inspect her grey pigeons. Each of the 250 royal pigeons wears a blue and gold leg ring stamped with her cipher, ER.

Racing Stables

The Queen is a keen horse-racing enthusiast. Her greatest unfulfilled ambition is to win the Derby at Epsom. Although that prize has so far eluded her, her stables do boast a number of trophies. Among her winners were Highclere, a filly that won the Prix de Diane at Chantilly in 1974, and Dunfermline, winner of the Epsom Oaks and the St. Leger in 1977. In 1982 she sold an outstanding filly called Height Of Fashion to an eager Arab purchaser for more than £1 million, which she used to buy a training stable in Berkshire, in the hope of producing that Derby winner she longs for.

The Queen Mother is equally enthusiastic about racing, although she prefers steeplechasers to flat racing. Her stables have brought in a number of winners. In 1965 she had installed in Clarence House a loudspeaker that can broadcast racetrack commentary. Explained a member of the Household, "She cannot always get to the races, and she does like to follow her horses' progress."

H & M Rayne

H & M Rayne is a firm of Bond Street shoemakers that produces the shoes worn by the The Queen, The Queen Mother and Princess Margaret. Margaret and The Queen Mother are both fond of platform shoes and high square heels, to increase their height. Princess Margaret also loves shoes with open toes and ankle straps. Rayne makes The Queen's sensible low-heeled shoes, which simply have to be comfortable, given the number of hours she spends on her feet at public functions.

Founded in 1889 by Henry and Mary Rayne, the firm has also made shoes and handbags for such luminaries as Lillie Langtry, Marlene Dietrich and Vivien Leigh. Still run by descendants of the founders, H & M Rayne, located at 15 Old Bond Street, will custom-make any pair of shoes in their catalogue—including shoes just like The Queen's—starting from £119.

Reading Royal Ears

There is a school of thought that says you can learn a great deal about a person by "reading" his or her facial features. According to one such expert, Kathy Thompson, protruding ears signify royalty—no surprise to fans of Prince Charles. Thompson also says that the small ears of Princess Diana predict "problems in middle years".

Ronald and Nancy Reagan

The Reagans were the first presidential couple ever invited to stay at Windsor; they paid a visit in the summer of 1982. The Queen went riding with the President, both of them dressed in sober tan (The Queen with her usual head scarf as well). Protocol was marred only once, on the Reagans' arrival. Nancy, never one to take a back seat, stepped forward with The Queen and President for the playing of the national anthems, rather than remaining a step behind with Prince Philip and Prince Charles.

The following spring, Queen Elizabeth and Prince Philip visited the Reagans in California (although actually they elected to stay on the *Britannia* rather than at the Reagan ranch). The royal couple hosted a dinner aboard the yacht for the Reagans, who were celebrating their thirty-first wedding anniversary. For the black-tie event, The Queen wore a tiara and knock-out sapphire necklace, earrings and bracelet as accessories, while Nancy was merely chic in a black and white print.

Red Boxes

The so-called "red boxes" are the official despatch boxes for the government papers sent to The Queen. Covered in red morocco leather, they are brought to The Queen several times a day, wherever in the world she might be. She spends up to three hours a day studying her papers, and often surprises her ministers with her up-

The Queen closing one of the "red boxes".

to-the-minute knowledge of current situations. Every day that
Parliament meets, the Vice-Chamberlain, who is an M.P., writes a
report on the day's business which The Queen reads the same
evening.

After Prince Charles came of age, The Queen began on occasion to
invite him to go over some of the papers in the red boxes with her, in a
tradition of royal apprenticeship that her father, King George VI, had
initiated with her. But The Queen never shares the red boxes with the
Duke of Edinburgh, however much she might value his opinion,
because he is not in the line of succession.

Red Crow

When Prince Charles visited Alberta, Canada in 1977, he was made an
honorary member of the Kainai Indian tribe and given the name Red
Crow.

Red Dragon of Wales

The Red Dragon of Wales is the personal emblem of Prince Charles.

Regency Act

The Regency Act was passed in 1937 to cover the contingency that
King George VI might die before his daughter Princess Elizabeth was
old enough to ascend the throne. The Regency Act specified that the
next adult in line of royal succession would become Regent until
Elizabeth's adulthood; that would have been the Duke of Gloucester.
After Elizabeth became Queen in 1952, the person who would
become Regent if she died before Charles reached adulthood was her
sister, Princess Margaret. In 1953 the Regency Act was amended to
make Prince Philip the Acting Regent if anything should happen to
Her Majesty. This change in the Regency Act was variously
interpreted as a sign of the The Queen's dependence on her husband,
as punishment of Princess Margaret for her involvement with
Captain Peter Townsend, and as Margaret's own wish to be free of
responsibilities that might keep her from marrying whom she
pleased.

The Regency Act also provides for the possibility that The Queen
might become incapacitated. In that case, royal business can be
transacted by Councillors of State appointed by The Queen: Prince
Philip, The Queen Mother, the Prince of Wales, Prince Andrew,
Prince Edward and Princess Anne.

"Mrs. Elizabeth Regina"

The Queen once bought a tractor on credit, and through a computer error, she was sent a collection letter regarding late payment of her instalment. The computer had addressed the letter to "Mrs. Elizabeth Regina".

Remembering the Monarchs

Schoolchildren have traditionally memorized the following mnemonic as a short-cut chronology of British monarchs, beginning with William the Conqueror:

> Willie, Willie, Harry, Stee,
> Harry, Dick, Harry Three,
> One, Two, Three Ned, Richard Two,
> Harry Four, Five, Six, Then who?
> Edward Four, Five, Dick the Bad,
> Harry twain and Ned the lad,
> Mary, Bessie, James the Vain,
> Charlie, Charlie, James again,
> William and Mary, Anna Gloria,
> Four Georges, William and Victoria
> Edward the Seventh next, and then
> George the Fifth in 1910.
> Edward the Eighth soon abdicated
> And so a George was reinstated.

HMS Renown

HMS *Renown* was the ship that the then Duke and Duchess of York (the future King George VI and Queen Elizabeth) boarded in January 1927 for their first extensive state visit, a six-month trip to Australia and New Zealand. There they were represented by King George in Canberra. The King knew that his second son, a model of domestic happiness with his pretty and loving wife, would make a favourable impression.

The Duke and Duchess were sad to leave their baby daughter Elizabeth, then only seven months old. The Duchess wrote of the future Queen, "The baby was so sweet, playing with the buttons on Bertie's uniform, that it quite broke me up." When they sailed back home, the *Renown* carried tons of toys for the little Princess.

Report Card for Prince Charles

At the end of Prince Charles's first term of school in 1957, Hill House sent the following school report to his parents:

READING: very good indeed; good expression
WRITING: good, firm, clear, well-formed
ARITHMETIC: below average; careful but slow, not very keen
SCRIPTURE: shows keen interest
GEOGRAPHY: good
HISTORY: loves this subject
FRENCH: shows promise
LATIN: made a fair start
ART: good, and simply loves drawing and painting
SINGING: a sweet voice, especially in the lower register
FOOTBALL: enjoying the game
GYMNASTICS: good

Cecil Rhodes

Cecil Rhodes was the man who created the nation of South Africa and later brought it into the British Commonwealth. On Princess Elizabeth's first trip to South Africa, in February 1947, she climbed to the top of one of the Matopo hills to see his grave. She made the climb without benefit of shoes; she had earlier lent her own sensible sandals to her mother, who had come out in the hill country on high heels and found that one of the heels broke. "So like Mummy," said her daughter fondly, "to set out in those shoes."

Ribena

Ribena annually buys blackcurrants from more than sixty acres at Sandringham, making The Queen their largest single supplier.

Sir John Riddell

Sir John Riddell has been Prince Charles's private secretary since 1984, succeeding Edward Adeane. Riddell was formerly a banker, and he lacks the family history of generations of connections with Buckingham Palace that have characterized many Household members. Many believe that he has encouraged the Prince to be more outspoken about current events, and particularly his belief that solving the problems of the inner cities with their high rates of unemployment must be a national priority.

Rift Among the Royals

Over the years there have been many rumours about royal rifts. But Princess Margaret firmly denies that any such thing exists. "In our family," she says forthrightly, "we do not have rifts. A very occasional row but never a rift."

Rockin' Royals

Princess Diana has attended concerts by Duran Duran and Genesis. A fan of Lionel Richie, she and Prince Charles danced at one of his London concerts. Her choice of a treat for her twenty-sixth birthday was to attend a rock concert by Genesis, led by her favourite singer, Phil Collins.

Viscount Linley and Lady Helen Windsor attended a Bruce Springsteen concert at Wembley stadium, wearing Bruce T-shirts.

At the age of twenty, Prince Andrew announced that his favourite rock group was Pink Floyd.

The Duchess of York is known to be a fan of Duran Duran, Phil Collins and the Rolling Stones. When she met David Bowie in 1987, she told him, "You are one of my favourite stars, and I love all your records."

The Queen Mother has had tea with Elton John and is known to like old Beatles hits.

Roses

The Queen Mother is especially fond of roses, and they bloom in profusion in the gardens of all her country houses. She admits that the bushes need pruning, but she can't bear to cut them back. Among her favourites are Pink Iceberg, a silvery pink; Silver Jubilee, which is a brilliant red; and Glenfiddich, the amber colour of a good Scotch malt whisky.

Rover

The Queen's personal car, which she drives when she is enjoying herself in the country, is a dark green 1971 Rover. She has it serviced regularly and intends to go on driving it until it is beyond mechanical help.

Royal Ascot

Royal Ascot is the name given to the opening week of racing in June at

Ascot, a racecourse only five miles away from Windsor. Since the reign of Queen Anne, Royal Ascot has frequently been attended by a large royal party, and in the days of King Edward VII it was one of the premier events on the social calendar. The Queen first attended Royal Ascot in 1945, wearing her Auxiliary Territorial Service uniform, and she has never missed a year since.

Each afternoon of the four-day week, the races are opened by a procession of royals in open carriages, coming from nearby Windsor Castle, where The Queen customarily entertains a house party. Like other spectators in the Royal Enclosure, the women of the Royal Family wear summery frocks and flowered hats, the men morning coats and grey top hats. Prince Philip has admitted that he sometimes conceals a transistor radio under his top hat, so he can follow the cricket matches while he watches the races. The royals then settle down to the serious business of watching the races and rooting for horses owned by various members of the Royal Family. In 1987 Princess Diana and the Duchess of York caused a furore at Royal Ascot when they carried their umbrellas like swords in front of them and jabbed some well-dressed patrons in the backside.

Royal Automobiles

The Queen owns four official maroon Rolls Royces. None of them has a licence plate, but there is a royal shield on the side of the vehicles and a small blue light on top to warn of her presence. The oldest of her cars is a Phantom IV, one of a total of twelve made for heads of state, that was given to her as a wedding present from the RAF. In 1954 she bought another Phantom IV second-hand. Two Phantom Vs were purchased in 1960 and 1961. Whichever car The Queen is riding in is equipped with her personal mascot, the silver emblem of St. George, on the radiator. All the Rolls Royces are hand washed by one of the ninety members of the Palace maintenance staff. Fifteen to twenty other cars are in the royal garage, including the old Rover in which The Queen likes to drive herself in Windsor Great Park.

The Royal Budget

It was the Duke of Edinburgh who first broke the news that the Royal Family was getting a bit strapped for cash. In 1969 he told a BBC interviewer that because the Civil List had not been revised for years, the Royal Family would "go into the red" the following year. He also joked that they might have to "move into smaller premises". After long debate, Parliament raised the Civil List, and it is now index linked to keep it in line with inflation.

A Royal Calendar of Birthdays and Anniversaries

February 19	Prince Andrew's birthday
February 22	the Duchess of Kent's birthday
February 29	James Ogilvy's birthday
March 1	Lady Rose Windsor's birthday
March 10	Prince Edward's birthday
April 6	Lord Frederick Windsor's birthday
April 21	The Queen's birthday
April 23	Lady Gabriella Windsor's birthday
April 24	the Ogilvies' wedding anniversary
April 28	Lady Helen Windsor's birthday
May 1	Sarah Armstrong-Jones's birthday
May 15	Zara Phillips's birthday
June 8	The Kents' wedding anniversary
June 10	Prince Philip's birthday
June 20	the Duchess of Gloucester's birthday
June 21	Prince William's birthday
June 26	the Earl of St. Andrew's birthday
June 30	Prince and Princess Michael of Kent's wedding anniversary
July 1	Princess Diana's birthday
July 4	Prince Michael of Kent's birthday
July 8	the Gloucesters' wedding anniversary
July 23	the Yorks' wedding anniversary
July 25	Lord Nicholas Windsor's birthday
July 29	the Waleses' wedding anniversary
July 31	Marina Ogilvy's birthday
August 4	The Queen Mother's birthday
August 15	Princess Anne's birthday
August 21	Princess Margaret's birthday
August 26	the Duke of Gloucester's birthday
September 15	Prince Harry's birthday
September 22	Mark Phillips's birthday
October 9	the Duke of Kent's birthday
October 15	the Duchess of York's birthday
October 24	the Earl of Ulster's birthday

November 3	Viscount Linley's birthday
November 14	the Phillipses' wedding anniversary
	Prince Charles's birthday
November 15	Peter Phillips's birthday
November 19	Lady Davina Windsor's birthday
November 20	The Queen and Prince Philip's
	wedding anniversary
December 25	Princess Alexandra's birthday
	Princess Alice's birthday

Royal Collections

Queen Mary was perhaps the greatest of recent royal collectors. She collected snuff boxes, dolls' house miniatures, jade figurines, family portraits and tea caddies, among other antiques.

Prince Charles claims to have a toilet-seat collection numbering more than one hundred items.

Prince Philip collects cartoons about himself. He then hangs them in the bathroom. One of the cartoons in his collection was drawn by Prince Charles; in it, the balding Philip is standing hopefully on a huge tin of hair restorer.

King George V had only one indoor hobby, collecting stamps. His stamp collection is said to be one of the most valuable in the world.

The Queen Mother has a large collection of Chelsea china, started for her by gifts from her husband, King George VI. She continues to add to it as fine pieces become available.

Royal Company of Archers

The Royal Company of Archers has been the Sovereign's bodyguard in Scotland since the time of King George IV. They attend The Queen when she makes state appearances at the Palace of Holyroodhouse.

Royal County of Berkshire Polo Club

The Royal County of Berkshire Polo Club is an exclusive club whose members include the Prince of Wales, Major Ronald Ferguson, father of the Duchess of York, and royal biographer Robert Lacey. A new addition to the club scene, it was opened in 1986 by Bryan Morrison, manager and promoter of rock stars, on 150 acres located between Ascot and Windsor. The clubhouse is superbly equipped, and in addition to all the amenities needed for playing polo the club also boasts tennis courts, a swimming pool, croquet lawns and a clay

pigeon shoot. Although the Berkshire is expensive, with a membership fee of over £5000 and annual dues of £1500, there is no shortage
of candidates for membership.

The Royal Family

The Royal Family is a film made about the daily lives of the royals in
1968-69. Once The Queen and Prince Philip agreed to the idea, they
were extraordinarily cooperative and let the film crew follow then
around for months. The director was Richard Cawston, who refused
to let The Queen see any of the footage as it was shot, for fear of
making her self-conscious or stilted. The film was first shown on the
BBC on Saturday night, 21 June 1969, and nearly caused a crisis in the
London waterworks because of the great number of toilets that were
flushed during the break in the middle of the showing.

A scene from the documentary film *The Royal Family*, filmed in 1968.

The Royal Family Pop-up Book

The Royal Family Pop-up Book by Patrick Montague-Smith, former editor
of *Debrett's Peerage*, was published in the UK in 1984 by Dean Books and

has become a collector's item. Six scenes of the Royal Family in a variety of settings have been designed by the world's leading expert in the genre, Vic Duppa-Whyte, from paintings by Roger Payne. Scenes include the wedding of Charles and Diana and the opening of Parliament complete with coaches and horses.

Royal Fingernails

The Queen keeps her nails sensibly short, like most countrywomen, but they are always beautifully shaped and carefully buffed to a shine. Princess Diana has the bad habit of biting her nails, so she must call in the manicurist before each public appearance to repair the damage. The Duchess of York has lovely nails and likes to wear bright red nail polish for evenings. Princess Margaret also sometimes wears coloured polish, but Princess Anne, like her mother, sticks to a conservative length and clear polish.

Royal Firsts

First princess to wear slacks in public	Princess Anne
First sovereign to allow television coverage of the coronation	Queen Elizabeth II
First royal to be photographed smoking a cigarette	King Edward VIII (as Prince of Wales)
First princess to wear her bridal veil covering her face	Princess Margaret
First royal to bring a McDonald's hamburger into Buckingham Palace	Princess Diana
First member of the Royal Family to travel behind the Iron Curtain	Lord Snowdon
First princess to wear coloured stockings in public	Princess Diana
First heir to the throne to attend public school	Prince Charles
First heir to the throne to parachute jump	Prince Charles
First royal to go snorkelling	Princess Margaret
First princess to wear a strapless gown in public	Princess Margaret

First sovereign to drive a car	King Edward VII
First sovereign to pilot a plane	King Edward VIII
First heir to the throne to be born in a hospital	Prince William
First queen to see her grandchild take the throne	Queen Mary
First royal bride to include her own family motto ("Dieu défend le droit") on her new coat of arms	Princess Diana
First sovereign to broadcast a radio speech	King George V
First sovereign to step from a plane bare-headed	King Edward VIII
First member of the House of Windsor to ride a winning horse in a flat race	Princess Anne
First royal to fly around the world	The Queen Mother

Royal Lodge

The Royal Lodge was initially a hunting lodge on the grounds of Windsor Castle. When King George IV undertook his extensive remodelling of Windsor, he turned the Royal Lodge into a comfortable home for the duration, in early nineteenth-century Gothic style. In 1931 it was given to the then Duke and Duchess of York to use as a country house. They restored the gardens and the house itself, covering the peeling outside walls with a cheerful coat of pink paint, the colour of strawberry mousse, and then surrounding it with a fragrant hedge of lavender. The Duke worked hard in the gardens, planting hundreds of azaleas and rhododendrons. Today it is the home of The Queen Mother when she is at Windsor. The interior is decorated in pale cool colours that make an attractive background for the frequent entertaining The Queen Mother does there.

Royal Marriages Act

The Royal Marriages Act, passed in 1772, specifies that members of the Royal Family may not marry without the Sovereign's consent until they reach the age of twenty-five. Thereafter, they may marry whom they please, provided they give one year's notice to the Privy Council. In that waiting period, Parliament may choose to disapprove of the marriage, in which case the royal will lose all government income as well as his or her place in the line of succession. In effect, the Royal Marriages Act means that royals don't get married without the full approval of both Sovereign and Parliament, as was demonstrated when Princess Margaret hoped to marry Peter Townsend.

Royal Mews

The Royal Mews at Buckingham Palace is open to the public at regular hours every week. Over seventy different kinds of carriages —phaetons, barouches, landaus and state coaches—are on display when they are not in active use. All are in working order. Carriage horses are also stabled there: the Windsor greys for state occasions and bay harness horses for more ordinary coaches. The Mews employs a total of eleven chauffeurs and around forty grooms and coachmen to keep everything in order and the vehicles ready for royal transport.

The Prince and Princess of Wales, after their marriage, in the 1904 State Landau.

Courtesy of the British Information Service.

The Royal Palaces of Britain

In the mid 1960s the Royal Family, largely at the urging of the Duke of Edinburgh, agreed to the making of a TV film called *The Royal Palaces of Britain*. A joint production of the BBC and ITV, the film was devoted to a close-up look at six of the royal palaces: Kensington Palace, Hampton Court, Holyroodhouse, St. James's Palace, Windsor Castle and Buckingham Palace. The Family was not actually shown, but there were intimate glimpses of the private rooms, with their pictures and flowers, and the views to which Family members wake up every morning. The film was narrated by Sir Kenneth Clark, later seen in the popular BBC series *Civilisation*, and was broadcast by the BBC on Christmas Day 1966.

Royal Regiment of Artillery

The Queen is Captain-General of the Royal Regiment of Artillery. The regiment has been in existence for nearly three centuries and has fought for the crown in many far-flung countries. The Queen dines with them about once every ten years, in a ceremony that is just the same as it was when her great-great-grandmother, Queen Victoria, used to visit. The regimental band plays "The Roast Beef of Old England" as the The Queen enters the dining hall at Woolwich, and the meal is served on glittering regimental silver that dates back to the reign of King William IV. Afterwards, there is the loyal toast and then the national anthem. As The Queen leaves, the band plays "The Posthorn Gallop".

The Royal Rent-a-Dogs

At Sandringham The Queen breeds black labradors, not as pets but as working dogs to accompany royal hunters. The Queen's labs often enter the field competitions of the International Gundog League, and she likes to attend if her schedule permits. Her Majesty has reared four field champions: Sandringham Ranger, Sandringham Slipper, Sherry of Biteabout and Sandringham Sydney. One journalist described the Sandringham labradors as "royal rent-a-dogs, happy to accompany any family member".

Prince Edward with one of the "royal rent-a-dogs".

The Royal Romance of Charles and Diana

A 1982 made-for-TV film, *The Royal Romance of Charles and Diana*, starred Catherine Oxenberg as Lady Diana Spencer, Christopher Baines as Prince Charles, Dana Wynter as Queen Elizabeth, Stewart Granger as Prince Philip, and Olivia de Havilland as The Queen Mother. Produced by Linda Yellin and directed by Peter Levin, the film recreates the love story from its earliest moment through the growing sense of attraction and ends with the wedding at St. Paul's. Expert intercutting of authentic wedding footage gives this charming fairy tale the feeling of reality.

The Royal Sceptre

The Royal Sceptre, part of the coronation regalia, is held in the monarch's right hand during the coronation ceremony. Surmounted by a cross containing a large amethyst, the Royal Sceptre also contains the Star of Africa, the biggest stone cut from the Cullinan Diamond. It weighs about 530 carats and can be detached from the sceptre for use as a pendant. In the coronation, this sceptre is considered the symbol of "Kingly Power and Justice".

Royal Standard

The Royal Standard is the flag of the British sovereign, which flies over any house in which The Queen is resident, or any vehicle in which she travels. It has changed many times over the centuries, as the kingdom itself was changed. The current Royal Standard is the same as it was at the accession of Queen Victoria: three gold lions of England on red in the first and fourth quarters; the lion rampant of Scotland in red and gold in the second quarter; and the gold harp of Northern Ireland on blue in the third quarter.

Royal Train

Until the 1970s, there were two royal trains to transport the Royal Family over Great Britain. One was for overnight trips and had twelve carriages. The amenities included a playroom for the children, separate sitting room and bathroom for The Queen and the Duke of Edinburgh, and bedrooms for at least three members of the Household who might accompany The Queen. The day-trip train was shorter, consisting of only six carriages.

The royal trains were given up in the interests of economy, and also because helicopters can now substitute for them on many short trips. When the Royal Family does want to travel by train—to go to Balmoral in the late summer, for example—B.R. simply make up a train for that occasion from special coaches.

Royal Travels

Characteristically, Elizabeth II was on one of her foreign trips at the moment when her father, King George VI, died and she became Queen. Since that time, Her Majesty has made over 150 state visits to ninety different countries. During her Silver Jubilee Year alone, she travelled nearly fifty-six thousand miles. She has been to Canada thirteen times, to Australia nine. In October of 1982, during her tour of islands in the South Pacific, she finally achieved her long-term goal of visiting every single country in the British Commonwealth.

Prince Philip is the royal who undertakes the largest number of engagements—over four hundred a year—and trips to foreign countries. A favourite Palace joke is, "It is reported that Prince Philip is to pay a state visit to Britain."

Before The Queen and her Consort leave on a trip, they send two or three members of the Royal Household to discuss all the necessary arrangements with their prospective hosts. Where possible, The

Queen prefers to stay on the royal yacht *Britannia*, which is sent out ahead to wait for her. In other cases, she stays at the residence of the British ambassador, or at a royal palace or presidential home.

The Queen travels with a staff of thirty to forty people, a large wardrobe for her public appearances, and a few of the things that are basic necessities for The Queen: a hot water bottle, a case of Malvern water to help her digest that strange foreign food, her current favourite camera and pair of binoculars, a big pile of white gloves, and a complete mourning outfit in case somebody dies while she is on tour.

"Royal Triangle"

The nickname "Royal Triangle" is given to the area in Gloucestershire that contains three royal country homes: Highgrove, the home of the Prince and Princess of Wales; Gatcombe, the home of Princess Anne and Mark Phillips; and Nether Lypiatt, the home of Prince and Princess Michael of Kent.

Royal Variety Performance

Every year, in late November, the royals attend a performance featuring variety acts designed to raise money for charity. The Queen and The Queen Mother attend in alternate years.

Royal Victorian Order

The Royal Victorian Order is an order of knights created by Queen Victoria in 1896. At that time, the recipients of all the other orders of knighthood were selected by the prime minister and his advisors, and The Queen felt the honours were becoming too political. Today, The Queen alone selects those who will receive the Royal Victorian Order, and it is a useful way for her to reward service to the Crown and the country.

Royal Walkabouts

In 1972, at the time of the Silver Wedding Celebration for The Queen and the Duke of Edinburgh, The Queen went on her first walkabout in Britain—an unannounced casual stroll through crowds of ordinary citizens of her realm. That first walkabout was such a success that it is now a feature of many of her state visits and appearances. Walkabouts are, of course, a nightmare for those responsible for The

Queen's safety, but Her Majesty always puts the need to be seen by her subjects ahead of any fears for her safety.

Royal Warrants

Royal Warrants are a mark of official recognition that a firm supplies goods and services to members of the Royal Family. The actual warrant itself is a formal document that a member of the Royal Family sends to a specific person in the business. Issued for a period of ten years but cancellable at any time, the Royal Warrant allows the recipient the right to use the term *By Appointment*, coupled with the coat of arms of the royal who grants the warrant. Only four members of the Royal Family may grant warrants: The Queen, The Queen Mother, the Duke of Edinburgh and the Prince of Wales.

A small number of companies hold Royal Warrants from all four; they include Harrods, the General Trading Company, Hatchards (the booksellers), and Savory & Moore, a firm of chemists. About 850 British firms possess Royal Warrants, for selling the Royal Family everything from diamonds to crackers to cattle-breeding services. New warrants are issued at the rate of twenty to thirty each year, and a similar number of firms drop off the list at each annual review.

Warrant holders are expected to maintain discretion about their association with the Royal Family. Any mention of specific items supplied to the royals, or publicity about details such as size or price, is frowned upon.

Royal Weddings:

Queen Victoria and Prince Albert

Queen Victoria and her beloved Albert were married on 10 February 1840 in the Chapel Royal at St. James's Palace. Victoria set new styles for wedding attire, many of which endure to this day. Her dress was white, and simple and in contrast to those of many earlier royal brides. It was made of satin trimmed with Honiton lace and had a low neckline, a fitted bodice and a full pleated skirt. She wore orange blossoms in her hair, a tradition that was popular in France but virtually unknown at that time in England. Another innovation was the way the Queen wore her veil, arranged so that it would not cover her face during the ceremony.

Princess Alexandra of Denmark and Prince Edward of Wales

At the time of their marriage on 10 March 1863, the groom, the future King Edward VII, was the Prince of Wales; his bride a princess

of the Danish royal family. The ceremony took place in the relatively
small St. George's Chapel at Windsor, in deference to Queen
Victoria's continued mourning over the death of Prince Albert two
years earlier.

The Prince of Wales wore a full dress uniform under his velvet
Garter robes and was attended by Crown Prince Frederick of Prussia
and the Duke of Saxe-Coburg. Princess Alexandra, who had captured
the fancy of the British public on her arrival from Denmark for the
ceremony, was dressed in crinolined white lace with a long silver
moiré train decorated with embroidered flowers and leaves and wore
a diadem centred with a huge sapphire. Eight bridesmaids were
dressed in tulle and decked in rosebuds.

Jenny Lind sang with the choir, while the future Kaiser Wilhelm
occupied himself by biting the royal uncles who were vainly trying to
keep the boy quiet. Queen Victoria refused to abandon her mourning
attire for this festive day. Concealed behind her black veil, she
watched the entire proceedings from a balcony and then left to visit
Prince Albert's tomb at Frogmore.

Princess May of Teck and the Duke of York
This couple's wedding took place under rather odd circumstances, in
the full glare of publicity. In 1892 the eldest son of King Edward VII
and Queen Alexandra, Prince Albert Victor (known as "Eddy"), died
of influenza. His death came only a few weeks before his expected
marriage to the German Princess May of Teck. Princess May was
chosen by Queen Victoria as suitable for the future Queen Consort.
Queen Victoria was loath to lose her from the family after the death
of the Duke of Clarence, and so a little over a year later, to Princess
May's embarrassment, it was announced that she would marry the
new heir to the throne, Prince George.

The wedding took place on 6 July 1893, in the Chapel Royal at St.
James's rather than St. George's Chapel at Windsor, where May (later
Queen Mary) had expected to be married to Eddy. The groom was in
full dress uniform covered with decorations. The bride wore a single
strand of pearls and a wasp-waisted satin brocade dress lavishly
decorated with lace and orange blossoms. In her hair she wore a
somewhat confused arrangement of orange blossoms and a small
tiara, holding back a token of a veil. She had five adult bridesmaids and
five little flower girls, and the full details of her trousseau were
published in the popular press.

Lady Elizabeth Bowes-Lyon and the Duke of York

The wedding of the second son of King George V and Queen Mary took place on 26 April 1923 at Westminster Abbey. For a royal wedding it was relatively quiet, since at that time it seemed unlikely that the future King George VI would ever ascend the throne. The fathers of the bride and groom were dressed in full military uniform, as was the groom himself. The bride was simply dressed, quite overshadowed by her magnificent mother-in-law, Queen Mary, who was wearing a six-strand pearl necklace, heavy lace gown, and a toque, in her usual style. When Lady Elizabeth walked down the aisle to the altar, a clergyman standing nearby fainted from the excitement, and the procession was delayed for some minutes before the man could be revived and removed. (Oddly, the same thing happened, at almost the same spot, fourteen years later when she walked down the aisle in her coronation procession.)

Six bridesmaids wore white and green gowns with silver shoes; two nieces bore Lady Elizabeth's train. The service was conducted by the Archbishop of Canterbury, and afterwards the Duke and Duchess of York returned to Buckingham Palace in the Glass Coach. After the traditional appearance on the balcony, the bride and groom and the wedding guests sat down to an eight-course wedding breakfast, featuring such delicacies as salmon, capons, tongue in aspic, fresh asparagus, fresh strawberries and bowls of grapes. The wedding cake was nine feet high and weighed eight hundred pounds.

The bride retired to change into a mushroom-coloured dress and a small hat with a big swoop of feathers at the back. An open carriage drove them to Waterloo Station, where they entered a special train carriage filled with white carnations, white roses and lilies of the valley. They spent their honeymoon at a country house in Surrey called Polesdon Lacey, lent to the couple by society hostess Mrs. Ronald Greville. Later they travelled to the Duchess's childhood home at Glamis, where her mother had redecorated a bedroom and sitting room for the young couple. There the newlywed Duchess came down with a bad case of whooping cough, which the Duke termed "not very romantic", although he looked after her devotedly.

Mrs. Wallis Simpson and the Duke of Windsor

Six months after King Edward VIII abdicated and became the Duke of Windsor, he married the woman for whom he had given up his throne. The wedding took place on 3 June 1937, the same day as his father's birthday. It was in France, near Tours at the Château de

Candé, the home of the Duke's friends Mr. and Mrs. Charles E. Bedaux. Wallis wore a dress that was the epitome of 1930s glamour, long blue satin cut to cling and drape, with a little matching jacket to cover the bare halter-top bodice. On her wrist was a huge diamond and sapphire bracelet that was her wedding gift from the Duke.

No member of the Royal Family was present, much to the groom's sorrow. Guests included Mr. and Mrs. Herman L. Rogers, with whom the Duchess stayed while she waited for the King to abdicate, and Baron Eugene Rothschild and his American-born wife.

Princess Elizabeth and the Duke of Edinburgh

Princess Elizabeth, the heir to the British throne, was married to Prince Philip of Greece, the newly created Duke of Edinburgh, on 20 November 1947. Winston Churchill commented, "Millions will welcome this joyous event as a flash of colour on the hard road we have to travel." Elizabeth's wedding dress was designed by Norman Hartnell, of white satin dotted with ten thousand seed pearls embroidered in patterns of York roses interspersed with crystal ears of corn. She wore her tulle veil off the face, held in place by her mother's sunray tiara. Her earrings were diamonds, there was a double strand of pearls around her neck (her private secretary had to dash back to St. James's Palace to retrieve the necklace from among the fifteen hundred wedding presents on display there), and her flowers were a spray of white orchids.

It is said that Prince Philip overslept that morning, but was nevertheless too early for his car; he had to go back inside and wait, passing the time with encouragement from his best man, David Milford Haven. He wore his regular naval uniform, with a sword that had belonged to his grandfather, Prince Louis of Battenberg.

Elizabeth set out from Buckingham Palace a 11.16 a.m., sitting beside her father in the Irish State Coach. Later King George VI wrote to his daughter, "I was so proud of you, and thrilled at having you so close to me on our long walk in Westminster Abbey. But when I handed your hand to the Archbishop of Canterbury, I felt that I had lost something very precious. You were so calm and composed during the ceremony and said your words with such conviction." On the way back down the aisle after the ceremony, the bride stopped and curtsied deeply to her mother and father, a gesture that nearly moved the King to tears.

The wedding was the first big post-war gathering of royals. Among the wedding gifts were fifty-three thousand packages of food from America and five hundred tins of pineapple from Australia, to help the

Courtesy of the British Information Service.

The formal wedding portrait of Princess Elizabeth and Lieutenant Philip
Mountbatten, 1947.

royals endure the privations imposed on Britain by post-war
rationing. The young couple then left from Waterloo Station aboard
the royal train to spend the first part of their honeymoon at Lord
Louis Mountbatten's country house, Broadlands. They were accom-

Courtesy of the British Information Service.

The newlywed Princess Elizabeth and Lieutenant Mountbatten on their honeymoon at Broadlands.

panied by Susan, the Princess's favourite corgi. They found the constant intrusion of the curious public too bothersome, and later fled to Birkhall in Scotland for several days of carefree privacy.

Princess Margaret and Antony Armstrong-Jones

Princess Margaret's engagement was announced in February 1960, just a few weeks after her nephew Prince Andrew's birth. Although her fiancé was two years younger than she and born a commoner, the country took the romance to their hearts. The wedding took place on 6 May 1960 in a Westminster Abbey that was full to bursting with fresh flowers. Silken banners along the route to the abbey bore the intertwined initials M and A. Guests who were too far from the altar to see the ceremony could follow it on closed-circuit television.

Princess Margaret made a ravishing bride as she rode in the Glass Coach, with a small round tiara crowning her huge fluff of veil that made her look like Disney's Snow White at her wedding to Prince Charming. Her dress was made of thirty yards of white silk organza, designed by Norman Hartnell. The wedding took place on the warmest day of the year, and according to the news reports, was all sunshine and sparkle. As Margaret and Tony drove off to embark on their Caribbean honeymoon, The Queen, The Queen Mother and Prince Philip ran alongside the car smiling and waving.

Princess Anne and Captain Mark Phillips

Princess Anne was married to Captain Mark Phillips on 14 November 1973. Buckingham Palace emphasized that the wedding was not a state function but a family occasion. To design her wedding dress, Anne passed over the traditional choice of Norman Hartnell and gave the commission instead to her own relatively unknown designer, Maureen Baker of Susan Small. Princess Anne stated forthrightly that she didn't want her wedding spoiled by "hordes of uncontrollable children", and so she had only two attendants: her youngest brother Edward and her niece Sarah Armstrong-Jones.

Nevertheless there was an aura of royal grandeur about the wedding: Princess Anne rode to Westminster Abbey in the Glass Coach, she wore a splendid tiara over her veil, military bands and sixteen trumpeters heralded the event, and a bevy of royals was in the crowd. The Princess carried a bouquet of white roses from Holland and orchids from Singapore. Her cake was as tall as she was, weighed 145 pounds, and was baked by the Army Catering Corps. The newlyweds made the expected appearance on the balcony of Buckingham Palace afterwards, and then they went on their honeymoon in the Caribbean, sailing out on the royal yacht *Britannia* as it headed out to await the next state visit of The Queen.

Lady Diana Spencer and Prince Charles

The wedding of Lady Diana Spencer to Prince Charles on 29 July 1981 marked the first time in more than three hundred years that an heir to the throne had married an Englishwoman. In a break with twentieth-century tradition, the wedding was held at St. Paul's, which was the preference of the bride and groom.

At 10.35 on a lovely British summer morning, Lady Diana emerged from The Queen Mother's home, Clarence House, where she had spent the night, and stepped into the Glass Coach for the formal procession to St. Paul's. Waiting for her at the altar was Prince Charles with his two "supporters", Prince Andrew and Prince Edward.

Fully veiled in a cloud of ivory tulle, Lady Diana walked down the long aisle on the arm of her father, the Earl of Spencer. Her young bridesmaids were Lady Sarah Armstrong-Jones, India Hicks (grand-daughter of Lord Mountbatten), Sarah Jane Gaselee (the daughter of Prince Charles's racing trainer), Catherine Cameron (daughter of a close friend of Prince Charles) and Clementine Hambro (a great-grand-daughter of Winston Churchill and a student at the nursery school where Lady Diana had been a teacher).

The wedding service, which lasted about one and a quarter hours, followed the alternative form that omits the bride's promise to obey her husband. After the singing of an anthem, "I Was Glad", Charles and Diana signed the register and then walked back down the aisle, observed by twenty-five hundred guests, to emerge on the steps of St. Paul's for their first appearance as husband and wife. The ride back to Buckingham Palace in the 1904 State Landau was cheered by thousands of enthusiastic royalists, as was the couple's appearance on the balcony, topped by a rather shy kiss.

After sitting through the wedding breakfast, cutting the 255-pound cake, and posing for the surprisingly informal official wedding portraits by Lord Lichfield, Diana changed into a coral dress covered by a matching jacket with lacy collar and cuffs and a coral hat with a big plume for the carriage ride (the groom's brothers had decorated it with balloons painted with Prince of Wales feathers and the traditional "Just Married").

At Waterloo Station, the Prince and Princess of Wales boarded a train to start their honeymoon. Later they flew to Gibraltar, where the royal yacht was waiting to take them on a long and very private cruise.

Courtesy of Emanuel.

A sketch of Lady Sarah Armstrong-Jones in her bridesmaid's dress, by Elizabeth and David Emanuel.

Diana's wedding dress can be seen on page 349.

Miss Sarah Ferguson and Prince Andrew

The wedding procession began at 11.00 a.m. on 23 July 1986, a beautiful English summer day. Sarah Ferguson had spent the night at Clarence House, The Queen Mother's residence, and then dressed with the help of the designer of her wedding dress, Lindka Cierach. On the arm of her father, Major Ronald Ferguson, she stepped into the Glass Coach for the ride to Westminster Abbey. Prince Andrew, who had been created Duke of York that morning, rode to the Abbey in the State Landau, accompanied by his younger brother, Prince Edward, who was his supporter.

The Royal Family on the balcony of Buckingham Palace after the wedding of the Duke and Duchess of York.

When Sarah arrived at the Abbey at 11.15, more than eighteen hundred guests were waiting for her—among them Prime Minister Margaret Thatcher, Nancy Reagan and Elton John. Her attendants were all children: Prince William; Princess Anne's children, Peter and Zara Phillips; her sister Jane's son Seamus Makim; her half-brother and half-sister, Alice and Andrew Ferguson; Laura Fellowes, the daughter of Princess Diana's sister Jane; and Lady Rosanagh Innes-Ker, the daughter of the Duke and Duchess of Roxburghe.

The marriage service itself was conducted by the Archbishop of Canterbury. Prince Charles read the lesson. Then it was back down the aisle and into the State Landau for the drive to Buckingham Palace. After the traditional wave on the balcony (and a big romantic kiss to thrill the nation), the bride and groom shared a wedding breakfast of lobster, salmon, chicken, assorted salads and wedding cake with 120 guests. At the end of the meal, the new Duchess of York slipped away to change into a blue and white flowered frock. Then the bridal couple (chaperoned by a huge teddy bear that was the gift of Prince Edward) drove to the grounds of the Royal Chelsea Hospital, where they stepped into a helicopter and flew away to begin their honeymoon on the *Britannia*, cruising the Azores in the Atlantic. A few weeks later Prince Andrew said publicly, "I know that the decision I made to marry Sarah was, and always will be, the best decision I have made, or ever will make, in my life."

Royal Wedding (the film)

In the romantic 1951 musical film *Royal Wedding*, Fred Astaire and Jane Powell played a brother-sister dance team in London at the time of Princess Elizabeth's marriage to Prince Philip. Authentic newsreel footage of the actual royal wedding and the wildly excited crowds was integrated into the "reel" adventures of Astaire, Powell and Peter Lawford.

The Royal Wedding Year 1981

Highlights from the year 1981:

January 4	Prince Charles's book *The Old Man of Lochnagar* hits the best-seller list.
February 25	Buckingham Palace announces the engagement of Lady Diana Spencer to Prince Charles.
February 26	Lady Di moves into Clarence House with The Queen Mother.
March 3	Buckingham Palace says Lady Di will be known as Princess Charles after her marriage.
March 4	Buckingham Palace says Lady Di will *not* be called Princess Charles, but Princess Diana, Princess of Wales.

March 10   Charles and Di (in a black strapless gown) make first public appearance at a benefit concert.

March 14   Prince Charles falls off horse playing polo.

March 18   Prince Charles falls off horse again.

March 28   Queen gives her official consent to the marriage.

April 14   Prince Charles tours Australia, nursing finger injured when falling off horse.

April 17   Palace attempts to stem rapid commercialization of royal wedding.

May 4   Prince Charles flies to Scotland for reunion with Lady Di.

May 5   British papers report that embarrassing phone calls were made from Charles in Australia to Di.

May 7   Palace gets injunction against publication of transcripts of phone calls.

May 9   German magazine *Die Aktuelle* publishes transcripts anyway; alas, they contain nothing sensational.

May 27   Palace says twenty-five hundred guests are invited to the wedding.

June 4   White House announces Nancy Reagan will attend royal wedding but the President will stay at home.

June 12   British Post Office issues stamp showing Charles a full head taller than Di.

June 18   Prince Charles visits New York City.

June 25   Palace announces newlyweds will live at Kensington Palace and Highgrove.

July 2   Press reveals that Lady Di is planning to omit *obey* from her marriage vows.

July 22   Spanish government announces King Carlos and Queen Sofia will stay away from royal wedding to protest British claim to Gibraltar.

July 27   Poet Laureate releases text of poem on wedding.

July 28   Fireworks display draws huge crowd in Hyde Park.

July 29   Royal wedding day arrives at last!

August 8   Newlyweds continue to cruise the Mediterranean.

September 12 Prince and Princess of Wales advertise for cook for Highgrove.

November 6   Princess of Wales expects baby next June.

Royal Weddings at Westminster Abbey

Until the twentieth century, royal weddings were basically private family events, and they were generally held in one of the private royal chapels at Windsor or Buckingham Palace. The first royal to be married at Westminster Abbey since the year 1269 was Princess Patricia, a grand-daughter of Queen Victoria, who married Sir Alexander Ramsey there in 1919. The choice of Westminster Abbey, rather than the Chapel Royal inside Buckingham Palace, made it necessary for the bride and her family to travel from Palace to Abbey in a carriage procession—which has been a feature of royal weddings ever since.

Royal Windsor Horse Show

The Royal Windsor Horse Show started in 1943, as a sort of compensation for the dreariness of wartime life. Originally a single afternoon of riding and driving competitions, it is now a five-day affair. The Household Cavalry puts on an exhibition of fancy riding, polo ponies go through their paces, show jumpers hurdle their horses and themselves over obstacles, and the Royal Family comes out to watch. Often they come to compete as well. Prince Philip drives The Queen's team of matched bay horses in the four-in-hand competition, and sometimes wins a ribbon.

Royal Worcester Porcelain

Royal Worcester started its association with the royals back in 1788, when King George III ordered a set of Worcester's Blue Lily china. The pattern was immediately renamed Royal Lily, and the word Royal added to the firm's name. Royal Worcester makes commemorative pieces of china for all royal occasions, and they are sought-after collector's items.

The Royal Yacht Britannia

The *Britannia* is an ocean-going private residence for the Royal Family. It was launched by The Queen in 1953, when she broke a bottle of Empire wine across its bow. The ship was a replacement for the previous royal yacht, the *Victoria and Albert*, and it incorporated some of the furniture from that yacht, commissioned by King Edward VII. The original cost of the *Britannia* was about £2 million, and since then refits have cost another £10 million or so. The *Britannia* weighs 5769 tons and can cruise at a speed of 21 knots. She requires 22 officers and 254 crew, all of whom are volunteers from the Royal Navy. It costs about £3 million a year to keep the *Britannia* on the high seas, an expense paid by the British government.

The Queen often makes official tours on the *Britannia*; it goes ahead, and she flies out to meet it. The royal apartments are comfortably furnished in the style of an English country house, although it seems that The Queen also uses it as a repository for some of the stranger gifts she receives. For example, she has hung a whale's tooth in one cabin, and on the dining table is a solid gold palm tree hung with ruby dates—a gift from the ruler of oil-rich Dubai.

A family reunion aboard the royal yacht *Britannia* after the Prince and Princess of Wales's 1985 tour of Italy.

Prince Philip's former private secretary once described the value of the *Britannia* to The Queen and to the nation:

> The dramatic effect is enormous of the royal yacht slowly leaving port with thousands of people watching The Queen go and cheering. This has a stupendous influence which a take-

The Prince and Princess of Wales ignore the rumours.

Photo by Snowdon, courtesy of the British Information Service.

off from an air terminal could not touch. People love to watch the great ship sailing away and they come in their thousands.

Her Majesty is able to entertain members of the Commonwealth country she is visiting, on board the yacht, in a way she could not do in a hotel or Government House. She can dine 60 people on board and hold a reception for 250.

Rubies

Royal rubies are once again in the public eye, thanks to Sarah Ferguson's engagement ring, with its central red stone encircled by ten sparkling diamonds. It was an especially suitable choice for a royal redhead, and we can expect to see more rubies in the new Duchess of York's jewel box.

Her aunt-in-law, Princess Margaret, also had a ruby engagement ring. When Antony Armstrong-Jones gave her the ring (which was an heirloom in his family), it was romantically described as "a rosebud set in a marguerite of diamonds". Rubies suit Princess Margaret's rather flamboyant personality, and she owns several pins conspicuously dotted with rubies.

The loveliest rubies in the Royal Family belong to The Queen Mother. For evening events, she often wears a necklace with fourteen large blood-red rubies each set in diamonds and the largest ruby of all mounted as a pendant, with matching drop earrings.

The Queen has two tiaras set with rubies but wears them infrequently; they tend to overpower her fair colouring and simple dignity.

Rumours

- That The Queen would abdicate in favour of her son Charles
- That The Queen would make her sister Margaret the Queen of Scotland
- That Princess Diana barely speaks to her stepmother, Raine
- That The Queen will offer Prince and Princess Michael of Kent a generous lifetime annuity if they will stay away from Great Britain
- That "Fergie and Di" are rivals who compete with one another for press headlines and the attention of the British public

- That Princess Diana is planning to divorce Prince Charles
- That the Queen and Prince Philip were estranged in 1957, when he embarked on a four-month tour of the Commonwealth

Courtesy of the British Information Service.

The Prince and Princess of Wales at La Scala opera house in Milan on 20 April 1985, during their visit to Italy.

S

St. Edward's Crown

St. Edward's Crown is the oldest of the monarch's crowns. Although it is called St. Edward's Crown, it was actually made (using some elements of an earlier piece) for the coronation of King Charles II in the seventeenth century. Traditionally associated with the coronation ceremony, it was not used by Kings George IV to Edward VII because it is heavy and awkwardly balanced. But King George V decided to reinstate its use during his coronation ceremonies, and his son and grand-daughter followed suit.

St. Edward's Crown has four golden arches that are depressed in the centre, signifying that it is the crown of a kingdom rather than an empire. It contains about 440 stones, although none is particularly large by royal standards. It is worn only briefly during the coronation ceremony. Before leaving Westminster Abbey for the return procession to Buckingham Palace, the Sovereign puts on the lighter Imperial State Crown, which weighs only 5lb.

Yves St. Laurent

The French designer Yves St. Laurent is the source of some of the Duchess of York's most striking outfits. According to published reports, she made her first visit to his Paris atelier in great secrecy, arriving in a British Embassy limo that took her into the private courtyard where she could enter unobserved. The reason for the hush-hush treatment apparently was the fear that Fergie would be criticized for patronizing French designers instead of English ones. But the success of her St. Laurent outfits forestalled criticism. Rumour has it that Princess Diana would love to shop at St. Laurent too, but the future Queen of England positively must buy British.

The Salmon's Revenge

In 1982 The Queen Mother choked on a salmon bone while dining with guests at the Royal Lodge in Windsor. Although she politely tried to continue making conversation, she had to be taken to a nearby hospital to have the bone removed. Later she joked that it was "the salmon's revenge".

Sandringham

Sandringham, deep in the Norfolk countryside, is one of The Queen's two privately owned residences, the other being Balmoral. Sandringham was purchased by her great-grandfather King Edward VII, when he was Prince of Wales and needed a country house. The purchase was made just months after his father, Prince Albert, died, and seeing it through was one of the ways Queen Victoria tried to follow what she thought her husband's wishes would have been.

Edward's first visit to the house came just after his marriage to Princess Alexandra of Denmark, and it was immediately apparent that the house was too small for a royal establishment. He first tried the conservative approach of erecting additional cottages and outbuildings to relieve the crowding in the old house itself, but Sandringham was still inadequate, especially as he and his wife began to have children of their own. In 1867 Edward tore down the existing house and, with the aid of architect A. J. Humbert, who designed Prince Albert's mausoleum at Frogmore, built a rather hideous red brick edifice trimmed with stone in its place. Supposedly Jacobean in style, with gabled roofs and brick chimneys, it succeeds in looking nothing less than high Victorian.

For a king's home, Sandringham is not large. There are few imposing rooms and many fairly modest ones; it's a good place for teatime chats, card games for children or adults, the jigsaw puzzle on a table in front of the fire. King George V, who called it "the place I love better than anywhere in the world", always kept the clocks at Sandringham half an hour fast, due to an obsession with punctuality. To make Sandringham more livable in the modern age, The Queen pulled down 91 of Sandringham's 361 rooms in 1977.

The grounds are glorious, with huge oaks planted by various royals beginning with Queen Victoria, and a wonderful garden of azaleas and rhododendrons created by King George VI. Sandringham houses part of The Queen's Stud, as well as the royal pigeon lofts and kennels for the Sandringham strain of black labradors, established in 1911 by

Queen Alexandra. The Royal Family usually goes to Sandringham after Christmas, and they greet the New Year there.

"Sandringham Slammer"

When Prince Edward attended a special performance of a play about wrestling, *Trafford Tanzi*, performed by the Cambridge Youth Theatre, he was given a small part as a wrestler called the "Sandringham Slammer". He downed his opponent with a hold referred to as the "Windsor Knot".

Sapphires

Sapphires have been one of the most popular choices for royal engagement rings. Lady Diana's sapphire ring became so famous that bargain-basement imitations are still advertised. Princess Anne, Princess Alexandra and the Duchess of Kent all have sapphire engagement rings as well. Perhaps the most magnificent of all is the engagement ring given to The Queen Mother by King George VI (then the Duke of York) in 1922. It is a huge Kashmir sapphire that resembles a serene reflecting pool, flanked by fiery diamonds.

The Queen owns a lovely sapphire brooch, a large stone surrounded by a circle of pearls, with an optional pearl drop pendant, which she frequently wears with a blue suit or silk dress for formal daytime appearances. She also owns a knock-out heirloom set of necklace, earrings and bracelet, which she occasionally wears in the evenings with a long gown.

The Queen Mother owns a square sapphire pin, set in a four-pointed diamond sunburst from which hangs a diamond chain, with a stone so fine and dark it is almost navy in colour. The Duchess of Gloucester owns a nice pair of sapphire and diamond earrings, and a diamond floral spray pin highlighted by sapphires. But in today's Royal Family, the biggest fan of sapphires is Princess Diana. She owns a pair of sapphire earrings that match her engagement ring, sizeable round stones surrounded by diamonds. Recently she has added a matching necklace, a gift from The Queen, that is a diamond-enclosed sapphire on a diamond chain, and a diamond bracelet set with a large sapphire in the centre.

David Sassoon

David Sassoon is one of Princess Diana's most practical fashion designers. He has worked with her to help her find new ways of wearing old favourites.

Scots Guards

The Scots Guards are a regiment of the Household Division. They wear no plumes on their bearskin hats. Their tunic buttons are grouped in threes. The Queen's cousin, the Duke of Kent, is their Colonel.

Sea Truck

The sea truck is an amphibious vehicle created for the British Army to get around in marshy or swampy terrain, and is used militarily in Bangladesh. A sea truck is always carried aboard the royal yacht *Britannia* in case of need. It was designed by Jeremy Fry, who was Prince Philip's room-mate at Gordonstoun and Antony Armstrong-Jones's first choice for his best man.

Sandra Seagram

Sandra Seagram was the last debutante to be presented at court. Traditionally, all young women who had a formal debut could also make an appearance at Buckingham Palace, to curtsey before the royals while wearing a long white frock and Prince of Wales feathers in their hair. In 1958 Queen Elizabeth decided to put an end to this tradition, and Sandra Seagram, a twenty-year-old deb from Toronto, was the last young woman to be presented at that last ceremony. According to press reports, after Sandra gave her required curtsey, she also gave Prince Philip a "little wink".

"Sea-kings' Daughter"

When Princess Alexandra of Denmark arrived in England in 1863 to marry the then Prince of Wales (later King Edward VII), her beauty and poise made her a public idol — rather like Lady Diana Spencer, the next young woman to marry a Prince of Wales. Alfred, Lord

Tennyson wrote a poem about her called, "A Welcome to Alexandra", a portion of which follows:

> Sea-kings' daughter, as happy as fair,
> Blissful bride of a blissful heir,
> Bride of the heir of the kings of the sea—
> Oh joy to the people, and joy to the throne,
> Come to us, love us, and make us your own.

A Seat for Princess Margaret

Princess Margaret, one of the shortest members of the Royal Family, sometimes has trouble with high-backed seats, because her hat brim brushes against the back of the seat, tilting her hat forward over her face. Therefore many royal vehicles, such as planes in The Queen's Flight, have been equipped with a certain number of seats of the "Princess Margaret type", meaning they have a low back and will allow small-statured royals to wear their hats unimpeded.

Carolyn Seaward

Carolyn Seaward was the 1980 Miss United Kingdom, who competed unsuccessfully in the Miss World pageant that year. She was also the first romantic attachment of Prince Andrew. While she held her beauty title, she visited the Royal Naval College at Dartmouth, where she met the Prince and started to go out with him. It was a short-lived romance.

"Seconds"

"Seconds" was the nickname given to Sarah Ferguson by her chums at boarding school, because she so often went back in the dining hall to queue for a second helping of food.

The Secret Meaning of Those Wedding Gifts

Among the gifts given to Prince Charles and Princess Diana at the time of their marriage were a number of fertility symbols, either overt or oblique. There were pictures of bunnies and mice, sometimes dressed as brides and grooms, as well as painted eggs. There was rice, of course, and also traditional love spoons from Wales. The Queen

Princess Anne competing in a show jumping event in 1971.

Courtesy of the British Information Service.

was the recipient of many of the same types of gifts, from her loyal subjects who either consciously or unconsciously hoped for an heir who would enable the House of Windsor to continue its reign.

Tessa Seiden

Mrs. Tessa Seiden is the corsetiere to The Queen.

Separation Announcement

On 19 March 1976 Buckingham Palace released the following official announcement: "Her Royal Highness the Princess Margaret, Countess of Snowdon, and the Earl of Snowdon have mutually agreed to live apart. The Princess will carry out her public duties unaccompanied by Lord Snowdon. There are no plans for divorce proceedings."

A Serious Fall

Although Princess Anne is a world-class rider, she has had her own troubles in staying on her mount. Her most serious fall came in 1976, when she fell off her horse Candlewick (owned by The Queen), which then fell on top of her. She suffered a hairline fracture of a vertebra in her neck and a concussion that put her in hospital for several days. A senior nurse at the hospital said Anne was an excellent patient. "She was no trouble at all to us, we treated her just like any other patient who may have been brought in with the same injuries."

Service of Remembrance

The Service of Remembrance, the annual ceremony led by The Queen to mark the nation's solemn remembrance of those who have fallen in battle, takes place on the Sunday nearest 11 November, the day World War I ended, at Whitehall. The Queen comes out of the old Home Office, accompanied by various other royals, and walks to the Cenotaph in Whitehall to lay a wreath to honour Britain's war dead. She always wears black, with the traditional spray of red poppies in her lapel.

17 Bruton Street

Queen Elizabeth was born at 17 Bruton Street, a private house in London's Mayfair. It was the town house of The Queen's grandparents, the Earl and Countess of Strathmore, who lent it to the Duke and Duchess of York at the time of their daughter's birth. The house was damaged in the bombing during World War II and was later demolished for commercial development of the site.

Kevin Shanley

Kevin Shanley is a hairdresser at Headlines in South Kensington and is one of Princess Diana's favourite stylists.

Michael Shea

Michael Shea was The Queen's press secretary from 1978 to 1987. He was formerly the deputy director of the British Information Services in New York. He resigned as press secretary to take a high-paying job as director of public relations for a large business firm.

During his tenure as press secretary, Shea lived in a beautiful grace-and-favour home near Buckingham Palace and often shared a joke with The Queen. It is rumoured that she gave him a china Miss Piggy doll after he accidentally revealed that her family occasionally called her by that nickname. The Gordonstoun-educated Shea writes mystery novels under the name Michael Sinclair. His rather frosty attitude towards "publicizing" The Queen was summed up in one quote: "I do not entertain people. I am not in the PR business."

Robin Janvrin was appointed as Shea's replacement.

Shiel of Altnaguisach

The Shiel (Gaelic for "little house") of Altnaguisach is a cosy little house on the grounds of Balmoral that Queen Victoria and Prince Albert created from a shepherd's cottage. They often went there for picnics and bouts of exhaustive domesticity.

Shoe Size

Princess Margaret is justly proud of her tiny feet; she wears a size $2\frac{1}{2}$ shoe.

The Queen Mother wears a $3\frac{1}{2}$.
Princess Diana wears a $7\frac{1}{2}$ AA.

Shooting Pudding

Shooting pudding has been a tradition of the Royal Family at Balmoral since the days of Queen Victoria. A dark, rich plum pudding, it is so heavy it looks almost as if it is made from the best agricultural mud. Only those who have been walking all day in the hills of Scotland could possibly eat it without fear.

Shopping in Bath

Bath is the city nearest the Waleses' country house, Highgrove. According to the locals, Diana often slips into town on Saturday morning and shops unrecognized in the trendy boutiques. One of her favourite shops is Habitat, for things for the house; she also likes to look in Laura Ashley's shop for clothes and home furnishings in traditional English prints.

Shopping Mistakes

In 1982 Princess Margaret attended the Fashion Gala sponsored by the Royal College of Art, at which a variety of outfits was modelled and sold. The Princess snapped up three outfits, cause of rejoicing by the college — until the following day when all three were returned, with the explanation that they were all too small for the Princess.

Silver Jubilee of King George V

In 1935 King George V celebrated his Silver Jubilee. Ever since he had fallen ill and nearly died of a lung abscess in 1928–29, his health had been frail. When he succeeded in reaching the milestone of twenty-five years as King, there was genuine rejoicing.

According to one account, here are some of the highlights of the Jubilee: there were two state dinners at the Palace and a Royal Command concert in the Albert Hall, ending at the King's request with community singing of "Jerusalem". Hitler sent a congratulatory telegram. There was a half-holiday at Maidstone Prison. The MP for Gloucester presented the city with a Bible containing signed photographs of the King and Queen. Six pigeons were released by the Duchess of Gloucester, bearing greetings from seventeen thousand schoolchildren in Scotland. There was a Jubilee Naval Review. The Duchess of Kent visited Sandringham.

A thanksgiving service was held at St. Paul's in May, and the King was deeply touched by the continual demonstrations of love and loyalty from his subjects. "I am beginning to think," he exclaimed, "they must really like me for myself." The King barely outlived his Silver Jubilee year, dying just before midnight on 20 January 1936.

Silver Jubilee of Queen Elizabeth

In 1977 Queen Elizabeth celebrated her Silver Jubilee, twenty-five

years on the throne. The theme of the celebration was one The
Queen enunciated in her Christmas speech of 1976. She wanted the
Silver Jubilee to be a special year "for people who find themselves the
victims of human conflict". Her Jubilee would be a time of
reconciliation. She undertook two tours that year, for a total of nearly
ten weeks of travel. On 4 May she received a tribute in Westminster
Hall from both Houses of Parliament.

A month later there was a thanksgiving service at St. Paul's
Cathedral, with a dazzling procession of carriages and royals.
Afterwards, The Queen and the Duke of Edinburgh walked to the
Guildhall for luncheon. She made a speech that referred to her pledge
at the time of her coming of age: "When I was twenty-one, I pledged
my life to the service of our people, and I asked for God's help to make
good that vow. Although that vow was made in my salad days when I
was green in judgement, I do not regret nor retract one word of it." In
the days after the speech, The Queen and her Consort rode out in all
four directions to meet The Queen's loyal subjects. Prince Charles
spent much of the year heading The Queen's Silver Jubilee Trust, an
organization aimed at encouraging young people to help others.

A film released in the Silver Jubilee year helped to show the real life
of The Queen. *Royal Heritage* demonstrated the trappings of monarchy
at their grandest and at their most human. There were the ceremonial
touches — the piper on the front lawn, the Company of Archers
protecting The Queen in Scotland. There was also Queen Mary's
exquisite dolls' house, and The Queen's own Little House at Windsor,
where she was shown playing with her grandson Peter Phillips and
her niece Sarah Armstrong-Jones. The cameras show redecorating in
the Palace, as in any other family's home, and they also show the
refurbishing of national treasures that just happen to belong to The
Queen.

Silver Wedding Anniversary

On 20 November 1972 The Queen and the Duke of Edinburgh
celebrated their silver wedding anniversary. There was a service at
Westminster Abbey, followed by a luncheon at the Guildhall. The
Queen began her speech by joking, "I think everyone will concede that
today, of all occasions, I should begin my speech with 'My husband
and I'." The Queen continued, "We—and by that I mean both of
us—are most grateful to you . . ." After the Guildhall The Queen and
the Duke visited the new Barbican site which was being built, and laid
the foundation stone of the Arts Centre.

Courtesy of Simpson Piccadilly.

Simpson's of Piccadilly at night.

Simpson's of Piccadilly

Simpson's of Piccadilly holds three Royal Warrants, as outfitters to The Queen, the Duke of Edinburgh and the Prince of Wales. It was the invention of Daks trousers that put Simpson's of Piccadilly on the fashion map. The patented Daks adjustable waistband did away with the necessity for braces or belt, held trousers up and shirt-tail down, and made the waistcoat a fashion option instead of a requirement.

There is still a Simpson family member on the board of directors, Georgina Simpson Andrews. She designs her own Georgina Simpson fashion collection for women and is married to actor Anthony Andrews of *Brideshead Revisited* fame. For further information, write to: Simpson's of Piccadilly, London W1.

Skiing

Many of the royals are enthusiastic skiers. Prince Charles and Prince Andrew, who both learned to ski in the Scottish Cairngorm Mountains while at school at Gordonstoun, have taken many skiing trips to Switzerland. The Prince used to go alone, queue for the ski lift, and stay at the Hotel Wynegg in Klosters; its proprietor, Ruth Guler, was a guest at his wedding. Princess Diana learned to ski when she was at school in Switzerland; in a pre-wedding interview, Prince Charles cited skiing as one of the things he and his bride-to-be had in common.

The Duchess of York had for years spent as much of her winter as possible in the skiing town of Verbier. In January, Fergie went on a skiing trip with some of her old friends (calling Andrew back at the Royal Navy base every night). A few months later she arranged to go back with her husband, renting a large house just outside Klosters. To make the trip more enjoyable, she also arranged for the Prince and Princess of Wales to join them there. The two couples celebrated Prince Andrew's birthday with a surprise champagne and fondue party, in the company of about twenty friends, and then made a midnight run down the torch-lit slopes.

In March 1988 a royal party was again at Klosters. The Prince of Wales led a party of highly competent skiers down a severe run and they went off-piste; an avalanche overtook them. Major Hugh Lindsay was killed outright, and Mrs. Patti Palmer-Tomkinson was in hospital in Davos for 128 days with both her legs shattered. There followed much speculation in the press as to whether Prince Charles should be "allowed" to take part in such "dangerous sports".

Prince and Princess Michael of Kent are also skiing enthusiasts; in fact, many of the younger generation of royals have learned to ski competently. Princess Anne skis, and she has already taken her children on a skiing holiday. (She goes on an ordinary package tour.) The Queen, however, has never been seen on the slopes.

Slipper

Slipper was the name of the Cairn terrier that the Prince of Wales gave to Wallis Simpson in 1934. Neither party ever mentioned whether the name came from the Cinderella story, but the ending was not a fairy tale. Poor Slipper, playing in the tall grass of a country house in France, suddenly gave out a howl and dropped dead. The only explanation anyone could ever put forward was that the dog had been bitten by a poisonous snake.

Sloane Rangers

The phrase "Sloane Rangers" was originated in 1975 by Peter York in *Harper's & Queen* magazine to describe Britain's young and privileged upper class. While the name is an inspired parody of an American cult hero, the Lone Ranger, "Sloane" refers to the area around Sloane Square, connecting Knightsbridge with Chelsea, which is where "Sloanes" live when in London and where they shop at Peter Jones, Harrods, The General Trading Company, and the like.

At the time of Lady Diana Spencer's marriage to Prince Charles in 1981, York and Ann Barr co-authored *The Official Sloane Ranger Handbook*. The book designated Princess Diana as "Supersloane" and described in witty and accurate detail the lifestyle of the Sloane Rangers, from their head scarves to their mating habits. (To order a copy, write to: Ebury Press, 27 Broadwick St., London W1V 1FR.)

Smelling Like a Royal

The Queen gets her fragrances from Floris and prefers old-fashioned floral scents.

In her teens, Princess Margaret wore "Shocking" by Schiaparelli.

Smiles

According to tradition, royals are not generally a smiley lot. Queen Victoria was only twice seen smiling in public, and her grandson King George V was equally solemn. The Queen never smiles unless she is genuinely amused by something, which has led to unfavourable publicity about the severe looks on her face during public appearances. She complains, "The trouble is that women are expected to be smiling all the time; it is terribly unfair. If a man looks solemn, it is automatically assumed that he is a serious person, concentrating, with grave things on his mind." The Queen often adopts a solemn look to avoid showing her emotions, as during the wedding of Prince Charles. By contrast, The Queen Mother is usually all smiles.

A thoughtful picture of The Queen, half-smiling.

Horace Smith

Horace Smith was a riding master who had a riding school at Windsor called Holyport. As a young girl The Queen learned horsemanship from him, and she was so admiring of his expertise and his methods that she later sent her daughter Anne, another excellent horse-woman, to learn from him as well.

Smoking

The only heavy smoker in the Royal Family is Princess Margaret, who continues to puff away in defiance of her doctor's warnings. She still sometimes likes to use her trademark long cigarette holders, a symbol of glamour left over from her younger days.

The Queen used to smoke, as did Prince Philip, but both have given it up in their later years. The new Duchess of York is known to have an occasional cigarette in private, but Prince Andrew doesn't smoke.

Prince Charles is an ardent non-smoker who dislikes any smoking in his presence. So vehement is he about non-smoking that when he buys a new car, he has all the ashtrays removed and the holes covered with leather patches.

The Queen Mother was known to have smoked in the past, although she no longer does, and her husband, George VI, smoked as many as eighty cigarettes a day, most likely the cause of his lung cancer. The Duke of Windsor was another of the Royal Family's heavy smokers.

"Something Must Be Done!"

Shortly after Edward VIII became King, he toured a Welsh mining district in which unemployment rates were unbelievably high. Visibly moved by the plight of the miners and their families, the King said firmly, "Something must be done!" His speech made the whole country optimistic about the commitment of the new King to his people, an optimism that was soon to crumble under the rumours of abdication.

Dr. Nigel Southward

Dr. Nigel Southward is The Queen's Apothecary. He is also Apothecary to the households of Princess Margaret, Princess Alice Duchess of Gloucester and the Duke and Duchess of Gloucester. His father, Sir Ralph Southward, is Apothecary to The Queen Mother's household. Dr. Southward strongly advises all his patients to refrain from smoking and drinking, and he believes in fresh air and healthy doses of exercise. The Queen follows his advice, with good results. She is rarely ill, except for occasional bouts of sinusitis, which are treated with homeopathic remedies.

The Spencers of Althorp

Lady Diana Spencer's family traces its lineage back to a Warwickshire landowner and sheep farmer in the reign of King Henry VI in the fifteenth century. Over hundreds of years, the Spencers became related by marriage to the Marlborough family and their most famous descendant, Winston Churchill; the Marquess of Halifax, from whom The Queen Mother is descended; and the Duke of Devonshire. Lady Diana's grandfather was the godson of King Edward VII; one of his sisters was a lady-in-waiting to The Queen Mother, and another was her lady of the bedchamber. Diana's father was an equerry first to King George VI and then to Queen Elizabeth, during the first two years of her reign.

The family home is Althorp in Northamptonshire, built in the early sixteenth century and completely remodelled in the late eighteenth century. Althorp is noted for its art collection, featuring pictures by Reynolds, Gainsborough, Titian and Stubbs, as well as its rare furniture and china, much of which came from the Marlborough home at Blenheim.

Spitting Image

Spitting Image, the television comedy programme that uses life-size puppets in satirical skits, uses royals as frequent targets. For example, in one sketch, Prince Philip (always depicted wearing a chestful of military decorations) donned a sheet and went to haunt Margaret Thatcher's bedroom. In another, Princess Margaret wanted to name the new baby of the Prince and Princess of Wales Gordon after the bottle of gin she held in her hand just before she fell down drunk. The Queen Mother peddled royal wedding souvenirs outside the Palace, and The Queen was seen telling her family about the "splendid bottoms" she had observed on nearly naked Maori warriors. The Queen puppet usually wears an old head scarf, Charles has huge ears, and Andrew has teeth bigger than the whole Osmond family put together.

Courtesy of Spitting Images Productions Ltd.

Spitting Image puppets of the Duke of Edinburgh, The Queen, and the Princess and Prince of Wales.

Although the Royal Family doesn't publicly admit to watching the show, insiders say they often laugh over some of the episodes. The Duchess of York has taped the segments about herself, which feature a puppet spray-painted with freckles.

Sporting Life

The publication *Sporting Life* is a favourite with The Queen. Every morning, newspapers are brought to The Queen's bedroom, along with Her Majesty's first cup of tea, and she reads *Sporting Life* in order to keep up her extensive knowledge of affairs in the world of horse racing and breeding. In fact, the publisher of the paper sends a copy by messenger straight from the presses as soon as it has been printed. Visitors have noted a bureau overflowing with press cuttings and have been told by The Queen that she is behind with her filing about horse breeding and form.

"A Sporting Week with the English Gentry"

In 1987 Mark Phillips announced that he would offer shooting lessons to well-heeled American tourists, under the auspices of a packaged tour (price: £6200) called "A Sporting Week with the English Gentry".

Sprig of Myrtle

All twentieth-century royal brides have included in their bridal bouquets a small sprig of myrtle from a tree at Windsor that was grown from a cutting taken from Queen Victoria's wedding bouquet. In the symbolic language of the flowers, myrtle stands for love.

Koo Stark (Kathleen Stark)

Koo Stark is the actress who was romantically linked with Prince Andrew in 1982, when he was twenty-two and she was twenty-six. Koo, star of a soft-porn film, met Andrew at the London club Tramps, when she approached him and a group of his friends and asked them to stop making so much noise. Their romance had just begun to flourish when he was sent to the Falklands during the war with Argentina.

On his return they began seeing one another again, and he took Koo to Balmoral to meet The Queen. Her Majesty reportedly commented, "She seems a very nice girl." Weeks later, Andrew took Koo on a holiday to Mustique, borrowing his Aunt Margaret's villa there for the occasion. Alas, journalists recorded their every move, and one of their friends ended up selling the story of the holiday to the newspapers. The publicity was distasteful to the Royal Family; and either out of deference to their feelings or because the romance had run its course, Andrew soon afterwards ceased to see Koo. She subsequently married Tim Jeffries, heir to the Green Shield Stamps fortune.

Start-Rite Shoes

All royal children wear the classic little strapped shoe that comes from Start-Rite. They come in various colours of leather, as well as black

Courtesy of the British Information Service.

Princess Diana, on the Buckingham Palace balcony, with her wedding bouquet containing the traditional sprig of myrtle.

patent for dress, and they fasten with a strap over the instep. The fastener may be a button (the classic model) or a buckle. The Queen and her sister both wore these shoes in their childhood, as did their children and now The Queen's grandchildren as well. For William and Harry, Princess Diana currently favours a slightly more stylish version made by Anthea More-ede in Kensington; they look like Greek fisherman's sandals.

State Coach

The Gold State Coach was built for King George III in 1762, and was first used on 25 November 1763 when he went to Westminster to open a new session of Parliament.

The gilded roof is supported by eight palm trees which branch out at the top to act as supports. The body is slung on leather straps decorated at each side by a triton. The panels, front and back as well as the sides, were painted by Cipriani from Florence, and show Britannia attended by Religion, Justice, Wisdom, Valour and Victory.

The coach was completely regilded for The Queen's Silver Jubilee in 1977 and the interior of crimson satin was renovated with specially woven material. It takes eight horses to pull this massive coach, and since King George VI's reign Windsor greys have been used. Even with eight horses, it can only go at a walk of about three miles an hour.

The Queen on her way to the State opening of Parliament.

Courtesy of the British Information Service.

State Opening of Parliament

This ceremony is one of The Queen's constitutional obligations. She always fulfils it in person, rather than delegating it to another royal.

When Prince Philip accompanies The Queen, an extra throne is borrowed from the Marquess of Cholmondeley, to give him a place to sit.

The State opening of Parliament usually takes place in late October or early November. The Queen travels to the opening of Parliament in the Irish State Coach. Once there, she dons her State Robes and the Imperial State Crown in the Robing Room. Her Majesty walks in a stately procession to the House of Lords, where she takes her seat on a heavily gilded throne and invites the peers to be seated. A member of The Queen's Household, the Gentleman Usher of the Black Rod, goes to summon the House of Commons. By tradition, as he approaches the door of their chamber, the door is slammed in his face; this symbolizes the independence of the Commons. After he has knocked three times, the door is opened and he is allowed in to deliver The Queen's summons. When the Members of Parliament at last arrive, The Queen dons her spectacles and reads the speech written for her by the party in power. The Queen first agreed to permit television coverage of the event in 1958.

Jackie Stewart Celebrity Challenge

To raise money for charity, former racing driver Jackie Stewart every year hosts a clay-pigeon shoot. Members of the Royal Family often compete. For example, in 1982 the event was won by a team consisting of Mark Phillips, the Duke of Kent, Angus Ogilvy and former King Constantine of Greece.

Stone of Scone

The Stone of Scone is one of the treasured relics of the monarchy in Great Britain. According to legend, the Stone was the pillow on which Jacob slept. Scottish kings venerated it as the Stone of Destiny and sat upon it to be crowned. In 1296 King Edward I of England stole it from the Abbey of Scone and took it to England, where he had a chair made to enclose it. That chair is now called King Edward's Chair, and it is always used in coronation ceremonies in lieu of an official throne of England.

A symbol of Scottish nationalism, the stone was the target of a plot in 1950 to "kidnap" it from Westminster Abbey as a protest against English rule over Scotland. It was recovered in good time for Queen Elizabeth's coronation.

The Strange Case of the Missing Photographers

Young Prince William has become so accustomed to being followed by a crowd of reporters and photographers that he finds it odd when they are not around. On his first day at school, he was, of course, the focus of enormous media attention, but on the second day, there was not a camera in sight. "Where have all the photographers gone?" he asked his mother plaintively. She answered firmly, "Don't be so grand, William."

Prince William on the other side of the camera.

Courtesy of the British Information Service.

Barbra Streisand

Barbra Streisand was presented to The Queen after a screening of *Funny Girl* attended by the Royal Family. Barbra, ever the brash Brooklynite, asked The Queen as they were introduced, "Why do women have to wear gloves to meet you, and the men don't?" The Queen was obviously taken aback by this direct question and answered, "Really, I don't know, it's a tradition, I suppose."

The Subjects of Queen Elizabeth II

Queen Elizabeth is Queen of the United Kingdom and its dependencies. She is also Queen of Antigua and Barbuda, Australia, Bahamas, Belize, Canada, Mauritius, New Zealand, Papua New Guinea, St. Lucia, St. Kitts-Nevis, St. Vincent and the Grenadines, Solomon Islands, and Tuvalu. Commonwealth countries, of which she is Head of State, include Bangladesh, Barbados, Botswana, Brunei, Cyprus, Dominica, The Gambia, Ghana, Grenada, Guyana, India, Jamaica, Kenya, Kiribati, Lesotho, Malawi, Malaysia, Maldives, Malta, Nauru, Nigeria, Seychelles, Sierra Leone, Singapore, Sri Lanka, Swaziland, Tanzania, Tonga, Trinidad and Tobago, Uganda, Vanuatu, Western Samoa, Zambia and Zimbabwe.

Sultan of Brunei

The Sultan of Brunei, who might possibly be the richest man in the world, is a devoted admirer of the Royal Family. He spent a year at the Royal Military Academy at Sandhurst before taking the throne, and was so happy at being a part of the Empire that he had to be pushed into independence. Prince Charles has been to visit the Sultan in Brunei, and they discovered they were both keen polo players.

Superhuman Traits of the Royals

According to Miss Iris Peake, a long-time lady-in-waiting to Princess Margaret, "The Princess simply doesn't feel the heat as we do." On her trips to hot climates in Africa and the Caribbean, said Miss Peake, "she takes no special precautions and wears no special make-up".

When The Queen Mother was a girl, her mother always used to tell her, "If you find somebody or something a bore, the fault lies in you."

Queen Mary, on overhearing a junior royal admit to being tired, replied firmly, "Stuff and nonsense. You are a member of the British Royal Family, and we are *never* tired."

When Buckingham Palace announced that The Queen would be getting inoculations for tetanus, polio, yellow fever and smallpox before she went to Brazil in 1968, they found it necessary to explain, "The Queen is not a fairy."

Aware of the mystique that surrounds her, The Queen herself once commented, "I have to be seen to be believed."

Sussex Commemorative Ware

Britain's largest and most comprehensive dealer in royal collectibles and memorabilia, Sussex Commemorative Ware offers a catalogue of hundreds of mugs, jugs, plates, medallions, teapots, figurines and the like celebrating royal personages and events dating back to Queen Victoria. Birth, death, wedding and anniversary mementoes include "1000 Years of English Monarchy: 973–1973", a Wedgwood mug printed with fifty-one full-length pictures of British sovereigns, and a bone china plate featuring Snowdon's colour portrait of "Prince William and His Parents". For further information, write to: 88 Western Road, Hove, Sussex.

Swaine Adeney Brigg and Sons Ltd.

Established in 1750 as whip-makers on the very spot in Piccadilly where they still conduct business, Swaine Adeney Brigg have held Royal Warrants from eleven British monarchs. Currently whip and glove makers to The Queen and umbrella makers to The Queen Mother, the firm, under the chairmanship of Robert Adeney, offers a wide variety of traditional goods with particular emphasis on country life, hunting and horse shows. Catering to men and women, the saddlery and dressage departments carry every conceivable type of riding equipment and accessory. The firm's Piccadilly Polo Room offers beginners' classes, with demonstrations and accompanying videos. Home video-cassettes on hunting, racing and dressage are also available. For further information, write to: 185 Piccadilly, London W1V 0HA.

Princess Anne tours Swaine Adeney Brigg & Sons Ltd. with Mr. Robert E. T. Adeney.

Courtesy of Swaine Adeney Brigg & Sons Ltd.

Courtesy of the British Information Service.

Prince William, four, taking an "angel" by the hand as he went to rehearse his part as a shepherd for a Nativity play at his London nursery school.

The Duchess of York, suitably attired in a flying jacket, shows off her private pilot's licence after it was presented to her at the Oxford Air Training School at Kidlington airport, near Oxford. To obtain the licence she had to put in a minimum of forty hours at the controls and pass written tests in aviation law, meteorology, principles of flying and navigation.

Courtesy of the British Information Service.

T

Table Manners

The Royal Family in general observes the conventional table manners of the British upper classes. Among the mealtime regulations:

- Dinner is eaten in the evening, luncheon in the middle of the day.
- The lap is covered with a "table napkin", never a "serviette".
- Port wine is passed to the left and never lifted from the surface of the table (so as not to disturb the aged contents of the decanter).
- Mustard is always presented in a silver holder.
- Stilton cheese must be sliced, never scooped.
- Formerly, the use of napkin rings was considered unacceptable in royal circles. "I quite refuse to use one," said King George V. "I like a clean napkin every day."

Tamarisk

Tamarisk is a modest cottage in the Scilly Isles, owned by Prince Charles, who is the Lord of the Isles. Various members of the Royal Family occasionally use it as a getaway spot, especially to take along the children, who can play on the beach and enjoy the salt air as well as the complete freedom of the isolated spot.

323

Taurus

The Queen was born under the sign of Taurus and shows many signs of a Taurean personality: a loving and loyal nature, coupled with a straightforward manner and great physical courage. A lover of physical beauty, the typical Taurus turns her aesthetic sense on making a comfortable and attractive home and knows how to keep it tranquil. Taurean women make the most steadfast friends and lovers.

According to one source, "Fleeting liaisons interest idealistic Taureans not a bit — the Bull girl is a one-man woman who, once committed, will never stray. A tender-hearted tower of strength to the needy, Taurus's clear-headed counsel and gentle guidance have turned many a person's life totally around..." According to the same astrologer, The Queen's magic colour is petal pink, and her most arousing erogenous zone is the back of her neck. The astrologer adds that a match between a Taurean woman and a Gemini man (Prince Philip's sign) can come to no good; Gemini's fickleness is more than the wholehearted devotion of Taurus can bear.

"Te Kotuku Rarenga Tahi"

In New Zealand, the Maori call Queen Elizabeth "Te Kotuku Rarenga Tahi", which means "Rare White Heron of Singular Flight".

Ten Good Books

For those who want to read more about the Royal Family, here is a list of ten good books on the subject:

1. Queen Alexandra of Yugoslavia, *Prince Philip*. A cousin gives an inside look at the family point of view on Philip and his marriage.
2. Cynthia Asquith, *The Life of Queen Elizabeth*. Rather precious look at Queen Elizabeth The Queen Mother dating from the late 1930s.
3. Stephen Birmingham, *Duchess: The Story of Wallis Warfield Windsor*. Fun and gossipy story of the royal romance and its rather dreary aftermath. Futura, 1987.

4. Marion Crawford, *The Little Princesses*. The first tell-all book from below stairs, a sentimental Valentine to the golden-curled Princess Elizabeth.

5. Trevor Hall, *The Royal Family Today*. Full of gorgeous colour photos by Patrick Lichfield. Colour Library Books, 1984.

6. Penny Junor, *Charles*. A close-up look at a prince who is doing his best to create a role for himself and develop the self-confidence to enact it in public. Sidgwick & Jackson, 1987; Pan, 1988.

7. Robert Lacey, *Majesty*. A fact-filled study of Her Majesty The Queen and her family. Sphere, 1986.

8. Elizabeth Longford, *The Queen*. Thoughtful analysis of The Queen's influence on the country.

9. Ann Morrow, *The Queen Mother*. A sunny biography of the warm-hearted Queen Mum. Granada, 1984.

10. *Sunday Express* Staff, *A Week in the Life of the Royal Family*. A book that has a documentary, slice-of-life feeling. Weidenfeld & Nicolson, 1983.

The Honourable Mr. and Mrs. Colin Tennant

In 1983 Colin Tennant became the third Baron Glenconner. The Baron and his wife, Anne, are among Princess Margaret's closest friends. Lady Anne Coke, the daughter of the Earl of Leicester, was a maid of honour at The Queen's coronation, and she married Colin Tennant in 1956. The Tennants have three sons and twin daughters, and their nanny, Barbara Barnes, was later passed along to the Prince and Princess of Wales. Lady Glenconner has served as an extra lady-in-waiting for Princess Margaret. One of Tennant's business interests was buying and developing the island of Mustique, where he and his wife formerly had a holiday home. He generously gave the Princess her home on that same Caribbean island as a wedding gift.

"Thank God for a Good King"

During the bleak days of World War II, King George made one of his frequent public appearances to inspect the damage done to England by Nazi bombs. One of his subjects shouted out, "Thank God for a good King." The King replied with dignity, "Thank God for a good people."

Margaret Thatcher

Mrs. Margaret Thatcher, Conservative MP for Barnet, Finchley, is the eighth prime minister of Queen Elizabeth's reign and the first woman ever to hold the position. She became Prime Minister in May 1979 and has won two subsequent general elections. She attended Oxford, worked as a research chemist while studying law, and became a barrister specializing in tax law in 1954. She was elected to the House of Commons five years later, and her meteoric rise in the traditionally male-dominated Conservative Party found her Party Leader by 1975. Insiders report that Mrs. Thatcher's relationship with The Queen is strictly business, but that the two strong-minded women in positions of leadership demonstrate considerable mutual respect.

"Thick as a Plank"

When Princess Diana visited a children's hospital in Surrey, teenage patients were playing Trivial Pursuit. One of them picked out a question for the Princess. She declined to try to answer, saying, "No thanks, I'm as thick as a plank."

"Thirty Years a Princess"

In 1984 Canadian radio stations frequently played a song called "Thirty Years a Princess", written about Princess Anne upon the birth of her brother's second son. By songwriter Nancy White, the song includes these words:

> Now don't you feel sorry for poor Princess Anne,
> She seems so sincere and she stands by her man,
> But as each year goes by, through no fault of her own,
> She moves another notch away from the throne.
> She can rise, she can curtsey
> And she's quite well-to-do,
> She can stand up for hours
> Without going to the loo.
> But from her place on the short list
> She's watched fate intervene
> Now it's thirty years a Princess
> And never a Queen.

Prime Minister Margaret Thatcher, with her husband, outside Number 10 Downing Street.

Photo from London Pictures Service, courtesy of the British Information Service.

Ian Thomas

Ian Thomas is the youngest and trendiest of The Queen's dress designers. Once an employee of Hartnell, he went out on his own, and The Queen became a customer. He specializes in feminine dresses

made of light silky materials that flatter the figure. The Queen has
said of his fashions, "I feel happy in these clothes. Once I put them on,
I can forget about them." As a mark of her favour, The Queen gave
Thomas a corgi named Frisky, and whenever she talks to him about
additions to her wardrobe, she asks warmly after Frisky's welfare.

Janet Thompson

Janet Thompson was the nanny who looked after Jane, Sarah and
Diana Spencer when they were children. She later recollected, "Diana
was not a difficult child, but she could be obstinate. She didn't like
walks, wouldn't eat the crusts of her bread. She wasn't keen on horses
and wouldn't fuss over our two dogs. She was very fond of pretty
clothes and keeping them neat. She loved flowered dresses ... As for
sweets, Diana always loved Smarties and fruit pastilles."

"Tiara Triangle"

Londoners call the area in which are located shops patronized by
English aristocrats—including, of course, the Royal Family—the
"tiara triangle". The tiara triangle is bounded on one side by Sloane
Street, the second side by Brompton Road, and the third side by
Beauchamp Place.

Tiaras

By tradition, unmarried women don't wear tiaras. Thus they are
often a gift to royal brides. Princess Diana has two tiaras. One, an
heirloom from her own Spencer family, has delicate swirls of
diamonds with a small heart in the very centre; it was the one she
wore with her long cloud of bridal veil at her wedding. The second
tiara was a gift from The Queen and formerly belonged to Queen
Mary. It has teardrop pearl pendants topped by delicate diamond
bows, and Princess Diana usually wears it with pendant teardrop
pearl earrings.

   The Queen Mother owns a magnificent Russian fringe tiara, which
she lent to her daughter Elizabeth to wear at her wedding. She herself
prefers a dainty flowery tiara that nestles snugly in her silver hair.
Palace insiders agree that The Queen Mother's jewellery collection is
probably the most beautiful in the Royal Family.

   The Queen has a varied tiara collection, some of which really are
miniature crowns. Most familiar from photographs is a tiara designed

Courtesy of the British Information Service.

The Queen in an elaborate tiara with matching necklace.

with diamond swags and Prince of Wales feathers. Another tiara features huge pearl drops within diamond circles, usually worn with matching earrings. In 1978 she had a new tiara made, using Burmese diamonds and rubies which make a set with the diamond and ruby necklace her father gave her as a wedding present.

"Tiaras if Possible"

Princess Alice of Athlone was a grandchild of Queen Victoria who married a brother of Queen Mary and lived to be a very old lady. When the Royal Family gave a party to celebrate her ninetieth birthday, the invitations requested "Tiaras if possible"—a commentary on the sad state of decline into which tiara wearing has fallen. She died in 1981 in her ninety-eighth year.

Titles of Prince Charles

- Duke of Cornwall
- Duke of Rothesay
- Earl of Carrick
- Baron Renfrew
- Prince of Wales
- Earl of Chester
- Lord of the Isles
- Great Steward of Scotland
- Personal A.D.C. to The Queen
- Commander of the Royal Navy
- Colonel-in-Chief of the Gordon Highlanders
- Colonel-in-Chief of the Royal Regiment of Wales (24th/41st Foot)
- Colonel-in-Chief of the 2nd King Edward VII's Own Gurkha Rifles
- Colonel in-Chief of the Cheshire Regiment
- Colonel in-Chief of the Parachute Regiment
- Colonel-in-Chief of Lord Strathcona's Horse (Royal Canadians)
- Colonel-in-Chief of the Royal Australian Armoured Corps
- Colonel-in-Chief of the Royal Regiment of Canada
- Colonel-in-Chief of 5th Royal Inniskilling Dragoon Guards
- Colonel-in-Chief of the Royal Canadian Dragoons
- Colonel-in-Chief of the Royal Pacific Islands Regiment
- Colonel-in-Chief of the Royal Winnipeg Rifles
- Colonel of the Welsh Guards
- Colonel Air Reserve Group of Air Command (Canada)
- Wing Commander of the Royal Air Force
- Great Master of the Order of the Bath
- Air Commodore-in-Chief Royal New Zealand Air Force
- Hon. Air Commodore RAF Brawdy

The Tornado

Some of the Palace staff have nicknamed young Prince William "The Tornado". Even his mother sometimes refers to him by that name.

Peter Townsend

Peter Townsend is generally believed to have been the real love of Princess Margaret's life. Born in Rangoon, the son of a British army officer, he followed his father into the Royal Air Force and achieved an excellent war record as a fighter pilot during the Battle of Britain. Group Captain Townsend was the kind of debonair gentleman who not only visited all his own crew members when they were injured, but also looked up in the hospital the crew members of the German planes he had shot down, bringing them oranges, cigarettes and good cheer. King George VI later chose Townsend to be one of his equerries; he went on to serve as Deputy Master of the Royal Household and then Comptroller. As a result of a war-time romance, Peter Townsend married Rosemary Pawle, with whom he had two sons. They were later divorced, an action she blamed on his absence due to his Palace duties.

Princess Margaret had turned to Group Captain Peter Townsend for comfort at the time of King George VI's death. Within a year, rumours about their romance were widespread. At first the rumours were denied, and then Townsend was abruptly named to the obscure post of air attaché in Brussels, and speculation increased that it was a move to break up the couple. The drama continued for several years. Newspapers took polls of reader opinion as to whether or not Margaret ought to be allowed to marry her hero, and members of Parliament spoke for and against it.

The key issue was Townsend's divorce, which meant that a second marriage to Princess Margaret would not be recognized by the Church of England. The Archbishop of Canterbury, spiritual head of the Church of England, was completely opposed to the marriage. As temporal head of the Church, Queen Elizabeth had to agree with him, despite the sympathy she felt for her sister's predicament. Margaret had the option of removing herself from the line of succession and marrying without The Queen's consent when she reached the age of twenty-five, but the Royal Family let it be known that they didn't approve of that course of action; the embarrassment of King Edward VIII's Abdication from his royal duty was still too fresh in everyone's mind.

At last, on Hallowe'en night in 1955, Princess Margaret issued a statement that put an end to the speculation. "I would like it to be known that I have decided not to marry Group Captain Peter Townsend. I have been aware that, subject to my renouncing my rights of succession, it might have been possible for me to contract a civil marriage. But, mindful of the Church's teaching that Christian marriage is indissoluble, and conscious of my duty to the Commonwealth, I have resolved to put these considerations before any others. I have reached this decision entirely alone, and in doing so I have been strengthened by the unfailing support and devotion of Group Captain Townsend. I am deeply grateful for the concern of all those who have constantly prayed for my happiness."

Trader Vic's

Like many visitors to San Francisco, The Queen and Prince Philip had dinner at Trader Vic's during their 1983 trip to California. Their party of fifty-five included Nancy Reagan. The Queen, in blue chiffon, diamonds and pearls, chose a gin martini in preference to the exotic South Seas concoctions for which Trader Vic's is famous. It was an unexpected evening in San Francisco for The Queen and Prince Philip. The weather had been so stormy that they had flown from the Reagan ranch instead of arriving by *Britannia*. This gave them an unscheduled evening and The Queen requested dinner at the famous restaurant.

Training for a King

When King Edward VIII announced that he was abdicating, the soon-to-be King George VI was distressed to think that he would have to reign without ever having been trained to be King. He said to Alex Hardinge, his private secretary, "I'm quite unprepared for it. I've never even seen a state paper. I'm only a naval officer; it's the only thing I know about." His secretary answered with a reassuring quote: "That was what your father said. There is no finer training for a king." King George V had suddenly found himself King when his father died in 1910, and he had felt overwhelmed by the responsibility.

Tramps

Tramps is the trendy nightclub in London where Prince Andrew first met Koo Stark. Royal watchers know that it later became a favourite spot of the Duke and Duchess of York.

Treaty of Portugal

The Treaty of Portugal was signed in 1387, binding Britain and Portugal in perpetual friendship. To commemorate the six-hundredth anniversary of that Treaty, Prince Charles and Princess Diana made an official visit to Portugal in February 1987. Although the weather was dreadful the entire time, Princess Diana's dresses made their usual headlines. The most memorable incident of the visit came at a state banquet, when the impeccably dressed Diana leaned over and playfully twanged the braces of Portugal's President.

Treetops

Elizabeth II was at Treetops, part of a safari lodge in Kenya, when she became Queen some time during the early morning hours of 6 February 1952, as her father (King George VI) died in his sleep. Her visit was to have been the start of a tour of Australia and New Zealand, which she undertook because her father's health was too frail to allow him to keep the commitment he had previously made for the trip.

King George was the one who suggested starting the trip in Kenya, as a combination royal appearance and holiday. After several days of official engagements in Nairobi, Princess Elizabeth and Prince Philip had driven to the Kenyan Highlands to stay at Sagana Lodge, a small house that had been their wedding gift from the people of Nigeria, and which they had never seen. Wearing bush slacks and a bright yellow shirt, Princess Elizabeth had climbed to the observation post called Treetops at the top of a nearby fig tree to survey the surrounding plain, which teemed with exotic animal life. Elizabeth stayed all day and all night too, making a film record of the sights, which she planned to take back to England to show the King, who had always loved Kenya.

The next day, Elizabeth returned to Sagana Lodge, where her husband shortly thereafter told her the news of King George VI's death. The new Queen boarded a plane and hurried back to London, to her grieving family and her new duties. The first member of the Royal Family to greet her was Queen Mary, who said gently, "Your

Courtesy of the British Information Service.

Queen Elizabeth returns to England after the death of King George VI in February 1952; Winston Churchill is waiting (right).

old Grannie and subject must be the first to kiss your hand." Elizabeth was just twenty-five when she shouldered the burden of the monarchy, a position in which her father predicted she would be "lonely forever".

Michael Trestrail

Commander Michael Trestrail was The Queen's bodyguard, responsible for her personal safety, from 1973 to 1982. He began his career in the London police force and rose to the rank of Commander. Then a scandal broke, in which a male prostitute told of a twelve-year homosexual affair with Trestrail. Trestrail confessed the truth, admitting, "I knew the terrible risks I was taking, but I just could not help myself." He then resigned, apologized to The Queen for the embarrassment he had caused, and vanished from royal life.

Trinity College, Cambridge

Trinity was the college which Prince Charles joined when he went to Cambridge University. He studied archaeology and anthropology in his first year and gained high honours (II.1) in the first part of the Tripos (degree examination). He decided to change to British Constitutional History for the remaining two years of his study, in spite of being urged by the Master of Trinity to study any subject he would like, as there was always time to learn the basis of his kingship later.

Royal duties began to get in the way of his university work, much to the concern of the College authorities. The summer term of his second year of study was spent learning the Welsh language at Aberystwyth University, and on 1 July of that year he was invested Prince of Wales. This was followed by a long tour of Wales. During his third year, study was again interrupted when he joined his parents for a long tour of the Pacific to celebrate the 200th anniversary of Captain Cook's voyage. He arrived back at Trinity College only four weeks before his Finals and yet he gained an Honours Degree (II.2).

Even when he was at Cambridge, life was not all work. He also performed in a student revue, called "Revulution". He wrote his own sketch, which opened with him walking on stage under a large umbrella, whispering, "I lead a sheltered life." He closed by walking off with a pretty girl, saying, "I like to give myself heirs."

His mentor while at Trinity was the Master of the College, R.A. (Rab) Butler, considered to be one of the ablest political figures of his generation and perhaps the most influential politician never to be appointed prime minister.

Trooping the Colour

The ceremony called Trooping the Colour takes place on The Queen's official birthday, which falls in June. (Her real birthday is 21 April, often a time of uncertain weather.) In over thirty years as Queen, Her Majesty has never missed a single Trooping of the Colour. The ceremony starts with The Queen's ride from Buckingham Palace to the Parade Ground; there she reviews the troops of the Household

Princess Elizabeth's first appearance at the Trooping the Colour ceremony in 1947.

Courtesy of the British Information Service.

Division. Each year a different regiment troops its colour, or flag, in a ceremony that is intended both to honour the regimental flag and to make sure that members of the regiment will be able to recognize it as a rallying point in the heat of battle. The Queen is accompanied by colonels of all the Household Division regiments, three of whom happen to be her husband, Prince Philip; her son, Prince Charles; and her cousin, the Duke of Kent.

About eight thousand people crowd the area to watch the colourful spectacle. The rest of the Royal Family watches from a little room in the arch that separates the Horse Guard Parade Ground from Whitehall. Later in the day, The Queen appears on the balcony of Buckingham Palace and watches the RAF fly over in tribute to her birthday.

In 1981 the ceremony was marred when a man fired at The Queen from the crowd in The Mall. Luckily, the gun contained only blanks. The Queen quickly recovered her composure and continued Trooping the Colour. Her horse, Burmese, also remained calm. In 1986 The Queen made her last parade on horseback. Thereafter, Burmese was retired and The Queen announced that she would inspect her troops while riding in an open carriage, as did her ancestor Queen Victoria.

Tuimalila

Tuimalila is a giant turtle that lives at the palace of Tonga and is greatly respected by the people of the country. Tuimalila is so old that he had met Captain Cook in his voyage of discovery through the Pacific Islands. He was in residence at the palace with Queen Salote when Queen Elizabeth visited there in late 1953, and he was one of the first citizens of Tonga to whom she was introduced. Pictures show Tuimalila as being a little the worse for wear, having been kicked by a horse and hit by a truck, but he appeared to be interested in his meeting with The Queen.

"Tum-Tum"

The rather portly King Edward VII was nicknamed "Tum-Tum", in friendly fashion, by his circle of intimates.

Tunnel of Love

On a state visit to Denmark in 1979, The Queen was taken to Copenhagen's famed Tivoli Gardens for lunch and a tour through the world-famous amusement park. When she and Prince Philip and their hosts, The Queen's distant cousin Queen Margrethe and her husband Prince Henrik, arrived at the Tunnel of Love, they stopped for a debate about whether or not to take the ride. Laughing, The Queen got into the first boat with Prince Henrik, followed by Margrethe and Prince Philip in the second boat. Throughout the so-called "romantic ride", screams of laughter could be heard from the tunnel. The security officers who took the ride with the royals made no comment about what happened in the tunnel.

The Two Ronnies

BBC TV's *The Two Ronnies*, featuring comedians Ronnie Corbett and Ronnie Barker, is one of The Queen's favourite television programmes.

U

"Uncle Dickie"

Members of the Royal Family called Lord Louis Mountbatten "Uncle Dickie".

United World Colleges

In 1962 Kurt Hahn, the founder of Gordonstoun, established Atlantic College, which subsequently became one of the United World Colleges. It was based on the idea of promoting peace through international education of young people. Atlantic College at St. Donat's Castle in South Wales was the first College. Lord Louis Mountbatten became chairman of the College in 1968 and held the post for ten years. Then Prince Charles took over, bringing his own energy and commitment to the post. It remains one of the causes dearest to his heart.

University of Keele

The University of Keele, in Staffordshire, was granted university status in 1962. Its first Chancellor was Princess Margaret, who attended the first degree-granting ceremonies in 1963.

Unusual Acts of Hospitality

In over thirty years of royal tours to all parts of the globe, The Queen has been confronted by many unusual acts of hospitality.

In Nepal, she patted little lambs on their woolly heads just before they had their throats slit in a religious ritual.

In India, she shot a tiger.

The Gambians presented her with a live baby crocodile in a silver tin.

Tribesmen of the Pentecostal Islands performed for her their traditional manhood ceremony, in which they dive off a high tower, stopped only inches before they hit the ground by a thin rope made of vines tied to their ankles.

In Fiji The Queen was given a large beaker of the national drink, Yaqona, which tastes exactly like soap. Etiquette demanded she down it in one swallow.

In Tuvalu she sat in a ceremonial canoe, borne high in the air by twenty-six men in skimpy native costume. She later commented, "It was a little queer."

In Tonga, on a boiling hot summer day, she was served an entire suckling pig that had been cooking in a pit full of warm stones for more than a week.

Diana relaxes during a visit to British troops stationed in West Germany. The Princess is wearing a tracksuit which she used during driving instruction in an armoured personnel carrier.

Courtesy of the British Information Service.

"Uptown Girl"

"Uptown Girl", one of Billy Joel's greatest hits, also happens to be the favourite pop song of Princess Diana. In fact, in early 1987 the Princess turned up in a London radio studio with DJ Graham Dene, and he ended his last early morning show by dedicating "Uptown Girl" to "Charles back in Kensington".

V

"The Vandy"

The Vanderbilt Racquet Club, usually called "The Vandy", is the exclusive tennis club in Shepherd's Bush that has become a favourite spot of young British aristocrats. Princess Diana goes there several times a week to play tennis, meet her girlfriends and share a chat. Charles Swallow purchased an existing club on the same site in 1985 and immediately transformed it into a social success. Membership is limited to eight hundred, and all applicants are rigorously screened and interviewed to see whether they will be "congenial". Those who pass inspection are allowed to pay £650 for membership and £550 for annual dues. The Vandy has eight courts, a fitness centre, jacuzzi, beautician, bar, restaurant and dry cleaner.

Celia Vestey

Celia Vestey is one of Prince Harry's godmothers. She and her husband, a meat tycoon, are neighbours of the Prince and Princess of Wales in Gloucestershire.

Veuve Cliquot Riche

The Queen Mother, like her grandson Prince Charles, adores champagne. Her favourite brand is Veuve Cliquot Riche, a hearty and full-bodied champagne with a hefty price tag.

Viscount Althorp

Viscount Charles Althorp is Princess Diana's younger brother. He became a contributing correspondent for the NBC TV *Today Show* in 1986, providing on-camera interviews and features from Britain.

341

Although cynics have suggested that his appointment was a means of getting an inside track with his royal connections, Charles—as he is called by his colleagues ("no titles, please")—has proved himself to be a thoroughly professional and engaging commentator whether he's explaining Stonehenge or demonstrating how a Savile Row tailor measures and fits someone for a bespoke suit.

Viscount Linley

David Albert Charles, Viscount Linley, is the son of Princess Margaret and the Earl of Snowdon, born on 3 November 1961. After attending Bedales School, he chose not to go to university but instead learned woodworking and carpentry in a two-year course at the John Makepeace School for Craftsmen, in Dorset.

In 1985, with a partner, Matthew Rice (a friend from Bedales), he opened David Linley Furniture, located in London on the New King's Road. The exclusive shop sells small wooden pieces as well as custom-made furniture of a very original design. The firm was an overnight success: they sold a huge table to New York's Metropolitan Museum for their trustees' room, and a folding screen to actor Sean Connery.

Linley's name has been linked with that of Susannah Constantine and Kate Menzies, but as of this writing he remains a bachelor and one of the most sought-after dinner guests at smart parties in London and New York.

Visiting the Troops in North Africa

King George VI insisted on visiting the British troops in north Africa in 1943, travelling 6700 miles, much of the time in desert heat, to get to a beach where three thousand soldiers were waiting to see him. Here is an eye-witness account:

> As he walked out on the veranda of his villa, first one man, then another, recognized him. And as if called by one voice, the thousands of men, most of them semi-nude, many of them still dripping with water, raced up the beach like a human wave.
>
> Then, as if the wave had suddenly frozen, they stood silently below the veranda, a solid mass of tanned and dripping men. There was one of those strange silences one sometimes gets among a huge crowd.
>
> A voice started "God Save the King". In a moment the

Courtesy of the British Information Service.

Viscount Linley in his furniture-making shop.

national anthem was taken up everywhere. It swelled deep-throatedly from a mass of soldiers. As the last notes of the anthem died out, the King suddenly turned, stepped down from the veranda. He stood there, surrounded by hundreds of men, talking to them, asking them about their experiences.

Then the men broke into song again, this time with "For He's a Jolly Good Fellow".

Courtesy of the British Information Service.

Official photograph
of Lady Sarah Armstrong-Jones,
daughter of Princess Margaret
and Lord Snowdon.

HRH Prince Edward.

Courtesy of the British Information Service.

Anna Wallace

Anna Wallace, grand-daughter of one of King George V's equerries, met the Prince of Wales in 1979 when they were both out with the Duke of Rutland's Belvoir Hunt. According to Palace insiders, Charles began a serious courtship that supposedly culminated in a proposal. But Anna never said yes.

She later became the Honourable Mrs. John Fermor-Hesketh and continues to hunt regularly with the Belvoir. She and Prince Charles have since established a friendly relationship.

Ruth Wallace

Ruth Wallace was engaged in the spring of 1987 to take over the care of Prince William and Prince Harry of Wales. She replaced Barbara Barnes, and is thought to have been given a mandate to exercise more discipline, especially over the somewhat temperamental Prince William, occasionally known as "William the Terrible". She and her under-nanny, Olga Powell, have been seen and heard in public giving young William what for, and most observers feel his behaviour has improved considerably.

Freda Dudley Ward

Freda Dudley Ward was the first of the sophisticated married women to whom the future King Edward VIII was attracted. Freda Dudley was the daughter of a rich cloth manufacturer. She married a Member of Parliament, and was one of the smart young hostesses of the 1920s; Cecil Beaton said she had "a hothouse elegance and lacy femininity".

The royal love affair was ended brutally in late 1934, after the Prince of Wales met Wallis Simpson. When Freda called him one day at Buckingham Palace, the operator told her that the Prince had left orders to put through no more calls from her.

Gerald Ward

Gerald Ward is one of the godfathers of young Prince Harry. He is a friend of Prince Charles from the polo field and a former neighbour of Princess Margaret in Mustique.

Stephen Ward

Stephen Ward was the London osteopath who became notorious at the time of the Profumo scandal in the 1960s. John Profumo, the Secretary of State for War, was meeting call girl Christine Keeler at the home of Ward, where she was simultaneously meeting a Soviet naval officer. There was a public outcry over the immorality, coupled with a fear that Christine was transmitting state secrets from Profumo to the Russian. Profumo had to resign from the government, but Ward was the only person brought to trial in the scandal. He was accused of living off the immoral earnings of the illicit amours of Christine and her friend Mandy Rice-Davies. During the trial he committed suicide by taking an overdose of sleeping pills.

Ward was also a competent artist and had been commissioned by the *Illustrated London News* to do a series of sketches of famous people, including members of the Royal Family. Among his royal subjects were Prince Philip, who had attended a party at Ward's flat, the Duke and Duchess of Kent, Princess Marina, Princess Margaret, Lord Snowdon and the Duke and Duchess of Gloucester. At the height of the Ward-Profumo scandal, the sketches were put on display at a public gallery. The potential embarrassment to the Royal Family was considerable. The *Illustrated London News* did the gentlemanly thing and

King George VI and Queen Elizabeth inspect World War II bomb damage at Madame Tussaud's.

sent a representative to buy all the sketches of the royals and remove them from public view for twenty-five years. They came to light again in a 1987 auction.

Wartime Bombing

During World War II, the Royal Family set an example of courage and imperturbability for the people of Great Britain. They never once considered the possibility of evacuating to safety, even though they were obvious targets for the enemy. When Buckingham Palace was bombed, they moved to Windsor Castle for the rest of the war. Every night during the worst of the Blitz, the King, the Queen and the two Princesses went downstairs to the air-raid shelter in the castle cellar when the first siren sounded and stayed there until the "all clear".

WE

When King Edward VIII began his romance with Wallis Simpson, he noted with pleasure that the initials of their first names — Wallis and Edward — formed the acronym WE. From then on, he used it constantly as a symbol of their love, writing it to her in letters and engraving it on the jewellery he gave her.

Wedding Bear

Following their wedding, the new Duke and Duchess of York found a gift from Prince Edward waiting for them in their carriage — a huge teddy bear festooned with ribbons. It accompanied them on their honeymoon. A mohair version of the bear has been created for sale by the Merrythought Toy Company of Shropshire.

Wedding Bouquet

As soon as a royal wedding is over, the bride's bouquet is ceremonially placed on the Tomb of the Unknown Warrior at Westminster Abbey. The custom was started by the present Queen Mother, who left her bouquet on the Tomb at her wedding in 1923. She had lost her brother Fergus at the Battle of Loos in 1915, and so great was the number of casualties and wounded in that war that almost every family was still affected at that time by loss and suffering.

Sketches of Lady Diana Spencer's wedding dress by Elizabeth and David Emanuel.

Courtesy of Emanuel.

Wedding Dress
Lady Diana Spencer

Lady Diana's wedding dress was a secret that the designers, David and Elizabeth Emanuel, managed to keep until the day of the wedding. The ivory silk taffeta dress was in the romantic style made famous by the Emanuels: low curved neckline, fitted and boned bodice, a tiny waist and full gathered sleeves trimmed with embroidered lace that had once belonged to Queen Mary. The very full skirt was held in shape by a many-layered petticoat of ivory tulle trimmed with lace; attached at the waist was a detachable twenty-five-foot-long train made of taffeta and trimmed with lace. A small blue bow was sewn into the waistband of the dress for "something blue". Her veil was ivory silk tulle hand-embroidered with ten thousand tiny mother-of-pearl sequins and held on by a Spencer family tiara.

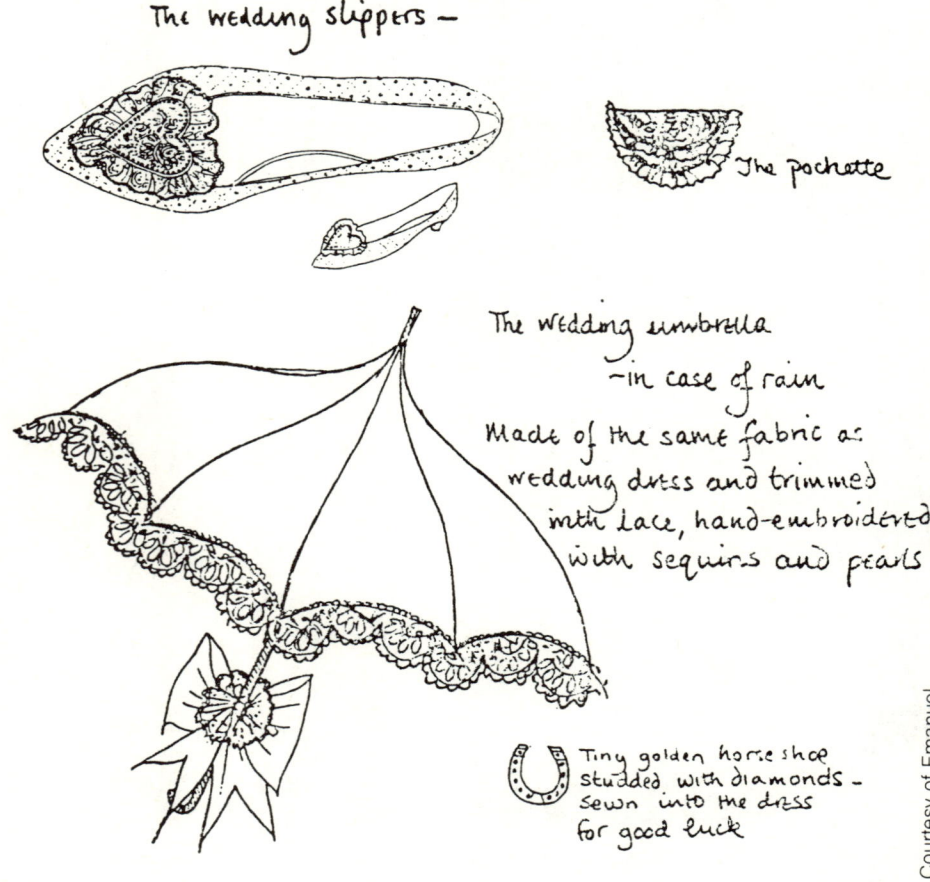

The wedding slippers —

The pochette

The wedding umbrella
—in case of rain
Made of the same fabric as wedding dress and trimmed with lace, hand-embroidered with sequins and pearls

Tiny golden horse shoe studded with diamonds — sewn into the dress for good luck

Courtesy of Emanuel.

Her low-heeled slippers were ivory silk trimmed with an embroidered diamond design and heart-shaped lace rosettes, designed by Clive Hilton. There was even a charming little parasol to match the dress, in case of rain. In her mixed bouquet of a shower design, she carried gardenias, a cascade of white orchids, and some of the new golden roses named after Prince Charles's great-uncle and idol, Lord Mountbatten.

Lady Elizabeth Bowes-Lyon

Lady Elizabeth Bowes-Lyon, now The Queen Mother, designed her own wedding dress, which was then made by seamstress Handley Seymour. A panel of silver lace ran down the centre of the dress, from the square neck to the hem. The sleeves were of Nottingham lace, quite simple but ready to billow dramatically when she moved her arms. This was a departure from tradition and deliberately chosen by the bride to help the Nottingham lace trade, which was suffering badly in the Depression. The only departure from the general simplicity of her wedding attire was a train of Flanders lace, a present from Queen Mary, who insisted it should be incorporated into the dress.

Miss Sarah Ferguson

Sarah Ferguson's wedding dress, designed by Lindka Cierach, was made (appropriately for a woman whose wedding would make her the Duchess of York) of Duchess satin, a shimmery ivory silk fabric. The fitted and boned bodice tapered to a dropped waist and was fully beaded; the neckline was edged with pearls. A fan-shaped bow at the back of the dress held a sweeping seventeen-foot train embroidered with a romantic motif for a sailor's bride, anchors and waves intertwined with hearts. Sarah's veil was made of pure silk also, scalloped with embroidered hearts along the edge and sequinned as well. Her sleeves and her satin pumps were covered with beadwork that incorporated bees and thistles, two of the devices on her own coat of arms.

Wedding Harness

The horses that pull the carriage in which royal couples ride in the procession after their marriage ceremony wear a special wedding harness. Made of patent leather, it has metal trimmings that jingle joyfully as the horses move along.

Courtesy of the British Information Service.

Their Royal Highnesses the Duke and Duchess of York at Madame
Tussaud's. The Duchess of York wears the only genuine replica of her
wedding dress made exclusively for Madame Tussaud's by her dressmaker
Lindka Cierach.

Josiah Wedgwood & Sons

Founded by Josiah Wedgwood in the eighteenth century, the
Wedgwood firm is world famous for fine china, earthenware,
decorative figures and crystal. To celebrate royal events, Wedgwood
traditionally issues commemoratives in limited editions. Examples

prized by collectors include portrait medallions, black basalt busts, sweet boxes and trophy plates. For further information, write to: Josiah Wedgwood & Sons, 32–34 Wigmore Street, London W1.

Courtesy of Josiah Wedgwood & Sons.

Wedgwood collector's items commemorating the marriage of the Duke and Duchess of York.

"Wellies"

Every member of the Royal Family has at one time or another been photographed wearing a pair of green Hunter Wellington boots, or "Wellies", named after the Duke of Wellington, the military commander who defeated Napoleon at Waterloo. This classic equestrian boot (it also comes in tan, but green is the preferred colour for royals) is rubber with a green cloth lining and top, ideal for slogging around the paddock or going down to visit the cows. Even fashion-conscious Princess Diana wears a pair around Highgrove on muddy days.

Welsh Guards

The Welsh Guards were formed by King George V in 1915, early in World War I, and are thus the junior regiment in the Household Division. They wear a plume of green and white feathers, and their tunic buttons are grouped in fives. Prince Charles, the Prince of Wales, is their Colonel.

Welsh Nugget of Gold

A romantic tradition in the Royal Family concerns a nugget of gold from Wales that has been used to make the royal wedding rings. A huge nugget found at Gwynedd in 1923 was first used for the wedding ring of The Queen Mother. The jeweller who made the ring, Mr. Bertolle, bought the nugget and then offered it to Princess Elizabeth at the time of her wedding to Prince Philip. Subsequently, wedding rings for Princess Margaret, Princess Anne and Princess Diana came from the same nugget. By the time Prince Andrew married Sarah Ferguson, the nugget had been used up. The Prince therefore bought a new nugget, which should provide royal wedding rings well into the twenty-first century.

West Heath

West Heath is the girls' school that Lady Diana Spencer attended. In those days she had long straight hair — dark rather than the highlighted blonde colour she later adopted. She excelled at swimming and tap dancing, which she took up after she grew too tall to be a ballet dancer. When Diana left school, she was given a special cup for her "helpfulness".

Wetherby School

Wetherby School, in Kensington, less than a mile from the Palace, is where young Prince William first went to school. The Prince and Princess of Wales chose Wetherby on the recommendation of Prince and Princess Michael of Kent, who sent their son Nicholas there. William started in January 1987 and made new friends quickly.

Prince William arriving for his first day at Wetherby School, with Princess Diana.

"What's Wrong? Do I Smell?"

Prince Charles has ruminated on the difficulty he has in sustaining interesting conversations. "Many people are too shy and overcome in the presence of royalty. Only the dignitaries seem to talk to me on well-tried subjects, usually of little interest. Unfortunately, the nicest people are those who won't come up and make themselves known. They're terrified of being seen to be friendly in case they'll be accused of sucking up or because they imagine, quite wrongly, that I won't want to talk to them. I used to think, 'Good God, what's wrong? Do I smell? Have I forgotten to change my socks?' I realize now that I have to make a bit of the running and show that I'm a reasonable human being."

When You Meet The Queen

When presented to The Queen, etiquette suggests an initial curtsey by women or bow by men. You do not shake her hand unless she offers her own; if she does, you are advised to make your handshake brief but firm, as she is well known to dislike limp handshakes. To be correct, you should not speak until spoken to. The first time you address The Queen, you should call her "Your Majesty". Thereafter, a simple "Ma'am" is proper.

Where to See the Royals in Person

When the Royal Standard is flying from Buckingham Palace, the Queen is in residence. And so it is at Windsor Castle, Sandringham, Holyroodhouse and Balmoral, the other royal residences. State visits can be detected by large flag poles in The Mall: The Queen may be welcoming some foreign head of state and driving with him or her, probably in an open carriage. For dates and times, ask the Tourist Office.

You can be certain that The Queen will be at the Trooping of the Colour on Horse Guards Parade (early June) — this is *the* great display of military ceremonial. On the Sunday nearest 11 November, The Queen attends the Remembrance Day Service at the Cenotaph. The one time each year when The Queen may be seen wearing robes and crown in the Irish State Coach is late October or early November, when the State opening of Parliament takes place.

Other clues for royal watchers appear in the Court columns of the major newspapers, which list such events as charity concerts, openings and visits. The rest is luck.

White Carnations

Every year on The Queen's wedding anniversary, she receives a bouquet of white carnations from Prince Philip — a floral tradition dating back to the morning of their wedding day.

White Lodge

White Lodge was the first home of the future King George VI and Queen Elizabeth after they were married. A gift to the then Duke and Duchess of York from his parents, who had started their own married life there, White Lodge was rather inconveniently located in Richmond Park. Passers-by could look right into the house, and it was difficult to travel to Richmond from London in those days. The Yorks lived there for three years, even though Elizabeth detested it. The house was gloomy and filled with large pieces of furniture. There was no central heating, and the kitchen was ancient and inconvenient.

The new Duchess of York did her best to make the place homelike, with elegant new furniture and bowls of fresh flowers. Even Queen Mary, whose parents were the previous tenants by a grant from Queen Victoria, admitted it was an improvement. The Yorks finally moved out in 1926, at the time of the birth of their first child, the future Queen Elizabeth, and into a house at 17 Bruton Street in London. White Lodge later became part of the Royal Ballet School.

White's

White's is a private club in London where Prince Charles's stag party was held before his marriage to Lady Diana Spencer. Twenty guests, all male of course, are known to have sipped his favourite champagne, Bollinger, but there was no report of other activities traditional to such bachelor flings.

Who Married the Plumber's Daughter?

According to Sir Anthony Wagner, the Garter King of Arms, in his book *English Genealogy*, one of The Queen's ancestors was a plumber's daughter.

In 1779, Mr. George Carpenter of Redbourn,
Hertfordshire, had the plumber down from London to repair
the roof of his house. With the plumber came his daughter,
and both remained at Redbourn some time. Mary Elizabeth
Walsh, the daughter, was then eighteen years of age, and Mr.
Carpenter upwards of sixty, yet notwithstanding the
disparity of their ages and positions, he married her. Their
daughter married the eleventh Earl of Strathmore.

That was The Queen's great-great-great-grandfather.

Who Says The Queen is Dowdy?

Malcolm Muggeridge, often a severe critic of the Royal Family's
behaviour, defended The Queen against those who call her dowdy: "It
is duchesses, not shop assistants, who find The Queen dowdy,
frumpish and banal."

"Will She Fit into the Soap Opera?"

British lyricist Richard Stilgoe explained to American readers of *People*
why there was such a fuss over Fergie. "We always worry when a
prince brings someone home — will she fit into the soap opera?" He
concluded, "Sarah has, very well."

Willie Wombat

Prince Charles likes to call his elder son "Willie Wombat", but many
people have pointed out that it is an unsuitably slothful name for so
active a child.

Harold Wilson

Harold Wilson (later Sir Harold) was the fifth prime minister of
Queen Elizabeth's reign. He was in office from 1964 to 1970 and from
1974 to 1976, when he resigned. He was the first of her prime
ministers who had not attended public school, but despite their
different backgrounds, Wilson and The Queen always got on well,
and she seemed exceptionally relaxed in his company.

Prime Minister Harold Wilson.

Windlesham Moor

Windlesham Moor was the country house near Sunningdale that Princess Elizabeth and the Duke of Edinburgh rented when they were first married. They entertained Prince Philip's friends from the navy there, and were able to pop over quickly to nearby Windsor to see the King and Queen.

Carlo Windsor

At the time that Prince Charles was studying at Aberystwyth in Wales, a satirical song about him became a popular local hit. Here's the first verse:

> I have a friend who lives in Buckingham Palace,
> And Carlo Windsor is his name.
> The last time I went round to his house
> His mother answered the door and said:
> "Carlo, Carlo, Carlo is playing polo today,
> Carlo is playing polo with his daddy."

Lady Helen Windsor

Lady Helen Windsor, the second child and only daughter of the Duke and Duchess of Kent, was born on 28 April 1964. She attended St. Mary's and Gordonstoun schools and then took a job with Christie's in their modern art department. The blonde Lady Helen is considered one of the beauties of the Royal Family, and she is rumoured to be planning marriage to David Flintwood, a London advertising executive.

Windsor Blue

Wallis Simpson's favourite colour was a medium blue that leaned a bit towards the pink side of the spectrum. She wore it often before her marriage, and her wedding dress when she married the then Duke of Windsor was in that shade. Naturally, it came to be called Windsor Blue.

Windsor Castle

Windsor Castle is one of the three official residences of The Queen. Its upkeep costs the Crown about £2.9 million a year. The castle itself was built by William the Conqueror after he won the Battle of Hastings in 1066; it was designed to be a fortress dominating the Thames Valley and the approach to London from the west. Over the nine hundred years of its existence, it has been altered many times, perhaps most notably in the 1820s by King George IV, who really created the castle we see today. His architect Jeffrey Wyatt raised the mediaeval tower and built a quadrangle linking the public suites (added during the reign of King Charles II) with the private part of the house.

Windsor is the final resting place of many of Britain's monarchs, including most recently George VI, the Duke of Windsor, and George V. In the beginning of the fifteenth century, the lovely little St. George's Chapel was begun, and completed in 1528. It stands in the Lower Ward of the castle, and this is where The Queen always attends church on Christmas Day. It is probably one of the finest Gothic buildings in the country.

The state apartments at Windsor are open to the public. Visitors can view King Henry VIII's huge suit of armour; art by Holbein and da Vinci, among others; and such wonders as a solid silver table presented to King Charles II by the Corporation of London. The gardens are extensive, with huge plantings of vegetables, big fruit orchards, and greenhouses for tropical orchids.

The private rooms of the castle have been extensively redecorated by The Queen. A family friend explains, "The decor is really jolly nice country house stuff." She likes strong pastel colours, soft-coloured carpeting, fresh flowers and large-print fabrics. Tables are covered with silver-framed snaps of the royals and little family mementos, such as a bowl made by Prince Andrew at school. The priceless royal art collection is casually placed on the walls, along with modern abstract paintings that are The Queen's own selection. To her, the castle is a place to live, and she tries to make it as cosy and homelike as possible. To the rest of the world, Windsor, with its site high atop a hill, its centuries of history, and its Royal Family treasures, is everything a castle ought to be.

Windsor Knot

After he gave up his throne, the Duke of Windsor made several contributions to sartorial elegance, among them the double-breasted dinner jacket and the fat symmetrical knot for a tie that is called the Windsor knot.

The "Windsor Wave"

All the royals do the "Windsor Wave", which is the stiff little motion of the hand with which royals acknowledge the cheers of the public. Apparently a full-blooded motion of the arm constitutes over-enthusiasm or causes too much wear and tear on the royal elbows.

Adam Wise

Squadron Leader Adam Wise was equerry to the Duke of York and is now an extra equerry, having returned to service duties.

Wood Farm

Wood Farm, a tenant home on the Royal Family's Sandringham estate, is a favourite getaway spot for Prince Philip. He goes there to shoot pheasant and then thriftily markets the birds with mention of their origin.

Woolton Pie

Woolton Pie was an austerity dish of World War II, made without meat but full of root vegetables such as parsnips, turnips, carrots and potatoes baked in a crust. Woolton pie was customarily served at Buckingham Palace during the war, to set a good example. Of course, at the Palace the Woolton pie did come to the table on vermeil platters and was carefully placed on delicate antique china.

Worldwide Butterflies

Worldwide Butterflies is located near Sherborne in Dorset, where there is a silk farm which provides silk for many royal occasions. Although England's climate is a difficult one in which to grow mulberry leaves, the farmers somehow manage the feat and then feed the leaves to silkworms, which spin the cocoons that are eventually turned into all-British silk. Previously known as Lullingstone Silk Farm, the silk was used for the coronation robes of King George VI, for the robe Prince Charles wore for his 1969 investiture as Prince of Wales, and for the wedding dresses of The Queen and Princess Diana.

World Wide Fund for Nature

The World Wide Fund for Nature is an organization dedicated to conservation of threatened wildlife and wildlife habitats all over the world. The Duke of Edinburgh serves as the WWF's international President and supports their work wholeheartedly, as does the Prince of Wales.

Worry About the Falklands War

In April 1982 Great Britain went to war with Argentina over that country's occupation of the Falkland Islands, administered by Great Britain since 1833. It was a tense time for the Royal Family, since Prince Andrew was serving in the Royal Navy and was actually assigned to a ship in the battle zone. As Queen, Elizabeth had a hot line to her bedroom to keep her abreast of the situation — even when she travelled to Canada to sign the new Canadian Constitution — and she worried about the British boys involved in the fighting. As a mother, she naturally worried about her own son, aboard the *Invincible*.

The Queen and Prince Philip, in his uniform of Admiral of the Fleet,

greeted Prince Andrew at the dock with a broad smile when the
Invincible returned safely with Andrew and the rest of the 820
Squadron in June 1982. As a joke for photographers, Andrew chose to
make his first appearance with a rose between his teeth.

Courtesy of the British Information Service.

The Duke of York during his visit with the Duchess of York to the island of
Mauritius in the Indian Ocean in 1987.

The Worshipful Company of Gardeners

This ancient guild in London supplies all the flowers for royal
occasions. They made the bridal bouquet for Lady Diana Spencer;
Sarah Ferguson's lovely spray of yellow roses, white lilies and
fragrant lilies of the valley; and "a riot of red flowers" for The Queen's
ruby wedding anniversary in 1987. On the day of The Queen's Jubilee

in 1977, marking the twenty-fifth anniversary of Her Majesty's accession, the Master of the Company presented her with a duplicate of her coronation bouquet, containing nothing but British flowers. The Company also arranges to clip sprigs of rosemary from The Queen's Christening Tree at Windsor each time one of her children gets married. Tied with a ribbon, they are tucked in with the going-away luggage, along with a note that says, "With every possible happy wish, rosemary for remembrance."

Courtesy of the British Information Service.

The Duchess of York during her visit with the Duke of York to the island of Mauritius in the Indian Ocean in 1987.

Y

William Butler Yeats on the Abdication

At the time of King Edward VIII's Abdication, William Butler Yeats wrote a sympathetic stanza:

Those cheers that can be bought or sold,
That office fools have run,
That waxen seal, that signature,
For things like these, what decent man
Would keep his lover waiting,
Keep his lover waiting?

York Cottage

York Cottage was the first home of the future King George V and Queen Mary after their marriage in 1893. Queen Victoria gave them what was then called the Bachelor's Cottage, built on the grounds of Sandringham by her son Edward, then Prince of Wales, during his rebuilding of the property.

George and Mary, at that time the Duke and Duchess of York, liked York Cottage so much that they spent their honeymoon there and continued to make it their principal country home for thirty-five years. All of their children except the eldest (King Edward VIII) were born there, and even after George became King he still clung to York Cottage, leaving his mother Queen Alexandra in the big house at Sandringham. It was not until 1925 that King George and Queen Mary left York Cottage for the big house, due primarily to the need for space for their family. York Cottage today is the estate office for Sandringham.

York House

York House is a grace-and-favour residence, meaning that the right to live there can be granted by The Queen at her pleasure. It is located in London on the north side of St. James's Palace, and currently is the home of the Duke and Duchess of Kent. Previous occupants include Edward VIII when he was the Prince of Wales, and war hero Lord Kitchener during World War I.

Young England Kindergarten

In 1980 Lady Diana Spencer became a teacher at the Young England Kindergarten, St. Saviour's Hall, St. George's Square, London. Run by Mrs. Wilson and Mrs. King, the school accommodates fewer than a hundred children. The curriculum is Montessori-based and includes swimming and dancing. During her employment, Miss Diana was known to be extremely popular with her young charges.

Z

Zara

Eyebrows were raised in 1981 when Princess Anne and her husband chose the unconventional name of Zara for their daughter. In a Royal Family dominated by male offspring, Zara is The Queen's first granddaughter. Like her older brother Peter, Zara thrives on life in the country, and she is known as a tomboy.

Christening of Princess Anne's daughter Zara.

Their Royal Highnesses the Prince and Princess of Wales, photographed by Lord Snowdon at Kensington Palace in London.

BIBLIOGRAPHY

Allison, Ronald, and Lemoine Serge. *Charles, Prince of Our Times*. London: Pitkin Pictorial, 1978.

Alexandra, Queen of Yugoslavia. *Prince Philip*. Indianapolis, USA: The Bobbs-Merrill Company, 1960.

Barker, Brian. *When The Queen Was Crowned*. New York: David McKay Company, 1976.

Barry, Stephen P. *Royal Secrets: The View from Downstairs*. New York: Villard Books, 1985.

Birmingham, Stephen. *Duchess: The Story of Wallis Warfield Windsor*. Boston: Little, Brown and Company, 1981.

Brown, Craig, and Lesley Cunliffe. *The Book of Royal Lists*. London: Routledge & Kegan Paul, 1982.

Cathcart, Helen. *Prince Charles*. London: W.H. Allen, 1978.

Clear, Celia. *Royal Children*. New York: Crown, 1987.

Collins, Anne. *The British Royal Family*. London: Heinemann, 1984.

Crawford, Marion. *Elizabeth The Queen: The Story of Britain's New Sovereign*. London: Greenwood, 1952.

Darbyshire, Taylor. *King George VI*. London: Hutchinson & Co., 1937.

Duncan, Andrew. *The Reality of Monarchy*. London: William Heinemann, 1970.

Graham, Tim. *On the Royal Road*. Boston: Little, Brown and Company, 1987.

Hall, Trevor. *Born to Be King: Prince William of Wales*. New York: Crown, 1983.

——.*The Royal Family Today*. New York: Crescent Books, 1984.

Hanmer, Davina. *Diana: The Fashion Princess*. New York: Owl Books, 1984.

Hoey, Brian. *HRH the Princess Anne*. London: Country Life Books, 1984.

Holden, Anthony. *Prince Charles*. New York: Atheneum, 1979.

——.*Their Royal Highnesses, the Prince and Princess of Wales*. London: Weidenfeld & Nicolson, 1981.

Judd, Dennis. *Prince Philip, Duke of Edinburgh*. New York: Atheneum, 1981.

Junor, Penny. *Charles*. London: Sidgwick & Jackson, 1987.

——.*Diana: Princess of Wales*. New York, 1983.

Keay, Douglas. *Royal Pursuit: The Media and the Monarchy in Conflict and Compromise.* New York: Dodd Mead, 1984.

King, Norman. *The Prince and the Princess.* New York: Wallaby, 1983.

Lacey, Robert. *Majesty.* New York: Harcourt Brace Jovanovich, 1977.

Lichfield, Patrick. *Lichfield on Travel Photography.* New York: Salem House, 1987.

Longford, Elizabeth. *The Queen: The Life of Elizabeth II.* New York: Alfred A. Knopf, 1983.

——.*The Queen Mother.* New York: Morrow, 1981

——.*The Royal House of Windsor.* New York: Crown, 1987.

Martin, Ralph G. *Charles and Diana.* New York: Putnam Publishing, 1985.

Morrison, Ian A. *HRH Prince Charles.* Loughborough: Ladybird Books, 1981.

Morrow, Ann. *The Queen.* London: Granada Publishing, 1983.

——.*The Queen Mother.* London: Granada Publishing, 1985.

Morton, Andrew. *The Royal Yacht Britannia.* London: Orbis Books, 1984.

Robinson, John M. *Royal Residences.* London: MacDonald & Co., 1984.

The Royal Family in Wartime. London: Odhams Press, 1945.

Shewell-Cooper, W. E. *The Royal Gardeners: King George VI and His Queen.* London: Cassell & Company, 1952

Sinclair, David. *Snowdon: A Man for Our Times.* New York: Proteus Books, 1982.

Spink, Kathryn. *Invitation to a Royal Wedding.* New York: Crescent Books, 1981.

Sunday Express Staff. *A Week in the Life of the Royal Family.* New York: Macmillan, 1983.

Talbot, Godfrey. *The Country Life Book of the Royal Family.* London: Country Life Books, 1981.

Thornton, Michael. *Royal Feud: The Queen Mother and the Duchess of Windsor.* London: Pan Books, 1986.

Various authors. *The Queen.* London: Penguin Books, 1977.

Wade, Judy. *Charles and Diana: Inside a Royal Marriage.* London: Angus & Robertson, 1987.

Winchester, Simon. *Their Noble Lordships: Class and Power in Modern Britain.* New York: Random House, 1982.

York, Peter, and Ann Barr. *The Official Sloane Ranger Handbook.* London: Ebury Press, 1981.

York, Rosemary (ed.). *Charles in His Own Words.* London: Omnibus Press, 1981.

Ziegler, Philip. *Diana Cooper.* New York: Penguin Books, 1981.

SPECIAL ISSUES AND COMMEMORATIVES

The British Parliament. Reference pamphlet, Central Office of Information, revised 1984.

Elizabeth II, 1952–1987: The Queen's 35th Anniversary of her Accession to the Throne. Souvenir edition, *Palace* magazine, 1987.

A Guide to the Riches of London. National Westminster Bank.

Historic Royal Homes. Department of the Environment and the Lord Chamberlain's Office, 1986.

The Monarchy in Britain. Reference pamphlet, Central Office of Information, 1986.

Radio Times, Coronation Supplement, 1937; Coronation Supplement, 31 May–6 June, 1953; Wedding Supplement, 16 Nov, 1947.

Royal Britain in Queen Elizabeth's Silver Jubilee Year. 1977.

The Royal Wedding: Official Souvenir. Pitkin Pictorial for the Royal Jubilee Trusts.

Royal Year 1986. The *Illustrated London News,* 1986.

Royal Year 1987. The *Illustrated London News,* 1987.

The Tower of London. Official Guide, Ministry of Public Buildings and Works, HMSO, 1967.

People, "The Wedding of Prince Andrew and Sarah Ferguson". 4 Aug 1986.

MAGAZINES

The following magazines contain regular and extensive coverage of the Royal Family and all their activities:

Majesty
Royalty Monthly
Tatler
Vanity Fair